BRITAIN'S EXPORT TRADE WITH CANADA

CANADIAN STUDIES IN ECONOMICS

A series of studies edited by V. W. Bladen, sponsored by the Social Science Research Council of Canada, and published with financial assistance from the Canada Council.

BRITAIN'S
EXPORT TRADE
WITH CANADA

BY

G. L. Reuber

UNIVERSITY OF TORONTO PRESS

Copyright, Canada, 1960
by University of Toronto Press
Printed in the Netherlands
Reprinted in 2018
ISBN 978-1-4875-7332-4 (paper)

To

M. L. J. R.

PREFACE

Most of the research for this study was done during the academic year 1954-5 when I was a research student at Cambridge University. The first version of the manuscript was subsequently completed at Ottawa as a part-time enterprise and accepted by Harvard University in 1956 in partial fulfilment of the requirements for a Ph.D. During the past two years this earlier draft has been revised, in some parts quite extensively, for publication.

It is a pleasure to acknowledge my heavy indebtedness to all those who have helped me. My greatest obligation is to Professor H. G. Johnson who spent several days of his very valuable time reading the penultimate draft of the manuscript. The twelve typewritten pages of critical comments and suggestions that emerged from this review resulted in some sections of the discussion being rewritten and in others being amended at numerous places. Even so, I cannot hope that Professor Johnson will be satisfied with everything that is said; but I am quite sure that the study has been greatly improved because of his criticisms. To avoid considerable repetition I have not acknowledged my indebtedness to Professor Johnson for specific suggestions in the course of discussion; suffice it to say here that there are many points which he brought to my attention.

Others whose help I should especially like to acknowledge include the following: Professor J. H. Williams, my thesis supervisor at Harvard; Professor Sir D. H. Robertson, my supervisor of studies at Cambridge; Mr. P. R. Fisk, now at the University of Aberdeen, who helped me greatly with statistical questions when I was at Cambridge; officials at Her Majesty's Treasury and the Board of Trade (including the United Kingdom Trade Commissioner's Office at Ottawa) who kindly consented to discuss the matters considered in this study, who supplied me with much documentary information, and who arranged a number of interviews with British business men; officials of various private trade associations and the Dollar Exports Council who generously gave me the benefit of their views; Messrs. E. Westbrook and W. Purcell of the Department of Trade and Commerce at Ottawa, who read an earlier draft of the manuscript and provided me with many useful comments; Dr. R. J. Wonnacott, who kindly read the manuscript at the proof stage; Miss M. James, at the Department of Finance library in Ottawa, to whom I turned repeatedly for books and periodical literature; and Dean V. W. Bladen, editor of this series, and Miss M. J. Houston, of the University of Toronto Press, who have been most helpful. I, of course, accept full responsibility for the book as it stands, and none of its deficiencies is to be attributed in any way to those who have assisted me.

Finally, I am most grateful to the Social Science Research Council of Canada and the Sir Arthur Currie Scholarship Fund for making my stay at Cambridge feasible financially, and to the Social Science Research Council of Canada for providing sufficient funds to make possible the revision and publication of the study. Acknowledgement is also due to the Harvard University Press for its kind permission to include in this book my note entitled "Anglo-Canadian Trade:

Prices and the Terms of Trade, 1924-54" which first appeared in the *Review of Economics and Statistics* XLI (May, 1959) pp. 196-9; to the Technology Press for permission to quote from Charles P. Kindleberger's *The Dollar Shortage*, published jointly by the Technology Press and John Wiley and Sons, Inc., and copyright by the Massachusetts Institute of Technology; and to the following associations and publishers for permission to quote from the publications indicated: Canadian Importers & Traders Association Inc., *Survey of British Trade Problems and Practices in the Canadian Market* (published 1957); the Board of Trade, Special Register Information Service reports; National Industrial Conference Board, *Studies in Business Economics*, no. 45; William Hodge & Company Limited, *The Theory of International Trade* by G. Haberler; Canadian Metal Mining Association, *Report of the Directors on the Mission to the United Kingdom* published in November 1955; Macmillan & Co. Ltd., "The Impossibility of Competition" by Mrs. Joan Robinson, in *Monopoly and Competition and Their Regulation* edited by E. H. Chamberlin; George Allen & Unwin Ltd., *American Investment in British Manufacturing Industry* by John H. Dunning; and the Royal Economic Society, "British-Canadian Industrial Productivity" by J. B. Heath, in the *Economic Journal*, December 1957.

G. L. R.

London, Ontario
December 1959

CONTENTS

TABLES

APPENDIX

BRITAIN'S EXPORT TRADE WITH CANADA

CHAPTER ONE

INTRODUCTION

POST-WAR DISCUSSIONS of international economics have devoted considerable attention to four closely related topics: the "dollar shortage"; the elasticity in demand and supply of exports and imports with respect to price and income changes; the relative shares in world trade supplied by various countries and changes in these shares; and the relevance for many contemporary problems of much of the theory of trade, based mainly as it is on assumptions of pure and perfect competition and cast largely in terms of three variables—price, income, and quantity. Underlying these issues has been the more general question of what are the main determinants of international trade in the modern (post-World War I) world and what is their relative importance.

The principal purpose of this study is to examine the main determinants of Britain's export trade with Canada since the 1920's and to evaluate their relative importance. Such a study may be considered significant for several reasons. In the first place, Britain's trade with Canada is important in its own right because of its size and composition. Since late in the nineteenth century Britain has been Canada's second most important trading partner. And although the relative importance of British trade with Canada has diminished in terms of Canada's general trading picture, which has come to be dominated by trade with the United States, the fact remains that about 15 per cent of total Canadian merchandise exports go to the United Kingdom at present and about 10 per cent of Canadian imports come from the United Kingdom. Looking at this trade from Britain's standpoint, one finds that since World War II Canada has usually ranked fourth or better in importance among all the countries with whom Britain has traded and second among Commonwealth countries. In 1957 the three largest buyers of British exports were the United States (£244 million), Australia (£236 million), and Canada (£195 million), followed by India (£176 million) and others; and the three largest sellers to Britain were the United States (£483 million), Canada (£320 million), and Australia (£248 million). In relative terms, Britain sold 6 per cent of her exports to Canada in 1957 and purchased 8 per cent of her imports from Canada. Both countries have derived considerable benefit from this trade because of the high degree of natural complementarity that exists between the two economies. This complementarity has been reflected in the composition of trade which has consisted mainly of an exchange of Canadian foodstuffs and raw and semi-processed materials against a wide variety of British manufactures.

The importance of Anglo-Canadian trade is further enhanced by the political significance sometimes attached to it. From time to time in the past public discussions have arisen in both countries, and particularly in Canada, concerning the desirability of increasing the flow of trade between Canada and Britain and possible methods of achieving this objective.

 Secondly, an examination of Britain's export trade with Canada is suggestive when one tries to evaluate the relative importance of various alleged limitations on Britain's ability to earn more dollars in the United States. This follows from the fact that there are important differences as well as similarities between the Canadian and United States economies. Accordingly, by studying Britain's export trade with Canada, one is in effect examining Britain's export trade with an American market stripped of certain features of the United States market— features that in some cases have been assigned considerable importance in post-war discussions of the dollar problem. Among the significant differences in this connection between Canada and the United States is, first of all, the difference in commercial policy. Compared with United States tariffs, Canadian tariffs facing British goods have, generally speaking, been considerably lower and less uncertain; and customs procedures have been less restrictive. In addition, the Canadian and United States economies differ greatly in terms of their size, self-sufficiency, and complementarity with the British economy. In sharp contrast with the United States, Canada is a relatively small country highly dependent on foreign trade; there has been relatively little tendency for Canadian output to replace imports; Canadian imports continue to be spread over a wide range of products rather than to be concentrated in a few primary commodity lines; manufactured products, not raw and processed materials, continue to make up a high proportion of Canadian imports; and changes in Canada's terms of trade have been significantly different from changes in the United States' terms of trade. Several similarities between the Canadian and United States economies are also especially noteworthy. The first is the highly dynamic and competitive nature of both economies and the emphasis on change and novelty in each.[1] Further, the pattern of business fluctuations in the two countries has been similar over the years, though the timing and magnitude of the fluctuations has never corresponded exactly. At the same time, both countries have experienced remarkable economic growth and prosperity since World War II, interrupted only briefly on a number of occasions by minor recessions.

 Thirdly, investigation of Britain's export trade with Canada is useful from the standpoint of forming a judgment about the sensitivity of Britain's export trade with Canada to price and income changes. On two occasions, 1931–5 and 1949–52, a major change in the level of British prices relative to the Canadian market has occurred because of currency revaluation. Furthermore, during the twenties and since 1945 Canadian incomes have risen rapidly, while during the thirties incomes fell very sharply. Attempts that have been made to measure elasticity by sophisticated statistical methods have been subjected to considerable criticism. Additional light might conceivably be shed on this question if, instead of trying to measure elasticity directly, one were to examine such quantitative and qualitative evidence as exists with a view to determining on the basis of past experience why trade might or might not be relatively sensitive to price and income changes and whether the degree of sensitivity is likely to be large or small. Such an approach cannot, of course, yield a numerical coefficient of elasticity. It may, however, be able to distinguish in broad terms between relatively high and low elasticity, which in many instances may be the important consideration anyway.[2]

 A fourth reason why an examination of the factors influencing Britain's export trade with Canada may be considered significant arises from the attention that has been given to the relative shares in world trade of various countries. In this connection, particular attention has been given to the decrease in Britain's share of world trade during the past century. In order to elucidate some of the reasons for this decrease, it is useful to try to explain the decrease in Britain's share of a particular market such as Canada's, which has been of significance and where the decrease in Britain's share of the market has been especially large, measured both as a proportion of all goods (that is, foreign and domestic) sold and of all goods imported.

And finally, consideration of Britain's export trade with Canada affords an opportunity to evaluate the significance of those factors emphasized by the theory of monopolistic competition in one particular market situation. Among these factors, special interest attaches to the role of non-price variables, the structure of the market, and the degree of competition entailed by this structure. In addition, the circumstances are such that one is also able to consider the implications of economic change together with the possibility that as between two trading partners there may exist different propensities to seek and accept economic change.

The discussion below has been pursued with these general considerations in mind. The particular approach that has been followed throughout the analysis has been, within limits set by the resources available to the writer, to try to explain in a systematic and comprehensive fashion the decrease in Britain's share of the Canadian market. Throughout the early chapters of this study two general questions lurk in the background, and are explicitly considered in chapter vi. The first is how during most of the period since World War II British exports were affected by British conditions of supply. The second is whether Britain should have devoted more resources to maintaining or increasing its share of Canada's market, or for that matter whether too great an effort was made to increase exports to Canada; it should be understood at the outset, however, that the primary purpose of this discussion is to explain the decrease in Britain's share of the Canadian market, not to evaluate business and governmental policies in relation to this phenomenon. Throughout the discussion merchandise trade only is considered.

At many points the analysis is open to criticism and requires qualification, partly because very little reliable information exists on certain important aspects of the subject, and partly because of the unsatisfactory nature of much of the information that does exist and the difficulty of gleaning it from a wide variety of sources and putting it to use in a meaningful way. In addition, the author cannot claim to have either special knowledge or first-hand experience of the many commodity markets relevant to the subject. Nevertheless, with the information available some general impressions emerge from the weight of evidence which clarify, in varying degree, the questions raised and give a clearer understanding of the subject as a whole.

RELATIVE SIZE AND GROWTH OF BRITISH EXPORTS TO CANADA

In 1958 British sales of merchandise to Canada totalled $527 million. This compares with about $300 million in 1948, $120 million in 1938, $190 million in

1928, well over $100 million in the years immediately preceding World War I, and about $40 million in 1868, the year when Canada emerged as a sovereign state.

The share of Canadian imports supplied by various countries since 1868 is indicated by Table I. During the decade from 1870 to 1879 an average of over 50 per cent of Canada's imports came from the United Kingdom; for the decade from 1948 to 1957 the corresponding figure is 10 per cent. During the same

TABLE I

SHARE OF CANADIAN IMPORTS SUPPLIED BY VARIOUS COUNTRIES, SELECTED YEARS, 1868-1957
(Percentage of total value of imports)

Year (fiscal)	U.K.	U.S.	All other			
1868	56	34	10			
1872	60	32	8			
1879	39	54	7			
1888	39	46	15			
1899	25	59	16			
1911	24	61	15			
1913	21	65	14			
Year (calendar)	U.K.	U.S.	Other Commonwealth	Continental Europe	Latin America	All other
1922	18	67				
1926	16	66	5	7	3	3
1929	15	69	5	7	3	1
1932	21	58	8	9	3	1
1935	21	57	10	7	3	2
1938	18	63	10	6	2	1
1948	11	69	8	3	8	1
1950	13	67	8	3	7	2
1957	9	71	4	6	7	3
1958	10	69	4	6	7	4

SOURCES: Dominion Bureau of Statistics, *Canada Year Book*, 1939, *Trade of Canada*, 1955, *Canadian Statistical Review*, 1957 Supp., monthly issues.

period the proportion of Canadian imports coming from the United States increased from an average of over 40 per cent to an average of over 70 per cent; and the proportion coming from all other countries increased from about 10 to about 20 per cent. As might be expected, these changes have manifest themselves in an irregular fashion. During the years associated with World Wars I and II and recovery from these wars Anglo-Canadian trade was very seriously disrupted. Apart from these periods, the years during which Britain's share of Canadian imports was generally declining most rapidly are roughly as follows: 1872 to 1879, 1888 to 1899, 1911 to 1914, 1925 to 1929, 1950 to the present. In the intervening years Britain's share was approximately unchanged or increased slightly.

Statistical information relating to the level of British sales in Canada and the level of Canadian imports is summarized in Table II. As indicated, the value of Canadian imports from Britain increased some fifteen times from 1869 to 1958 compared with over an eighty fold increase in total Canadian imports. The periods when imports from Britain have increased coincide roughly with those periods when total Canadian imports and the Canadian economy generally were expanding. Excluding World Wars I and II and the immediate post-war years, six periods of major expansion in imports from Britain are apparent: 1869 to 1873 (when Canadian imports from Britain increased by 93 per cent and

TABLE II

CANADIAN IMPORTS: INDEX NUMBERS, SELECTED YEARS, 1869-1957
(1900 = 100)

(fiscal)	Value		Volume		
	Total(a)	from U.K.(a)	Total(a)	from U.K.(b)	from U.K.(c)
1869	37	80	28	48	
1873	72	154	52	73	
1879	46	70	44	63	
1883	71	117	60	111	
1888	58	88	61	104	
1897	62	66	74	82	
1906	164	156	153	186	
1913	389	313	353	298	
(calendar)					
1922	442	309	265	156	156
1929	752	440	554	271	258
1932	262	211	267	158	148
1935	319	264	325	207	178
1938	392	269	385	201	172
1948	1,527	676	709	253	183
1950	1,838	913	773	402	261
1954	2,370	887	1,004	353	228
1957	3,257	1,179	1,299	514	319
1958	3,007	1,190	1,198	499	307

SOURCES:
(a) Dominion Bureau of Statistics, *Canada Year Book*, various issues, *Trade of Canada*, 1955, *Canadian Statistical Review*, 1957 Supp., monthly issues; K. W. Taylor and H. Mitchell, *Statistical Contributions to Canadian Economic History* (Toronto: Macmillan, 1931), vol. II, table III.
(b) Value of U.K. exports to Canada (incl. Newfoundland after 1938) deflated by price index of U.K. exports: Central Statistical Office, *Annual Abstract of Statistics, Monthly Digest of Statistics; Times Review of Industry* (London & Cambridge Economic Bulletin no. 26), June 1958; Albert H. Imlah, *Economic Elements in the Pax Britannica* (Cambridge: Harvard University Press, 1958), table 8, pp. 94 ff.
(c) Value of U.K. exports to Canada deflated from 1929 to 1954 by price index of U.K. exports to Canada, Appendix below; from 1954 to 1958 by price index of U.K. exports to dollar area: Central Statistical Office, *Monthly Digest of Statistics.*

total Canadian imports increased by 95 per cent); 1879 to 1883 (67 and 54 per cent respectively); 1897 to 1913 (374 and 527 per cent respectively); 1922 to 1929 (42 and 70 per cent respectively); 1932 to 1937 (58 and 79 per cent respectively); and 1948 to 1957 (74 and 113 per cent respectively). During some of these years the increases shown represent recovery rather than growth beyond previously established peaks; the latter measured in terms of value is confined to 1870 to 1873, 1906 to 1913, 1922 to 1929, and 1948 to 1958.

It is evident from the statistics that since the turn of the century at least the periods when Canada's imports from Britain were at comparatively high levels and increasing most rapidly coincide roughly with the periods when Britain's *share* of Canadian imports was shrinking. This means that generally during these years total Canadian imports were increasing even more rapidly than imports from Britain. The question raised for further consideration, therefore, is why British suppliers have not participated fully in the expansion of Canadian imports during these major periods of growth. In addition, one is warned against over-emphasizing relative shares as a basis for judging export performance.

Another interesting point revealed by the figures is that the volume of British goods sold in Canada during much of the period since World War II has apparently been less than the volume of sales immediately before World War I.[3] Only since 1957 does the volume of British exports to Canada appear to have risen significantly above the 1913 level. This is to say that in 1956, for example, the volume of British sales in Canada was roughly the same as immediately before World War I in spite of the fact that the volume of total Canadian imports from all countries had increased almost four times and Canada's gross national product, adjusted for price changes, had increased some four and a half times. Thus, the large increase in the value of British exports to Canada which occurred between 1913 and the mid fifties is mainly a reflection of rising prices; the volume of goods sold seems to have been approximately the same.

How does this general picture of Britain's export trade with Canada compare with the picture of Britain's export trade with other countries? Statistics roughly indicating the share of world exports provided by the United Kingdom and the United States are shown in Table III. According to these estimates Britain's share of world exports of manufactures decreased from 40 per cent in 1870 to

TABLE III

APPROXIMATE SHARE OF WORLD EXPORTS OF MANUFACTURES
(Percentage of total value of exports)

	U.K.	U.S.
1870	40	3
1899	33	11
1913	30	13
1929	24	21
1937	24	21
1950	27	31
1956	20	31

SOURCES: Estimates for 1870 based on G. D. A. MacDougall, "Britain's Foreign Trade Problem," *Economic Journal*, LVII (March 1947), p. 80; League of Nations, *Industrialization and Foreign Trade* (Geneva, 1945), pp. 157 ff; 1899-1929, H. Tyszynski, "World Trade in Manufactured Commodities, 1899-1950," *Manchester School of Economic and Social Studies*, XIX (Sept. 1951), Table VIII, p. 286; 1937-56, Stephen Spiegelglas, "World Exports of Manufactures, 1956 vs. 1937," *Manchester School of Economic and Social Studies*, XXVII (May 1959), Table 2, p. 114.

about 30 per cent prior to World War I, and to about 20 per cent in recent years. The United States' share, on the other hand, increased substantially after 1870, until in 1950 it stood at over 30 per cent of world exports.[4] There is, therefore, a resemblance between changes during the past century in the relative position of the United Kingdom and the United States in the world market, on the one hand, and in the Canadian market, on the other.

A rough similarity is also apparent in changes in the level of exports. From 1869 to 1957 the value of total British exports increased seventeen and a half times—compared with a fifteen fold increase in the value of British exports to Canada. During the same period the value of total United States exports increased over seventy-five times. This basic difference in the average rate of growth of British and United States exports during the past century is apparent not only from the aggregate trade figures but also from figures relating to the major geographical areas—Europe, South America, Asia, Africa, and Oceania. British exports to Europe and the outer sterling area have increased more than those of the United States since 1945; but then United States exports to these areas were seriously restricted for many of these years. Finally, it is interesting to observe that the volume of British exports to the world since 1913 has not increased much more than the volume of British exports to Canada. As far as one can tell from the statistics, the volume of total British exports in 1954 was about 10 per cent above the 1913 level. Consequently, in the case of both total British exports and British exports to Canada price changes mainly account for the increase in the value of exports that occurred between 1913 and 1954.

TABLE IV

UNITED KINGDOM AND UNITED STATES EXPORTS: INDEX NUMBERS, SELECTED YEARS, 1869-1957
(1913 = 100)

| | U.K. (a) | | | U.S. (b) |
	Value	Volume	Average value	Value
1869	36			11
1913	100	100	100	100
1929	139	86	162	212
1938	90	61	147	126
1948	300	84	359	
1954	509	109	467	617
1957	633	133	476	849

SOURCES:
(a) Werner Schlote, *British Overseas Trade* (Oxford: Basil Blackwell, 1952), Appendix, Table 5; *Times Review of Industry* (London & Cambridge Economic Bulletin no. 26), June 1958.
(b) U.S. Dept. of Commerce, *Historical Statistics of the United States, 1789-1945; Statistical Abstract of the United States, 1958.*

One general conclusion that emerges from all this is that the decline in Britain's position in the Canadian market does not appear to be an exceptional development mainly attributable to some special factor such as Canada's geographic location near the United States, important as this undoubtedly has been.

Rather, the foregoing evidence suggests, *prima facie*, that the change in Britain's position in the Canadian market can be viewed merely as a more vivid manifestation of the change in Britain's general position in world trade. Since 1870, and especially since 1914, Britain's relative position in world trade generally has decreased. The decline in Britain's relative position in Canada seems merely to have occurred somewhat in advance and to have proceeded somewhat further than the decline elsewhere.

TABLE V

BRITISH EXPORTS TO CANADA AND THE UNITED STATES, SELECTED YEARS, 1912-58

	Index numbers (1926 = 100)		Share of total imports	
	Canada	U.S.	Canada	U.S.
1912	81	71	21	17
1926	100	100	16	9
1932	57	19	21	6
1938	72	31	18	6
1948	182	76	11	4
1954	238	131	10	5
1957	317	200	9	6
1958	320	226	10	7
Increase 1938-58(%)	341	629		

SOURCES: U. S. Dept. of Commerce, *Statistical Abstract of the United States*, various issues; Dominion Bureau of Statistics, *Review of Foreign Trade*, 1958.

Finally, it is interesting to compare changes in the level of British exports to Canada and to the United States, and to consider also how Britain's share of the total imports of these two countries has changed. As is evident from Table V, Britain's share of Canadian imports has declined more during the past few decades than her share of the United States market—though the former share is still somewhat larger than the latter. Secondly, since 1938 British exports to Canada have increased significantly less than British exports to the United States. To some extent this reflects the relatively greater decrease in British exports to the United States during the thirties. Compared with 1926 British exports to Canada have increased about three-quarters more than British exports to the United States; but then total Canadian imports during this period increased some two and a fifth times more than total United States imports. Admittedly a wide variety of factors, such as changes in commercial policy, may affect this comparison. Without attempting to sort out the various influences at work, it nevertheless remains true that in aggregate statistical terms the trend of Britain's export trade with Canada from several viewpoints compares unfavourably with the trend of Britain's export trade with the United States since the twenties.

CHAPTER TWO

INCIDENCE OF STRUCTURAL CHANGES

1. The Pattern of Canadian Demand

THE DEMAND for goods and services within an economy arises from three major sources: consumers, investors, and governments. The supply of goods and services by which this demand is satisfied is provided from domestic production and from foreign production imported from abroad.

Within this framework it is readily apparent that the share of total demand satisfied by imports from one foreign country, relative to the share satisfied by domestic producers and imports from other foreign countries, can be altered simply by changes in the pattern of demand. Country A may continue to command the same proportion of each commodity market in country B and still find that its share of B's total market has decreased. This would happen if B's demand for those commodities in which A had the strongest position expanded less than B's demand for other commodities where A's share of the market was smaller. In this section an attempt is made to evaluate the degree to which Britain's share of the Canadian market has been impaired by long-run structural changes of this sort.

In addition, the consequences of Britain's decline as an entrepot are briefly examined. It is possible that country B at one time imported a considerable volume of goods from country C via country A. Subsequently, because of long-term changes in shipping routes and communications as well as other economic and political relationships, country B may acquire most of its goods from C by direct import rather than indirectly through A. As a result, A's share of B's market will have decreased even though domestic producers of goods in A retain as large a share of B's market as before.

It can be argued, of course, that the reason why structural changes of this sort arising out of changing conditions in demand reduce the share of trade accruing to one country is because this country does not adjust its industrial structure quickly enough to the changing conditions. Were rapid adjustments forthcoming, the share of trade would decrease much less and conceivably might even increase. Nevertheless, the fact remains that economic adjustments entail a cost and it does not necessarily follow that a country would be better off if it did seek to adjust quickly in order to maintain its market share. Moreover, the incidence of structural changes in demand is most unlikely to be the same for all countries; some are likely to find the change more unfavourable than others. Thus, the burden of adjustment as well as the time required to allow adjustment to take place may differ greatly for different countries. Consequently, even though an ability and willingness to adjust to new circumstances may allay some of the effects of changes in demand, it is still important to consider whether, in general, changes in demand have been such as to favour an increase or decrease in a country's share of trade and to gain some impression of the relative importance of this factor.

Perhaps the single most impressive characteristic of Canadian demand since 1926 has been its rapid growth. From 1926 to 1956 total expenditure on Canada's gross national product increased about six times when valued in current dollars and over three times when valued in constant dollars. This growth has been accompanied by some change in the proportion of total expenditure forthcoming from various sectors of demand, as indicated by Table VI.

TABLE VI

PERCENTAGE DISTRIBUTION OF GROSS NATIONAL EXPENDITURE, 1926-8, 1937-9, 1954-6
(Current dollars)

	1926-8 average	1937-9 average	1954-6 average
Personal expenditure	70	73	64
Government expenditure	10	12	18
Business gross fixed capital formation	15	11	20
Inventory change	3	2	1
Exports	30	27	21
Imports	—30	—25	—24

SOURCE: Dominion Bureau of Statistics, *National Accounts, Income and Expenditure, 1926-1956*, pp. 26-7.

The patterns of personal expenditure in the late twenties and in the early fifties are shown in Table VII. During these thirty years expenditure (in constant dollars) on food, shelter, clothing, and the category including fuel and a variety of services, in total, decreased about 10 per cent in relative importance. This was compensated for mainly by increased expenditures on tobacco, drink, and automobiles. Classified in another way, the figures show that expenditure (in current dollars) on services and non-durable goods decreased in relative importance at the same time that the share of personal expenditure on durable goods increased about 5 per cent.

The composition of investment expenditure in selected years since 1926 is shown in Table VIII. The figures indicate that well over half of Canadian investment expenditure during this period has been for construction. Furthermore, investment expenditure on repairs and maintenance has generally exceeded one-fifth, and at times two-fifths, of total spending. The figures also reveal that the four most important sectors (utilities, manufacturing, housing, and government) have in most years since 1926 accounted for between 70 and 75 per cent of total investment. Finally, investment in primary mining has increased more rapidly than in any other sector, although the size of investment in the primary mining sector remains relatively small.

Two questions follow naturally from this brief review of the pattern of Canadian demand. How large an area of Canadian demand might be regarded as largely inaccessible to British supplies; and how has the size of this area of

TABLE VII

PERCENTAGE DISTRIBUTION OF PERSONAL EXPENDITURE, 1926-9, 1952-5

	1926-9 average	1952-5 average
A. *In constant dollars*		
Food	30	27
Tobacco and drink	5	9
Clothing and personal furnishings	14	12
Fuel, electricity, gas, telephone, household supplies, insurance, moving expense, repairs to furniture and appliances, domestic service, home furnishing	10	8
Furniture and home appliances	4	4
Shelter	13	10
Purchase and operation of automobile	7	11
Other transportation	2	2
Personal and medical care	6	7
Miscellaneous	9	10
B. *In current dollars*		
Durable goods	8	13
major durable goods*	7	11
miscellaneous durable goods	1	2
Non-Durable goods	54	52
Services	38	35

SOURCES: Dominion Bureau of Statistics, *National Accounts, Income and Expenditure 1926-1956*, pp. 88-9; Royal Commission on Canada's Economic Prospects, *Consumption Expenditures in Canada*, prepared by David W. Slater, p. 4.
* Including house trailers, new and used automobiles, home furnishings, furniture and appliances, radios and television sets.

TABLE VIII

PRIVATE AND PUBLIC INVESTMENT IN CANADA, CURRENT DOLLARS
(Percentage of total annual investment)

	1926	1929	1932	1938	1948	1957
A. *By industry*						
Agriculture, fishing	9	8	7	10	10	6
Primary woods operation	1	1	1	1	1	1
Primary mining	2	3	2	4	3	6
Construction industry	2	2	1	1	2	3
Manufacturing	20	21	14	14	20	18
Utilities	27	27	26	23	22	26
Trade, finance, and commercial services	7	9	8	8	8	8
Housing	18	14	15	17	18	15
Institutions	4	3	5	3	4	4
All other, mostly government*	10	12	21	19	12	13
B. *By type of investment*						
Construction	56	57	62	58	55	63
Machinery and equipment	44	43	38	42	45	37
Total new investment	65	72	55	60	68	78
Total repairs and maintenance	35	28	45	40	32	22

SOURCES: Department of Trade and Commerce, *Private and Public Investment in Canada 1926-1951*, Tables 15, 19-23, 26, 41, 66, 70, and 73; *Public and Private Investment in Canada, Outlook 1958*, Table I, p. 11.
* Residual.

demand changed since the twenties? The answers to these questions are very roughly indicated by Table IX. It has been assumed that British suppliers are unable to cater to Canadian demand for food, services, fuel, and major durable goods (house trailers, new and used automobiles, home furnishings, furniture, appliances, radio and television sets). To the extent that this assumption overstates the share of the market that tends to be inaccessible to Britain, it is par-

TABLE IX

SOME CANADIAN MARKETS CLASSED AS RELATIVELY INACCESSIBLE TO BRITISH SUPPLIERS
($ millions)

	1926-7 average	1937-8 average	1948-9 average	1955-6 average
Personal expenditure				
Food	964	970	2855	4369
Services	1454	1422	3285	6520
Major durable goods	241	273	858	2067
Fuel	134	133	275	389
Sub-total	2793	2798	7273	13345
As % of total personal expenditure	75	72	69	74
Government expenditure	510	643	1962	5023
Business investment in fixed assets				
New residential construction	203	156	702	1452
New non-residential construction	270	179	868	2199
Sub-total	473	335	1570	3651
As % of total fixed investment	62	55	56	62
Total	3776	3776	10805	22019
Total above, as % of total personal, government, and business expenditure	76	73	71	76

SOURCE: Dominion Bureau of Statistics, *National Accounts, Income and Expenditure, 1926-1956*, Tables 2 and 47.

tially at least compensated for by the omission of any adjustment for personal expenditure on cotton textiles, drink and tobacco of domestic origin, and the value added locally to products imported from the United Kingdom. All government expenditure, the second major sector of demand, has been included in Table IX. Although a portion of government demand may be open to British value added locally to products imported from the United Kingdom. All government expenditure is on defence requirements which for strategic and other reasons are mainly met by North American suppliers. Further, non-military government expenditure consists largely of expenditure on services and construction. In addition, as indicated in chapter v below, governments generally tend to favour domestic over foreign producers when making their purchases. As for investment, the third major sector of Canadian demand, it has been assumed that all expenditure on construction is beyond the reach of British suppliers. This assumption also is too stringent; but again the bias thus introduced is in part compensated for by the fact that no allowance has been made for the portion of the market for machinery and equipment that is relatively inaccessible to British suppliers or for the value added domestically to machinery and equipment imported from Britain.

In view of the arbitrary nature of these assumptions, it is clear that Table IX gives only a very rough impression of the proportion of the Canadian market that might be regarded as comparatively inaccessible to British supplies. With this qualification, the figures suggest two main conclusions. First, about three-quarters of the Canadian market comprising personal, government, and business expenditure (excluding inventories) might be viewed as more or less inaccessible to British goods. Secondly, this proportion of the market apparently did not increase from 1926 to 1956; considering the bias in the assumptions, it probably decreased. As a share of gross national expenditure, total Canadian imports decreased from 29 per cent in 1926-7 to 25 per cent in 1955-6. On the basis of these figures, then, it would seem that Britain's share of the Canadian market has not been greatly undermined because of faster-than-average growth in those sectors of Canadian demand that are less accessible to British supplies.[1]

So much for Canadian demand generally. Changes in the pattern of Canada's import demand over the years can be clarified with the help of the various classifications of imports. Table X shows Canadian imports classified by component material. It will be noted that in 1957 almost half of Canada's imports consisted of metallic products, about one-fifth of farm and wood products, a further fifth of non-metallic minerals and chemicals, and the remainder of fibre products and miscellaneous goods. The figures also show changes in the relative importance of these various categories of goods. In 1926, farm, wood, and fibre products together accounted for about 50 per cent of imports; in 1957 these products made up about one-quarter of Canadian imports. During the same period imports of metal products, chemicals and miscellaneous goods have grown substantially

TABLE X

CANADIAN IMPORTS CLASSIFIED BY COMPONENT MATERIAL*
(Percentage of total value of annual imports)

	1926	1929	1932	1935	1938	1948	1951	1954	1957
Agricultural & vegetable products	22	18	22	21	18	13	13	13	12
Food	12	11	14	13	12	10	9	10	10
Non-food	10	8	9	8	7	3	4	3	2
Animal & products	5	6	4	4	4	3	3	2	2
Fibres & textiles	19	16	15	16	14	13	12	8	7
Wood, wood products, paper	5	5	6	4	4	3	3	4	4
Iron & its products	20	27	17	19	26	30	33	32	38
Non-ferrous metals & products	5	6	6	5	6	6	7	9	9
Non-metallic minerals & products	15	13	18	20	17	23	17	15	14
Chemicals	3	3	5	6	5	5	5	5	5
Miscellaneous goods	6	5	8	6	6	4	7	12	9

SOURCES: Dominion Bureau of Statistics, *Canada Year Book*, annual issues; *Review of Foreign Trade*, 1957.
* Minor discrepancies due to rounding.

more important, and imports of non-metallic mineral products (including petroleum products) have remained of about the same relative importance.

Table XI shows imports classified by degree of manufacture. According to these figures, Canadian imports of manufactured products have increased from about two-thirds of total imports prior to World War II to about three-quarters at present; and imports of raw materials and semi-fabricated products have decreased during this period from one-third to one-quarter of total imports. Imports of raw materials and semi-fabricated products from the United Kingdom have, of course, remained relatively small during the past thirty years. The relative importance of imports of raw and semi-fabricated products from the United States has decreased from a quarter to an eight of total imports at the

TABLE XI

CANADIAN IMPORTS CLASSIFIED BY DEGREE OF MANUFACTURE*
(Percentage of total value of annual imports)

	Total	U.S.	U.K.	Other
Raw materials:				
1928-9 average	24	19	1	4
1938-9	27	18	2	8
1948-9	26	16	2	9
1954-5	19	10	—	9
Partially manufactured:				
1928-9 average	9	5	1	3
1938-9	9	3	2	4
1948-9	7	2	1	4
1954-5	5	2	1	2
Fully manufactured:				
1928-9 average	67	43	14	10
1938-9	64	41	15	9
1948-9	66	51	10	6
1954-5	75	61	8	7

SOURCE: Dominion Bureau of Statistics, *Trade of Canada*, 1955, vol. I, p. 94.
* Minor discrepancies due to rounding.

same time that imports of these goods from other areas have increased in relative importance. Imports of manufactured goods from Britain—accounting for most of Canada's imports from Britain—have decreased significantly in relative importance since the twenties and imports of manufactured goods from the United States have become more important.

Canadian imports are classified by end use in Table XII. Some of the main points emerging from the figures can be summarized as follows:

(*a*) Consumer goods, including automobiles and parts, accounted for about 30 per cent of Canadian imports in 1957, fuels and lubricants about 10 per cent, industrial materials about 25 per cent, and investment goods about 33 per cent.[2]

TABLE XII

CANADIAN IMPORTS CLASSIFIED BY END USE*
(Percentage of total value of imports)

	Total			From U.K.			From U.S.		
	1929	1937	1955	1929	1937	1955	1929	1937	1955
Food, drink, tobacco	19	17	12	4	3	—	7	5	6
Furs, hides, skins, leather, textile products	18	17	9	6	7	2	8	6	5
Capital goods and consumer durables	24	23	40	1	2	3	22	20	36
Industrial metals for manufacture of durables	15	16	12	1	3	1	12	10	8
Chemicals	3	5	6	—	1	—	2	3	5
Fuels and lubricants	11	13	11	—	1	—	9	10	5
Miscellaneous goods, mainly for consumers	10	10	11	2	2	1	7	7	9
	100	100	100	15	19	8	69	61	73

SOURCE: Royal Commission on Canada's Economic Prospects, *Canadian Imports*, prepared by David W. Slater, Appendix D, Tables III, IV.
* Minor discrepancies due to rounding.

(*b*) During the past thirty years, imports of foods, textile products, and industrial materials have generally decreased in relative importance while imports of durable goods and chemicals have increased greatly in relative importance. Imports of fuels and lubricants and miscellaneous consumer goods have remained of about the same relative importance.

(*c*) British exports to Canada prior to World War II were highly concentrated in those sectors of Canada's import market which have become less important or remained of about the same relative importance. United States exports to Canada, on the other hand, were more highly concentrated in those sectors of the import market which have expanded most rapidly.

(*d*) In the static and declining sectors of Canada's import market, British trade has decreased more in relative importance than United States trade.

(*e*) In those sectors of Canadian import demand which have increased in relative importance, Britain's relative position remains small even though it has increased substantially and has become somewhat more significant by comparison with that of the United States.

To what extent is the change in Britain's share of the Canadian market explained by changes in Canadian demand, and to what extent does it reflect the substitution of one foreign supplier by another? The summary figures presented in Table XIII indicate that the first of these possibilities has indeed been operative. About 80 per cent of Britain's exports to Canada in the late twenties, classified by end use, was in those commodity groups that have expanded less than the average for all imports, about 20 per cent in the group that has expanded at the average rate or more than average. The corresponding figures for the United States are 54 and 46 per cent respectively. A similar pattern is evident when Canadian imports are classified by component material:

TABLE XIII

INCIDENCE OF CHANGES IN DEMAND

A. *Classified by component material*

	Percentage change in Canadian imports			Percentage of imports in 1929* from	
	1929*-38*	1938*-48	1948-57	U.K.	U.S.
Total	—37	230	113	100	100
Agricultural & vegetable products	—37	139	86		
Animals & products	—58	180	47	73	32
Fibres & textiles	—47	222	17		
Wood & products	—42	115	207		
Iron & products	—40	274	173		
Non-ferrous metals & products	—38	231	211		
Chemicals	—2	221	148	21	52
Miscellaneous goods	—28	134	355		
Non-metallic minerals & products	—18	343	28	6	16

B. *Classified by degree of manufacture*

	Percentage change in Canadian imports		Percentage of imports in 1929* from	
	1929*-38*	1938*-55	U.K.	U.S.
Total	—37	490	100	100
Raw materials	—23	290		
Partially manufactured	—27	233	11	34
Fully manufactured	—42	615	89	66

C. *Classified by end use*

	Percentage change in Canadian imports		Percentage of imports in 1929 from	
	1929-37	1937-55	U.K.	U.S.
Total	—38	482	100	100
Food, drink, tobacco	—43	294		
Furs, hides, leather, textile products	—42	218		
Industrial metals for manufacture of durables	—33	322	79	54
Fuels and lubricants	—28	391		
Miscellaneous goods, mainly for consumers	—27	556		
Capital goods and consumer durables	—42	932	21	46
Chemicals	—7	597		

SOURCES: Dominion Bureau of Statistics, *Trade of Canada, Canada Year Book, Review of Foreign Trade,* various issues; Royal Commission on Canada's Economic Prospects, *Canadian Imports,* Appendix D, Table III.

* Fiscal year ending March 31.

British trade has been concentrated more heavily than United States trade in those classifications that have expanded least. On the surface at least, the picture is considerably different when imports are classified by degree of manufacture. In these terms, British trade has been very heavily concentrated in the sector of trade that has expanded most—finished manufactures. This classification is very broad, however, and, as indicated below, much of the increase has occurred in lines of products where Britain's share in the twenties was relatively small.

In order to see beyond these aggregative figures, Table XIV has been prepared showing the fate of the most important Canadian imports from Britain during the mid-twenties. It will be noted that Canadian imports of many of these items have increased less than Canadian imports generally. This is particularly true of such items as textiles, fibres, leather, sugar, distilled spirits, tea,

TABLE XIV

Changes in Value during the Past Thirty Years in Some of the Most Important Canadian Imports from Britain in 1924-7*

Rank 1924-7	Commodity	Imports 1924-7* average $ million		Percentage change 1924-7* to 1954-6	
		From U.K.	Total	From U.K.	Total
1	Wool products, manufactured	31.0	37.3	56	73
2	Distilled spirits	19.8	22.2	—54	—28
3	Cotton fabrics	15.0	26.1	—64	105
4	Rolling mill products	7.1	42.8	87	260
5	Wool, raw and manufactured	6.5	10.6	140	204
6	Miscellaneous textiles	6.3	25.1	43	116
7	Hard fibres and products	5.6	14.6	—5	55
8	Tea	4.9	12.2	—57	103
9	Chemicals (ex. drugs)	3.3	24.9	479	829
10	Non-farm machinery	3.8	31.8	824	1425
11	Anthracite coal	3.1	35.8	3	—13
12	Pottery and china	2.9	4.2	293	271
13	Synthetic fibres	2.6	4.6	62	974
14	Silk and manufactures	2.5	24.3	—84	—69
15	Leather and products	2.0	7.8	280	135
16	Cotton yarns and threads	1.5	4.2	200	114
17	Books, printed matter	1.8	12.3	78	493
18	Electrical apparatus	1.4	15.3	1507	1407
19	Containers	1.3	2.9	138	210
20	Glassware	1.3	7.5	408	475
21	Paper	1.2	9.8	58	439
22	Drugs and medical preparations	1.1	2.9	100	769
23	Hardware	1.0	3.6	230	472
24	Sugar and products	1.0	43.1	400	53
Total, all imports		158.1	912.1	169	430
Above commodities as percentage of total imports from area		81	47		
Above commodities as percentage of total imports		14	47		

Sources: Dominion Bureau of Statistics, *Canada Year Book, Trade of Canada*, various issues.
* Fiscal years ending March 31.

rolling mill products, pottery and chinaware, and coal—commodities that together accounted for about 70 per cent of Canadian imports from Britain during
this period. Table XIV also reveals that structural changes are not a complete
explanation of the decline of Britain's relative position in the Canadian market.
Imports from Britain of some of the products listed have lagged behind imports from other areas. Accordingly, even in these traditional commodity lines,
Britain's share of Canadian imports has been decreasing. The conclusion follows that not only has the sector of the Canadian market on which Britain has
traditionally been most dependent expanded less than other sectors, but also
within this traditional sector British sales have not kept pace with such market
expansion as has occurred.[3]

Increases in imports from Britain in those sectors of the Canadian import market
that have expanded most are shown in Table XV. Canadian imports from
Britain in some of these commodity lines have increased greatly—in some instances
substantially more than imports from other countries. Most of these larger in-

TABLE XV

SOME CANADIAN IMPORTS THAT HAVE INCREASED MORE THAN AVERAGE SINCE THE TWENTIES
($ millions)

	1924-7* average		1954-6 average		Percentage increase	
	From U.K.	Total	From U.K.	Total	From U.K.	Total
Synthetic fibres and manufactures	2.6	4.6	4.2	49.4	62	974
Books, printed matter	1.8	12.3	3.2	73.0	78	493
Aluminum and manufactures	.2	4.3	5.8	50.0	2800	1063
Precious metals	.7	2.2	19.0	35.6	2614	1518
Electrical apparatus	1.4	15.3	22.5	230.5	1507	1407
Petroleum products	.1	42.8	.1	380.6	—	790
Farm machinery	.1	12.6	4.3	184.5	4200	1364
Non-farm machinery	3.8	31.8	35.1	484.8	824	1425
Tubes, pipes, and fittings	.4	3.5	12.1	77.7	2925	2120
Engines and boilers	.6	11.0	13.6	111.2	2167	811
Vehicles and parts	.5	39.2	28.6	398.8	5620	917
Tools and hand implements	.2	2.0	3.0	27.7	1400	1485
Hardware and cutlery	1.1	3.6	3.3	20.6	200	472
Stamped and coated products	.2	1.7	.4	13.4	100	688
Rolling mill products	7.1	42.8	13.3	154.0	87	260
Aircraft and parts (ex. engines)	—	—	8.2	109.9		
Scientific equipment	.2	3.5	1.8	37.6	800	974
Chemicals and drugs	4.4	27.8	21.3	256.5	384	823
Above commodities as percentage of total imports from area	16	29	47	56		

SOURCE: Dominion Bureau of Statistics, *Canada Year Book, Trade of Canada*, various issues.
* Fiscal years ending March 31.

creases, however, reflect the fact that imports from Britain during the twenties
were very small; and despite the increases that have occurred Britain's share
of Canadian imports of many of these products remains comparatively small.
In commodity lines where imports from Britain were more significant during
the twenties, the increase in imports from Britain during the past thirty years
generally compares less favourably.

The incidence of changes in the pattern of Canadian demand on British sales in Canada can be more precisely indicated by asking oneself the following hypothetical questions:

(a) What would Britain's share of Canadian imports now be assuming (i) the proportion of imports supplied by Britain in particular product lines to have changed as in fact it has since the twenties and (ii) the pattern of Canadian import demand to have remained unchanged?

(b) What would Britain's share of Canadian imports now be assuming (i) the proportion of imports supplied by Britain in particular product lines to have remained unchanged from the twenties and (ii) the pattern of Canadian demand to have changed as in fact it has?[4]

An attempt has been made to answer these questions statistically using 1929 and 1955 for purposes of comparison. One difficulty in carrying out this exercise stems from the qualitative changes in various product categories since 1929. A further complication arises from changes in the statistical classifications between 1929 and 1955. Moreover, to make the task manageable it has been necessary to rely upon trade classifications incorporating some degree of aggregation. Subject to these qualifications, the estimates derived are as shown

TABLE XVI

PROPORTION OF CANADIAN IMPORTS SUPPLIED BY BRITAIN, 1929 AND 1955

	1929 %	1955 %	Decrease 1929-55
Actual	15.1	8.5	6.6
Hypothetical			
(a) assuming the 1929 pattern of imports unchanged	15.1	11.5	3.6
(b) assuming Britain's 1929 share of particular product lines unchanged	15.1	11.3	3.7

SOURCE: Derived from Royal Commission on Canada's Economic Prospects, *Canadian Imports*, Appendix D, Table IV.

in Table XVI. The figures suggest that about half of the decrease in Britain's share of Canadian imports from 1929 to 1955 is explained by changes in the pattern of Canadian demand and about half by a reduction in Britain's share of particular product lines.

Thus, although the change in relative importance of the various products purchased by Canadians has been an important factor, it is not a complete explanation of Britain's decreasing share in the Canadian market. Apart from the possibility that some of the incidence of changes in the pattern of demand might have been avoided by adjusting to them more quickly, the evidence indicates that even had there been no change in the broad pattern of Canadian demand, Britain's market share would still have decreased significantly.

There is also the question of the degree to which the decrease in Britain's share of the Canadian market reflects the general decline of the United Kingdom as an entrepot for certain primary products. Various writers have recognized that Britain's entrepot trade has become less important over the years in response to many factors such as new developments in transportation and communications, changing economic and political alignments in the world, and the impact of foreign investment and economic development on primary producing areas.[5] For a number of reason it is difficult to say how significant this decline has been in terms of British exports to Canada. The figures shown in Table XVII suggest that it has been a factor contributing to the decrease in Britain's share of Canadian imports. In this connection, it is also noteworthy that during the twenties Britain supplied about 75 per cent of all Commonwealth exports to Canada and that this ratio has decreased to an average of

TABLE XVII

DECLINE IN BRITAIN'S ENTREPOT TRADE

	1927-28	1937-38	1956-57*
A. Indexes: (1927-28 = 100)			
Total U.K. Exports	100	69	453
Total U.K. Re-Exports	100	56	115
U.K. Exports to Canada	100	73	545
U.K. Re-Exports to Canada	100	49	193
B. Canadian Imports of Certain Products:			
		(% share imported from U.K.)	
Cocoa	18	19	4
Coffee	8	7	2
Spices	39	35	12
Tea	45	32	10
Hard Fibres	43	45	24
Raw Wool	49	27	50

SOURCES: Board of Trade, *Annual Statement Relating to the Trade of the United Kingdom,* various issues; Dominion Bureau of Statistics, *Canada Year Book, Trade of Canada,* various issues.
  * Incl. Newfoundland.

less than 70 per cent in recent years. All things considered, however, the decrease in Britain's entrepot trade has probably been a relatively minor factor contributing to the decrease in Britain's share of Canadian imports during the period under consideration. For one thing, in the late twenties total British exports of primary and semi-processed products to Canada accounted for only 2 per cent of Canadian imports. The comparable figure recently has been one per cent. Only a small part of this decrease of one per cent can be ascribed to the decrease in Britain's entrepot trade in primary products; about half, for instance, is accounted for by the decreased importance of British coal exports to Canada. Furthermore, as indicated by Table XI, Canada's import demand for raw and semi-processed materials has grown significantly less during the past thirty years than Canadian demand for manufactured products.

From the foregoing description of the pattern of Canadian imports it is apparent that, for one reason or another, Britain's ability to supply some of the goods that Canada imports is obviously very limited. This is especially evident in those instances where Britain herself depends entirely or to a very important degree upon foreign imports. Any attempt to determine how large a proportion of Canadian imports might be regarded as beyond reach as far as Britain is concerned is necessarily rather arbitrary. It may nevertheless be helpful to try to arrive at some notion of the approximate order of magnitude in question.

Among those Canadian imports which, because of limited resources and productive capacity, Britain can hardly be expected to supply one would include almost all agricultural, vegetable, animal, and wood products. (Some significant exceptions within these categories are preserved fruits, confectionery, bakery products, alcoholic beverages, leather and its products, books, and special papers.) One would also include most raw natural fibres, of which the most important are raw cotton and raw wool. For the same reason, most raw and semi-processed non-ferrous metal and non-metallic mineral products would be included (for example, bauxite, petroleum, base metals, sulphur, and certain stone products). Apart from these products, one would probably also include most parts and components that are imported to supply Canadian industries manufacturing American type products and to provide repairs for such products sold in the past. The single most important item here is automobile parts which in 1956 accounted for about 5 per cent of total Canadian imports. In addition there are certain other products such as air conditioning and heating equipment for houses where British production seems limited. Finally, one might include various "non-commercial" items such as settler's effects, tourist purchases, and goods for diplomatic missions.

On this basis the trade statistics indicate that at present some 40 to 50 per cent of Canadian imports, by value, can be dismissed from consideration as far as British export trade with Canada is concerned, particularly in the short run. It is also apparent from the figures that this ratio has not changed greatly since the twenties; to the extent that it has changed it may have become slightly smaller. Thus it does not seem that Britain's share of the market has been impaired because those sectors of trade in which Britain has less chance of participating have become larger.

Subsequent chapters will be mainly concerned with the 50 to 60 per cent, approximately, of Canadian imports from which Britain is less obviously excluded. This sector comprises mostly manufactured products, especially textiles, chemicals of various kinds, and all types of metal manufactures, machinery and equipment.

2. Foreign Investment

When foreign investment is on the scale that it has been in Canada during the present century, its influence necessarily permeates all sectors of the economy in varying degree. Consequently, it is important to consider the role that foreign investment has played in shaping Canada's import demand, since in many cases foreign investment has been a root cause influencing developments at the surface level.

The prominent role it has played in Canada's economic development is clearly apparent from Table XVIII. Although the greater part of Canadian investment has been domestically financed, the proportion financed by foreigners has been very high. Moreover, the relative importance of foreign investment has generally increased since 1945; and in 1956-7 it accounted for a larger share of net capital formation than at any time since World War I.

TABLE XVIII

FOREIGN FINANCING OF TOTAL CANADIAN INVESTMENT
(Percentages)

	1926-30	1946-9	1950-5	1956-7
Net use of foreign resources as				
Percentage of gross capital formation	n.a.	—	17	27
Percentage of net capital formation	about 25	—11	19	33
Direct foreign financing as				
Percentage of gross capital formation	n.a.	19	25	32
Percentage of net capital formation	about 50	24	32	42

SOURCES: Dominion Bureau of Statistics, *The Canadian Balance of International Payments,* 1957, p. 31; Royal Commission on Canada's Economic Prospects, *Canada-United States Economic Relations,* prepared by Irving Brecher and S. S. Reisman, p. 96.

The broad pattern of foreign investment in Canada is shown by Table XIX. Since 1930 the value of United States investment in Canada has increased from about three-fifths to about three-quarters of total foreign investment. Britain's share, on the other hand, has decreased from over one-third to less than one-fifth. The substantial increase in United States direct investment, relative to indirect investment, is also apparent. At present more than half of this direct investment is located in manufacturing and the petroleum, natural gas, mining,

TABLE XIX

LONG-TERM FOREIGN INVESTMENT IN CANADA
(Percentage of total foreign investment)

	U.K.			U.S.		
	1930	1945	1956	1930	1945	1956
Government securities	6	2	1	16	20	12
Manufacturing—total	4	4	5	15	19	23
—direct	2	2	4	12	17	20
Petroleum & natural gas	—	—	—	2	2	13
Other mining & smelting	1	1	1	3	4	7
Public utilities	19	13	6	18	15	6
Merchandising	1	1	1	2	2	3
Financial institutions	3	3	2	3	4	6
Other enterprises	—	—	—	1	1	1
Miscellaneous	2	1	1	1	2	3
Total investment	36	25	17	61	70	76
direct	5	5	7	26	32	47
indirect	31	20	10	35	38	28

SOURCE: Dominion Bureau of Statistics, *The Canadian Balance of International Payments,* 1957, pp. 48-9.

and smelting industries. In addition, the decline in the relative importance of British investment is almost entirely accounted for by the relative decrease in British investment in public utility and government securities. This largely explains why most of the decrease in the relative importance of British investment in Canada reflects a decrease in indirect investment. Finally, the figures demonstrate the great difference in size between United States and United Kingdom direct investment in Canada. This difference is greatest in the manufacturing, petroleum, and mining categories; it is smallest in the categories of public utilities, merchandising, financial institutions, other enterprises, and miscellaneous. Total United States direct investment in Canada in 1956 was about seven times greater than Britain's direct investment.

Because of its qualitative features, foreign investment in Canada exercises a greater influence on the Canadian economy than is indicated simply by its quantitative importance. Two qualitative aspects are especially significant. First, much of the non-resident investment in Canada, particularly United States investment, is concentrated in strategic sectors of the economy—notably manufacturing and resource development. The degree to which these sectors are controlled abroad is shown in some detail in Table XXXIV below. Secondly, the inflow of direct investment from the United States has been accompanied by a particularly rich inflow of United States technology, risk-bearing, and entrepreneurial talent. These characteristics together with the strategic location of much of the investment have contributed greatly to the growth of United States investment in Canada during the past thirty years.

How has foreign investment in Canada affected Canada's import demand? Other sections of this study examine some of the manifestations of foreign investment in detail. Suffice it to say here that there is little doubt that the heavy inflow of investment and its accompaniment of technology, risk-bearing, and entrepreneurship from the United States have considerably increased Canadian demand for United States imports over what this demand would have been had (a) United States investment in Canada consisted less predominantly of direct investment and (b) had the investment been of domestic or non-American origin. In the first place, the high proportion of United States direct investment has greatly enhanced Canadian imports of United States techniques, equipment and engineering advice, adherence to United States engineering standards and measurements, and familiarity with United States products and suppliers. In addition, the Canadian market has come more and more to demand United States standards of distribution, especially in such matters as delivery dates, the ready availability of spare parts and service, packaging, and sales promotion. Moreover, given the present importance of United States investment in Canada and its reliance upon imports from the United States, a large replacement demand for United States type of products is now deeply entrenched in the Canadian market. Further, the heavy flow of foreign investment, technology, risk-bearing, and entrepreneurship into strategic areas of the Canadian economy has served to make the Canadian market more competitive. As a consequence, sellers who have been at some disadvantage with respect to prices and other market variables have found the Canadian market more difficult than would otherwise have been the case and a higher premium has been placed on the ability to adjust quickly in response to changing conditions. Also, Canada's economic development fostered by foreign investment has increased the competition between local production and imports.

One important reason for these and other influences on Canadian demand is that United States investment has frequently resulted in some element of common control over certain important segments of United States and Canadian business. This, combined with various other factors such as the physical proximity of the two countries and the similarity of preferences, has resulted in a close integration of production and distribution facilities between the two countries, much closer than has been usual in the international economy. One consequence of this economic integration has been to augment the exchange of goods at various stages of production—for example, the export of Canadian raw and semi-processed materials and the re-export of these from the United States in the form of parts and components for assembly in Canada or as finished goods.[6] It is noteworthy that about one-eighth (depending upon one's classification) of Canadian imports consists of parts and components, both for investment and consumer purposes; and most of these come from the United States. Moreover, the trade figures indicate that those sectors of investment goods imports that have grown most rapidly have in many cases been closely related to areas where United States investment has also been growing most rapidly.

Another consequence of the integration between the two countries has been to increase specialization in the production of final goods—for example, Canada produces and exports to the United States certain kinds of farm machinery and relies upon United States production, in part or wholly, for other types of farm machinery. In addition, because of the long distances along the Canada—United States border the same goods may be exchanged between the two countries on an inter-regional basis—one region along the border can be more economically supplied from a Canadian plant while another region can be more economically supplied from an American plant. Admittedly, integration and the specialization associated with it reflects a variety of natural economic forces and would probably have proceeded a considerable distance even in the absence of United States investment. It is certain, however, that the process has been carried further as a result of United States investment in Canada and the co-ordinated control frequently arising from this investment over business in both countries. Business enterprises operating in both countries to some degree tend to be organized and run on a continental rather than a national basis and specialization is reflected in their internal administration and organization. The degree to which businesses are organized on a continental basis, of course, varies greatly and is influenced by many factors such as commercial policy and transportation costs.

Because of these and other considerations, it is generally agreed that the flow of investment from the United States to Canada has increased the share of Canadian imports purchased in the United States. It is interesting to compare statistically changes in Britain's relative importance as a supplier of capital and as a supplier of goods to Canada. In both respects Britain has become substantially less important, as shown in Table XX. And although it may be appropriate to recall the logical fallacy of *post hoc, ergo propter hoc*, it never-

TABLE XX

British Long-Term Investment in Canada and British Exports to Canada

	1926	1939	1948	1954	1956
British investment in Canada ($ mm.)					
Manufacturing	234	257	340	657	840*
Merchandising	49	55	76	136	158
British investment as percentage of total long-term foreign investment					
Manufacturing	20	18	15	15	
Merchandising	33	29	27	24	23
British exports to Canada					
1926 = 100 (value)	100	69	182	238	294
Percentage of total Canadian imports	16	15	11	10	8

Sources: Dominion Bureau of Statistics, *Review of Foreign Trade*, 1957, p. 49; *Canadian Balance of International Payments*, 1957, p. 48; *Canada's International Investment Position, 1926-54*, p. 78-9.

* Rough estimate only.

theless seems reasonable that the decrease in Britain's importance as a supplier of capital to Canada has not been unrelated to the decrease in the proportion of Canadian imports purchased from Britain.

Granting this general conclusion, one must immediately add that the importance of United States investment as an explanation of the increased share of Canadian imports purchased in the United States can be exaggerated. United States investment has contributed greatly to the high rate of growth in total Canadian demand. Admittedly, because of the nature of United States investment in Canada, part of this increase in demand has perhaps been virtually predestined to fall into the hands of United States suppliers for reasons already indicated. Much of it, however, has been free to satisfy itself from any supplier satisfactorily catering to it. Even in the case of United States subsidiaries, it does not follow that they must necessarily rely upon American and Canadian suppliers. Insofar as these subsidiaries are guided by principles of profit maximization—and most United States direct investment in Canada has been made by large profit-conscious companies—their business decisions will be based on satisfactorily meeting requirements at the lowest cost and there will be little consideration of nationality as such. In addition, the growth of United States direct investment has to some extent resulted in a substitution of Canadian production for imports, (for example, of fuels and consumer durables such as automobiles). The incidence of substitution has probably fallen more heavily on imports from the United States than on imports from Britain. Accordingly this has been a factor tending to increase Britain's share of Canadian imports. Finally, the influx of United States investment and the establishment of United States subsidiaries in Canada has been accompanied by some artificial restrictions on United States-Canadian trade through tariff restrictions—imposed to aid infant industries such as the electrical and automotive industries mainly controlled in the United States—as well as through patent-licensing arrangements, market-sharing agreements, and interlocking financial and administrative relationships.[7]

These considerations, then, suggest some reasons why United States investment in Canada may not have reacted as adversely on Britain's share of Canadian imports as is sometimes claimed. It remains to add that if one considers the level of British exports to Canada—in many respects more important than the share of imports—it is certain that British exports to Canada at present are greater than they would have been had total investment, including foreign investment, in Canada been significantly less than in fact it was. Investment, including foreign investment, has been a primary factor accounting for the rapid growth in Canadian demand during the past thirty years.

CHAPTER THREE

PRICES AND COSTS

ACCORDING to elementary economic principles based on assumtions of pure and perfect competition the flow of international trade is determined in the first instance by differences in money costs and prices. In such a competitive world both the composition of trade and its geographic pattern faithfully reflect the gravitational forces engendered through price incentives. The real world is, of course, more complicated and many factors other than price must be taken into account. Nevertheless, even though price may not always be as important as sometimes stated or implied, the price variable undeniably can be and frequently is important. Hence, no one can hope to analyse the question in hand adequately without examining Britain's competitive price-cost position vis-à-vis the Canadian market.

Despite the unique place that price holds in the history of economic theory and analysis, an investigation of comparative prices continues to be fraught with a host of conceptual and statistical problems. For a number of reasons it is exceedingly difficult to obtain reliable price information; and when obtainable the information is exceedingly difficult to interpret. Accordingly, it is necessary to draw on as wide an assortment of information as possible in the hope that the weight of evidence will compensate to some extent for the obvious deficiencies in each single piece.

A comparison of prices may take the form of a comparison of price changes over time or, alternatively, a comparison of absolute price levels. If one wishes to explain changes in the flow of trade one is principally interested in relative price changes. Moreover, a comparison of price changes, as indicated by price index numbers, has a number of important advantages over absolute price comparisons: for example, information is available on a more comprehensive basis and is more reliable; problems relating to the comparability of goods are rather less formidable; and relative price movements are somewhat less difficult to interpret. At the same time, a major limitation of this approach—aside from a variety of statistical problems such as weighting, the comparability of the series, and so on—is that no inferences can be drawn about differences in price levels. And it is price differentials—account having been taken of various supplementary costs such as transportation, insurance, tariffs, and sales taxes—that are important in influencing the direction in which trade will flow. Hence a comparison of price index numbers might show that a country's relative price position had improved; but in absolute terms many of its goods might still be at a considerable, though diminished, price disadvantage. Since, therefore, each approach has certain points in its favour and neither is entirely satisfactory by itself, both have been here pursued.

1. COMPARATIVE PRICE CHANGES

In comparing price changes in different countries over an extended period of time a wide variety of well-known statistical problems present themselves. For example, indexes relating to different countries are bound to differ in composition and structure: the weighting is sure to be different, and no two series will be found relating to exactly the same basket of goods. Moreover, during the past thirty-five years there have been appreciable shifts in the relative importance of various products included in each series as well as changes in the nature of the products themselves. Also, when considered for long periods of time during which large price fluctuations occurred, price index series may be importantly influenced by weights differing in a way related to price movements. For these and other reasons that need not be reviewed here, the comparisons that follow should be interpreted with considerable caution.

In Table XXI various price index series are presented with 1926 put equal to 100. This year has the advantage of being statistically convenient.[1] In addition, it is a year when prices in North America were close to their inter-war peak (disregarding the years immediately following World War I) and when prices in the United Kingdom had already fallen considerably because of the sustained deflationary policy in the United Kingdom resulting from Britain's return to the gold standard in 1925.[2] Thus, the choice of 1926 as a base year means that subsequent years are related to a year when British producers were in a relatively strong price position compared with North American suppliers.

In preparing Table XXI it has also been necessary to take into account changes in foreign exchange rates, transit costs (including freight, insurance, and handling charges), and tariffs. Adjustments for changes in foreign exchange rates are a relatively simple matter. For the entire period changes in the official exchange rate can be used for making adjustments since this was the price at which the individual Canadian buyer could freely obtain foreign exchange (war years excepted). This is true almost without exception as far as sterling is concerned. It is also true of most other foreign currencies except for United States dollars during the period from 1946 to 1950. Yet even the controls designed to conserve United States dollars became increasingly lenient after 1948 and the foreign exchange rate for United States dollars became more and more significant as a price. It is important to note that in so far as these post-war foreign exchange controls do introduce a bias into the figures, it is a bias that understates the strength of Britain's comparative price position during these years relative to other years when there were no restrictions.

It is much more difficult to take account of changes in transit costs and tariffs. Canadian imports, as shown in official Canadian statistics, are mostly valued f.o.b. at point of shipment in the exporting country. Variations in transit costs and tariffs might, therefore, cause the laid-down price in Canada to change somewhat differently from the f.o.b. price. In most cases, of course, transit costs and tariffs make up a comparatively small part of the laid-down price of imported products. Consequently, deviations in movements between f.o.b. and laid-down prices are necessarily limited. Nevertheless, these deviations might still be significant.

Unfortunately there is really no way of adequately adjusting for relative changes in transit costs and tariffs. It is practically impossible to measure accurately the height of a tariff and changes therein. As for shipping costs, information is very incomplete and difficult to interpret. Data relating to various other costs such as insurance and handling charges scarcely exist at all. In view of these difficulties, the question arises whether it might be feasible to omit making an adjustment for these costs. Failure to make such an adjustment would imply that the transit costs and tariffs, taken together, of various suppliers had remained in roughly the same relative relationship to each other over the period. At a minimum, one should like to know the likely direction of the bias introduced into the comparisons by omitting to make an adjustment. In view of the general conclusions indicated by the statistics below, it is particularly important to know whether the omission of an adjustment is likely to mean that during the past thirty years British prices have increased more, relative to North American prices, than shown by the figures.

Such evidence as the writer has been able to find suggests that by omitting to make such an adjustment one probably does not represent changes in Britain's competitive price position in an unduly favourable light. The opposite, in fact, seems somewhat more likely. Figures on duty collections indicate that Canadian tariff reductions since 1926 have probably been as great on imports from Britain as on imports from the United States. Relative to 1926 the average ad valorem duty collected on all imports from Britain had decreased about one-third by 1937-8 and almost an additional third by 1956-7. The average ad valorem duty collected on United States imports, on the other hand, was about the same in 1937-8 as in 1926 and about one-quarter less in 1955-6. In addition, the administration of Canadian customs duties, government purchasing policies, and various other factors favoured British over other foreign suppliers after World War II, and, to a degree, after the Ottawa Agreements in 1932, thereby enhancing any price advantage that Britain may have gained.[3] As for shipping charges, available estimates indicate that relative to 1926 ocean freight charges were lower in 1937-8 than rail freight charges. Since World War II, ocean rates, with the exception of 1951, have apparently increased less, compared to prewar, than rail rates.[4] Handling charges and certain other costs of this kind are highly labour-intensive. Not only are wages, converted at the official exchange rate, considerably lower in Britain than in Canada and the United States, but they have also risen less rapidly in Britain, as shown below.[5] All things considered, therefore, it seems feasible (despite the rather unsatisfactory nature of the foregoing evidence) to proceed with a comparison of various relevant price index numbers without adjusting for tariffs and transit costs.

Table XXI shows various price index series for Canada, Britain, and the United States along with data indicating changes in exports to Canada and Canada's domestic output. An advantage of the wholesale price series is that they include not only those goods that actually have been traded but also those goods that might have been traded but, for one reason or another, were not. The various export price series shown, on the other hand, include only those products that actually have been traded. It bears repeating that comparison of price movements as indicated by any of these price series is limited by various qualifications, some of which have been referred to above (different weights, reference to somewhat different baskets of goods, difficulties of inter-temporal com-

	Canadian Prices		United Kingdom Prices			
				Exports		
	Wholesale manufactures(a)	Imports(b)	Wholesale manufactures(c)	All areas(d)		All exports to Canada(e)
				Total	Manufactures	
1926	100	100	100	100	100	100
1927	96	95	96	95	107	98
1928	95	94	95	95	106	99
1929	93	91	93	93	105	98
1930	87	80	81	88	100	90
1931	75	68	69	77	87	77
1932	70	66	56	61	68	65
1933	70	63	66	69	78	76
1934	73	67	73	76	85	90
1935	71	66	73.	75	84	87
1936	72	67	78	77	87	91
1937	78	74	89	84	93	98
1938	78	68	83	85	95	99
1939	77	68	79	80	88	n.a.
1946	104	111	124	144	160	n.a.
1947	122	128	129	155	171	n.a.
1948	145	145	147	170	186	236
1949	150	149	156	163	178	237
1950	159	160	136	141	151	216
1951	182	183	153	163	174	275
1952	173	160	146	158	172	224
1953	172	159	144	155	170	238
1954	169	159	143	150	166	233
1955	169	160	149	154	169	236
1956	174	164	156	159	175	244
1957	179	170	156	150	176	242
Percentage change						
1929-38	—16	—25	—11	—9	—10	1
1938-48	86	113	77	100	96	138
1948-57	23	17	6	—12	—5	2
1929-57	92	87	68	61	68	147

SOURCES:

(a) Fully and Chiefly Manufactured Goods—Dominion Bureau of Statistics, *Canadian Statistical Review*, 1957 Supp., and monthly issues.

(b) Dominion Bureau of Statistics, *Canadian Statistical Review*, 1957 Supp., and monthly issues.

(c) 1926-48 covers materials, semi-manufactured goods, and finished products; 1949-57 relates to all manufacturing industries except fuel, food, and tobacco—*Times Review of Industry* (London & Cambridge Economic Bulletin no. 26), June 1958.

(d) Average value all exports; value of manufactures exports ÷ volume of manufactures exports—*Times Review of Industry* (London & Cambridge Economic Bulletin no. 26), June 1958.

United States Prices			Value of exports to Canada(h)				Canada(i)	
Wholesale ex. farm & food(f)	Exports all areas(g)		Total		Manufactures		Gross national expenditure	Industrial production, manufactures
	Total	Manufactures	U.K.	U.S.	U.K.	U.S.		
100	100	100	100	100	100	100	100	100
94	93	90	111	106	105	118	107	101
93	96	89	116	123	115	125	115	113
93	96	89	118	134	122	162	116	118
85	85	84	99	98	119	159	105	98
78	68	70	66	59	94	109	86	85
80	62	69	57	39	66	63	71	74
78	64	63	59	32	50	39	67	80
77	67	62	69	44	60	38	76	93
78	71	64	71	47	65	48	82	101
80	72	65	75	55	65	53	89	111
85	76	68	89	73	72	70	101	127
82	71	67	72	63	83	89	99	117
84	73	68	69	74	66	77	108	126
115	121	109	122	210	126	283	227	221
133	137	122	115	295	118	416	260	242
145	146	129	182	270	180	365	295	251
146	140	127	187	292	189	409	311	252
160	143	130	245	318	234	430	344	265
171	158	140	256	421	242	603	406	282
155	147	131	219	445	222	670	439	286
156	146	133	275	482	280	759	462	306
156	143	129	238	443	242	693	460	292
162	147	133	243	516	246	816	508	314
168	152	139	294	622	301	985	564	333
169	153	143	317	598	331	946	593	326
—12	—26	—25	—39	—53	—32	—45	—15	—1
77	106	93	153	329	117	310	198	114
17	5	11	74	121	84	159	101	30
82	59	61	169	346	171	484	411	176

(e) Appendix; 1954-7: value of exports to dollar area ÷ volume of exports to dollar area—Central Statistical Office, *Monthly Digest of Statistics*, various issues.

(f) All commodities other than farm products and foods—U.S. Dept. of Commerce, *Statistical Abstract of the United States*, 1957.

(g) U.S. Dept. of Commerce, *Statistical Abstract of the United States*, various issues.

(h) Dominion Bureau of Statistics, *Trade of Canada*, 1956, vol. I; *Review of Foreign Trade*, 1957. Figures on the export of manufactures relate to the fiscal year ending March 31 of the year indicated from 1926 to 1939; thereafter the figures relate to calendar years.

(i) Dominion Bureau of Statistics, *Canadian Statistical Review*, 1957 Supp., and monthly issues; *Monthly Review of Business Statistics*, Feb. 1944.

parisons). Subject to these and other qualifications, what are some of the main points indicated by the figures?

With only a few exceptions, the price series shown leave the impression that, compared with Canadian price changes, price movements in Britain have not been such as to impair Britain's competitive selling position. If anything Britain's prices appear to have generally become more competitive during the thirty-year period covered by the figures, and evidently were significantly more so after the devaluation in 1949 and to a lesser extent during the early thirties. On the other hand, Britain's competitive price position appears to have become relatively weaker during the late thirties and the years immediately after World War II.

Secondly, British price movements are less favourable in comparison with price movements in the United States, but the periods when they were more competitive coincide roughly with the periods when they were also more competitive with Canadian prices.

Thirdly, the prices of British exports to Canada seem to have risen substantially more over the years than the prices of British exports to other countries and British wholesale manufactures. Furthermore, the price trend shown for British exports to Canada compares much less favourably with the trend of Canadian and United States prices than does the trend indicated by Britain's wholesale and total export price index series. For instance, from 1926 to 1957 prices of British exports to Canada increased, on average, about twice as much as prices of total Canadian imports. From 1926 to 1938 the Canadian index decreased about 30 per cent more than the British; and from 1938 to 1948 the British index increased about 25 per cent more than the Canadian. However, since 1948 the price index for all Canadian imports has increased some 15 per cent more than the index relating to the price of British exports to Canada.[6]

Finally, there is no significant correlation between relative price movements in the three countries (as shown in Table XXI) and Britain's sales record in Canada.

Generally speaking, during the years since 1926 incentives created by differential price movements in the three countries considered have evidently been swamped by many cross-currents of a non-price nature. From 1946 to 1949, when British prices were high compared to years after 1949, Britain's share of the Canadian market was generally larger than in most years after 1949. Moreover, since 1949 Britain's share of the Canadian market has been substantially smaller than pre-war despite the apparent improvement in Britain's price position. At the same time, it should be recognized that the increase in Britain's share of the Canadian market in the early thirties coincided roughly with some improvement in her competitive price position. Also, from 1938 to 1946 when Britain's price position deteriorated, her position in the Canadian market deteriorated. In both of these periods there were, however, other important factors at work (a depression, tariff changes, a world war) which probably exercised a more important influence than relative price changes did.

There seems to have been relatively little response in the distribution of British resources in favour of the Canadian market as a consequence of the increases in prices of British exports to Canada relative to domestic British prices and prices of British exports to other countries. Despite the relatively high prices apparently obtainable in the Canadian market, exports continued to flow into other world markets at about the same rate (as shown in Table XXXVIII below). This situation cannot be adequately explained simply on the basis of peculiarities in the commodity composition of British exports to Canada. Again apparently there was little response to incentives arising from relative price changes.

In some instances changes in British prices of manufactured goods not sold in Canada—that is, potential exports—have compared more favourably with the price changes of North American goods than the price movements of British goods actually sold in Canada. The price index series for British wholesale prices and all British exports decreased more during the depression than the index for British exports to Canada, and both of the former increased less than the latter after 1938. To some extent this difference in movement may reflect differences in the relative importance of the various products included in each series, though it is doubtful if the differences in price movements—particularly between the total export series and the exports-to-Canada series—can be entirely accounted for in these terms. Furthermore, an explanation in these terms rather begs the question. If relative price changes were more favourable for British products having a comparatively small weight in the export-to-Canada index, one might have expected the weight of these products to have increased over time as more were sold because of relatively favourable prices. At the same time, one might have expected sales to lag, relatively, of those products for which price changes have been less favourable. Since the foregoing figures relate only to price changes one cannot legitimately draw conclusions regarding absolute price margins. Nevertheless, it is conceivable that at times Britain may in some instances have been exporting the wrong commodities to Canada, or at any

TABLE XXII

Selected Price Index Numbers Expressed in Canadian Currency:
Canada, United Kingdom, United States

A. WHOLESALE PRICES: MATERIALS AND MANUFACTURES, 1926 = 100

		1929	1938	1948	1950
Iron & steel	Can.	94	101	154	175
	U.K.	93	128	178	155
	U.S.	96	100	155	186
Coal	Can.	96	91	138	150
	U.K.	68	82	163	126
	U.S.	91	78	131	154
Chemicals	Can.	95	80	121	125
	U.K. (1930 = 100)	100	96	159	131
	U.S.	95	77	136	134 (1949)*
Non-ferrous metals	Can.	99	73	108	107
	U.K.	97	76	159	128
	U.S.	107	73	158	158
Cotton products	Can.	91	74	164	168
	U.K.	98	65	191	156
	U.S.	100	66	207	194
Wool products	Can.	96	74	194	225
	U.K.	99	74	165	139
	U.S.	89	77	156	171

* Using post-devaluation exchange rates.

B. U.K. EXPORT PRICES; CANADIAN WHOLESALE AND IMPORT PRICES;
U.S. WHOLESALE PRICES, 1950 = 100

	1938	1948	1950	1954	1957
1. *Metals and engineering products*					
U.K., exports:					
Metals & engineering goods	69	122	100		
Metals			100	111	125
Engineering goods			100	110	120
Canada:					
Iron and non-ferrous metals					
and products, wholesale	54	90	100	114	130
Iron & products, import	52	86	100	103	119
Non-ferrous metals, import	45	93	100	112	127
U.S., wholesale:					
Metals & products	53	86	100	104	121
Machinery & motive products	56	86	100	103	119
2. *Textiles*					
U.K., exports:					
Textiles & clothing	43	120	100		
Textiles ex. clothing			100	100	99
Canada:					
Wool cloth, wholesale	33	86	100	88	88
Cotton cloth, wholesale	40	89	100	95	98
Hosiery and knit goods, wholesale	48	95	100	113	111
Fibres and textiles, import	30	92	100	92	83
U.S., wholesale:					
Cotton products	33	98	100	81	80
Wool products	45	85	100	87	86
Apparel		98	100	91	91

C. U.K. EXPORT PRICES; CANADIAN IMPORT PRICES, 1948 = 100[†]

		1948	1950	1957
Rubber products	U.K.	100	76	89
	Can.	100	159	147
Chemicals	U.K.	100	75	72
	Can.	100	103	111
Machinery	U.K.[‡]	100	82	112
	Can.	100	114	137
Electric machinery and	U.K.	100	80	94
apparatus	Can.	100	105	142
Vehicles	U.K.[§]	100	80	91
	Can.	100	114	127
Pottery, glass, abrasives	U.K.	100	81	91
China tableware	Can.	100	99	115
Glass	Can.	100	120	149
Synthetic fibres	U.K.	100	73	63
	Can.	100	100	96

[†] All series are average value series; U.K. series from 1948 to 1950 are only very approximately comparable with those from 1950 to 1957.

[‡] Including electric machinery 1948 to 1950, excluding electric machinery 1950 to 1957.

[§] Including vehicles, aircraft, locomotives, and ships, 1948 to 1950; road vehicles and aircraft 1950 to 1957.

D. WHOLESALE PRICE CHANGES, 1949 TO 1957, SELECTED COMMODITIES

	Index numbers for 1957		
	Canada (1949 = 100)	U.K.// (June 1949 = 100)	U.S. (1949 = 100)
China & earthenware	112	89	121
Glass (other than containers)	165	96	120
Dyes and dyestuffs	120	94	113
Sulphuric acid	141	117	122
Soda ash	126	109	127
Drugs & pharmaceuticals	162	70	116
Soap	109	83	111
Iron castings	122	104	132
Iron & steel			
sheets	152	108	133
tin plate	134	107	123
tubes	121	104	141
Hand tools	152	103	145
Cotton cloth	107	80	91
Serge cloth	100	95	92
Worsted yarn	133	112	95
Rayon fabric	122	77	69
Rayon yarn	123	87	84
Carpets and rugs	135	116	124
Boots and shoes	127	83	111
Rubber footwear	187	96	128
Tires and tubes	122	124	142

// Index for June 1957.

SOURCES: Series shown in section C have not been published and have been obtained privately from the Board of Trade and Dominion Bureau of Statistics; some of the series shown in section D have been obtained privately from Dominion Bureau of Statistics and the Bureau of Labour Statistics. All other series are based on indexes available in one of the following publications: Dominion Bureau of Statistics, *Canadian Statistical Review, Prices and Price Indexes;* Central Statistical Office, *Statistical Abstract for the United Kingdom, Monthly Digest of Statistics;* Board of Trade, *Board of Trade Journal,* Feb. 14, 1958, *Report on Overseas Trade;* U.S. Dept. of Commerce, *Statistical Abstract of the United States;* Bureau of Labour Statistics, *Monthly Labour Review, Prices and Price Relatives for Individual Commodities in the Revised Index, 1947-50.* In many cases it has not been possible to find series that are very closely alike for the three countries. At best, the series are only very roughly comparable.

rate may have been exporting commodities to Canada in the wrong proportions, judging solely on the basis of relative price movements.

Further analysis along this line requires a comparison of the price trends of specific commodities and commodity groups. In Table XXII various detailed price statistics are summarized. It is evident that the comparative position of British prices since 1926, as indicated by the aggregate figures so far discussed, is generally reflected in the more detailed figures. The general trends suggested by the aggregate index numbers cannot be put down as a statistical fluke arising out of the averaging process. Thus, even if some of the differences in movement between the aggregate series can be attributed to differences in weighting, the more detailed figures suggest that part, at least, of the differences represents a genuine difference in price movements.

The favourable showing of British prices in the early thirties and since 1949 is, of course, partly due to the devaluations of 1931 and 1949. This raises the question of how effective these very substantial devaluations (about 30 per cent in 1931, and about 25 per cent in 1949 followed by a further depreciation of 8 per cent to 1952 as the market-determined value of the Canadian dollar appreciated) were in stimulating sales to Canada. Unfortunately, it is impossible to answer this question conclusively since both occasions were marked by confusion arising from the many additional changes in the economic scene taking place at the same time; for example, the 1931 devaluation came in the midst of a great depression and a move to imperial preference and protection; the 1949 devaluation preceded the Korean War and its aftermath by some eight months. Notwithstanding these complications, the statistics shown in Table XXIII have been prepared in order to give some impression of the efficacy of this action in increasing Britain's share of Canadian imports.

TABLE XXIII

VALUE OF BRITISH EXPORTS TO CANADA DURING PERIODS

OF LARGE EXCHANGE RATE VARIATIONS, 1930-5, 1948-52

A. THE DEVALUATION OF 1931 AND SUBSEQUENT APPRECIATION

(fiscal years)	1930/1	1931/2	1932/3	1933/4	1934/5
Sterling in Can. funds (cents)	485.75	447.88	398.19	484.35	493.73
(1931/2 = 100)	108	100	89	108	110
U.K. exports to Canada	141	100	81	99	105
U.K. exports to all countries*	146	100	94	94	102
Can. imports from all countries	157	100	70	75	90
Can. gross national product*	111	100	82	68	64
U.K. exports to Canada	(percentage of total Canadian imports)				
Total	17	18	21	24	21
Vegetable products	23	23	20	22	18
Animals & products	8	11	16	16	15
Fibres & textiles	38	36	42	44	45
Wood & products	10	12	17	17	15
Iron & products	9	14	20	24	19
Non-ferrous metals & products	10	12	18	15	16
Non-metallic minerals & products	8	10	14	16	13
Chemicals	13	13	18	22	22
Miscellaneous	13	16	17	18	21
confectionery	57	62	72	79	82
alcoholic beverages	83	84	81	88	86
leather products	19	19	30	33	32
cotton products	24	27	31	29	31
wood products	75	75	83	83	83
rolling mill products	19	31	51	60	51
tubes, pipes, fittings	13	16	39	34	24
engines and boilers	7	4	6	6	6
hardware and cutlery	25	28	42	43	36
machinery (ex. agricultural)	9	11	14	16	13
vehicles	2	3	4	5	2
wire	50	59	57	71	71
electrical apparatus	10	11	14	9	9
clay products	41	46	57	51	47
coal	11	13	26	27	21
glass products	13	12	12	19	18

B. THE DEVALUATION OF 1949 AND THEREAFTER

(calendar years)	1948	1949	1950	1951	1952
Sterling in Can. funds (cents)	403.00	375.69	304.41	294.69	273.40
1949 = 100	107	100	81	78	73
U.K. exports to Canada	97	100	131	137	117
U.K. exports to all countries	88	100	122	144	144
Can. imports from all countries	96	100	115	148	146
Can. gross national product	95	100	111	130	141
U.K. exports to Canada	(percentage of total Canadian imports)				
Total	11	11	13	10	9
Vegetable products	4	6	6	4	5
Animals & products	11	8	11	10	12
Fibres & textiles	42	36	31	29	24
Wood & products	4	4	4	3	3
Iron & products	6	9	15	9	9
Non-ferrous metals & products	13	12	18	15	15
Non-metallic minerals & products	4	5	5	5	4
Chemicals	6	6	9	8	7
Miscellaneous	20	13	11	9	7
sugar & products	2	2	5	4	6
alcoholic beverages	56	56	54	52	48
leather products	47	37	50	50	42
cotton products	21	15	11	11	8
wool products	72	70	67	59	69
rolling mill products	2	5	15	11	10
tubes, pipes, fittings	9	9	16	22	18
engines & boilers	13	17	12	10	8
hardware & cutlery	17	15	19	14	13
machinery (ex. agricultural)	5	6	8	7	9
vehicles & parts	14	22	31	13	10
wire	3	5	34	24	21
electrical apparatus	10	8	11	12	13
clay products	43	41	40	39	36
coal	1	3	3	2	3
glass products	18	22	22	20	14
soda & sodium compound	11	11	23	26	16

SOURCES: Dominion Bureau of Statistics, *Canada Year Book*; *Trade of Canada*, various issues; *Canadian Statistical Review*, 1957 Supp.; exchange rates as reported by Dominion Bureau of Statistics, mimeo.
  * Calendar year.

The 1930's situation is particularly difficult to evaluate because of the variety of concomitant economic developments. Although Britain's share of the Canadian market increased from 1930 to 1935, much of this increase occurred from 1933 to 1935 when the pound was again appreciating—by about 20 per cent. This increase in the proportion of Canadian imports coming from Britain, occurring in the face of an exchange rate appreciation, must be attributed largely to the impact of the depression on the composition of Canadian imports, as well as to other factors such as the increased tariff margins granted the United Kingdom at Ottawa in 1932. Moreover, some of these other factors, such as the depression, were operative before 1933 and partly account for the increase in Britain's share from 1930 to 1933.

The 1949 episode is also overlaid with complications. On balance, it seems that the devaluation of 1949 resulting in relatively lower British prices coincided with some diversion of British output to the Canadian market and some increase in Britain's share of Canadian imports of certain commodities. The trade figures suggest that these changes are partly accounted for by other developments such as the speculative buying, the shortage of United States supplies (for example, automobiles and certain capital goods), and the very rapid rise in the price of woollen goods following the outbreak of the Korean War. At the same time, in some product lines an increase in Britain's share of Canadian sales probably occurred mainly because of Britain's stronger price position.

What general conclusions can be drawn from these two episodes, as far as the effect of devaluation on British share of the Canadian market is concerned?[7] The figures, at the aggregative as well as at a more detailed level, are consistent with the view that devaluation in both instances resulted in some substitution of imports from Britain for imports from elsewhere. On both occasions, however, other important factors were tending to increase Britain's share of Canadian imports anyway and it is doubtful whether such increases in this share as did occur can be mainly attributed to substitution effects arising from devaluation. It is evident then that the percentage change in Britain's share of Canadian imports during these two periods was appreciably less than the percentage change in relative prices resulting from devaluation. Moreover, for the 1949 devaluation at least the effectiveness of devaluation in increasing Britain's share of Canadian imports over the longer term is not apparent. Since 1950 Britain's share has consistently been smaller than it was from 1946 to 1949. All this seems to suggest that although devaluation in 1931 and 1949 may have served somewhat to enhance Britain's share of Canadian imports their influence, especially in the longer term, has been largely overshadowed by other market factors.[8]

It can be argued, of course, that without devaluation Britain's share of Canadian sales would have decreased even more since 1949 than in fact it has. This may well be true, even though unverifiable. Such a contention, however, only serves to underline the relative importance of other factors in this situation compared with price incentives. It also leaves open the question whether, as far as increasing Britain's share of Canadian sales is concerned, measures operating directly on these other factors might not have been at least as effective as a realignment of price relationships.

There is one further matter to be mentioned in connection with these periods of sharp variations in the value of the pound. It is sometimes said that the effect of a devaluation is not only to increase the sale of goods already exported but also to bring new products into the flow of trade. A survey of the 1931 devaluation by Charles P. Kindleberger found little, if any, evidence of new goods entering Britain's export trade with Canada:

An attempt to find an example which would bear usefully here has stopped far short of the point at which firm conclusions could be drawn. Yet the writer, with the assistance of Sidney Chernick, has examined the change in British exports to Canada between the 12-month period ended September, 1931, when the average exchange rate was $4.88, and the subsequent 12-month period, when the rate was $3.44. Rough allowance had to be made, of course, for the fact that Canadian national income fell by approximately 20 per cent over the period, although this was short of the 30 per cent depreciation.
Numerous examples were found of expanded British sales to Canada at the expense of U.S.

sales. For these competitive goods already imported, depreciation brought about an increase of British exports. No example appeared, however, of an article imported from Britain after September, 1931, which was not imported before. It is recognized, however, that the period is short, and the situation not free from confusion.[9]

The writer has compared the Canadian trade returns for the years 1948 and 1949 with those of 1951 and 1952. Since one's estimate of the appearance of new items depends upon the degree of detail in which the trade returns are classified, it is very difficult to measure this sort of phenomenon with any assurance. On the basis of the figures shown in the *Trade of Canada*, volume III— the most detailed figures published—it is evident that some new items entered Britain's export trade with Canada during this period. Nevertheless the evidence for 1949, like that for 1931, suggests that in terms of the size of the devaluation which occurred the effectiveness of devaluation in drawing new items into trade during these periods can be judged small.

2. COMPARATIVE PRICE LEVELS

Absolute price comparisons are very difficult both to make and to interpret. Not only are the data almost inevitably inadequate, but also the conceptual framework into which this data can be fruitfully fitted leaves much to be desired. A basic assumption underlying most reasoning in economics is that if, in a competitive situation, individuals are given a clear choice between two identical commodities, they will invariably buy the cheaper commodity. That is to say, it is assumed that individuals would rather pay less than more for the same product. From this it follows that identical products will sell at identical prices if sales are to be made at all. Consequently, the fact that two specimens of a particular commodity sell in the market place at different prices means, by assumption, that these two items are not comparable in every respect; the very fact that prices are different means that the commodities in question are also different.[10]

Suppose now that one is given the following information: A careful survey of shoe prices indicates that Canadian-made shoes of a certain type, quality, location, and so on, sell at $20.00 per pair in Montreal; and "comparable" shoes made in Britain sell at $15.00 per pair. Obviously the shoes are not comparable in every respect or they would sell at precisely the same price. What meaningful conclusion can, therefore, be drawn from this factual information?

Can one say, first of all, that the price of the Canadian-made shoes is too high? No. More Canadian-made shoes than British shoes may be sold even though the Canadian-made shoes sell at $5.00 more than the British product. If this is so, it means that for a majority of buyers it is the British-made shoes that are more expensive even though they sell at $5.00 less than the Canadian product. Most buyers value the greater "attraction" or some other quality of Canadian shoes at more than the $5.00 difference in price. To offset the non-price features of the Canadian product it would be necessary for the British product to sell at more than $5.00 below the price of the Canadian product—perhaps very much more. But the most profitable way to increase sales of British shoes might not be to reduce prices at all. It might be more profitable to raise prices and to use part of the additional revenue to alter the design, quality, salesmanship, and other variables relating to the British product. In short, to increase the sale of British shoes it might be necessary to rejuggle the whole set of price and non-price variables until a new combination had been found where sales were higher. Does it then follow that this should be done?

No: it may of course be the case; but then again it may not. Given the conditions of market supply and demand, British producers may be making the best of the market which confronts them, even though they command only a relatively small portion of that market. In other words, given the market conditions, British producers are maximizing their profits by selling at $15.00 per pair the type of shoes they are selling in the manner and at the place they are selling them. On the other hand, British producers may not be maximizing profits. The only way one could conclusively answer this question would be through a series of trial-and-error experiments in which each producer individually could vary those variables under his control and thus determine whether his profits increased or decreased as a result.[11] In principle, it is not clear whether a decrease in a seller's share of sales reflects a change in market demand and supply conditions or a change in the wrong direction of the variables at the disposal of the individual producer, or both. Clearly, then, the prospects of using only absolute price data to come to a conclusion that prices are too high or too low in terms of maximizing returns are nil. It is conceivable that the article selling at the low absolute price is too expensive while the article selling at a higher absolute price is too cheap, given the market conditions in which the goods are sold and the seller's position with respect to such factors as costs, scale, and alternative markets.

So much for what one cannot conclude from an absolute price comparison. Are there any positive conclusions that one can draw from such price information? In the first place, it is clear that if the $20.00 shoes in the example above sell more readily than the $15.00 shoes, the $20.00 shoes must be more attractive in terms of some non-price factor. This is merely a truism, but one that can be used to some advantage. For if one found, as a result of comparing the absolute prices of numerous products, that over a broad range of goods British goods in absolute terms sold at prices that were lower than Canadian or United States goods, one would have some indication of whether British goods were relying upon lower prices to overcome disadvantages with respect to non-price factors. Alternatively, one might find that sellers were relying upon advantageous non-price factors to overcome high prices. Further, by comparing various sectors of trade one might gain some notion about the sectors in which this reliance tended to be greater and those in which it tended to be less. In no case, however, would there be any indication of whether British goods are in a strong or weak position.

Secondly, if one were to find any evidence relating to the size of *changes* in absolute prices, one might, by relating this information to sales data, obtain some impression of the degree of substitutability between functionally similar British, Canadian, and American products; though to draw this inference one would have to be able to assume that the non-price characteristics of the goods remained constant.

With these limited objectives in mind, the following information relating to absolute price levels has been assembled. In doing so, the general objective has been to compare the prices at which British goods are available with the conventional price ranges within which most sales are made in Canada of functionally substitutable North American products. Such a comparison is necessarily imprecise and is subject to considerable margins of error, given the information that is available. At what point in the producer-to-consumer pipeline are price quotations taken? What are the conventional price ranges? What precisely are functionally substitutable goods? What proportion of these goods are sold within conventional price ranges? Simply mentioning some of these questions—and others might readily be added—indicates the tentative nature of the comparisons made below and is intended to emphasize the caution that should be attached to them. In order to obtain any evidence at all on comparative price levels, it has been necessary to assume that when, in the sources referred to below, British prices are compared with North American prices, the comparison is sufficiently valid to be significant—that is, that goods which are close substitutes functionally have been compared and that British prices have been related to the conventional price range within which North American products are sold.

No attempt has been made to make a strictly statistical comparison because of the virtual impossibility of obtaining adequate statistics for more than a few standardized and simple products. Instead, this comparison is based on more general information that has been collected mainly from three sources. One source is the variety of market reports prepared by United Kingdom Trade Commissioner's office in Ottawa for the Special Register Information Service of the Board of Trade. Secondly, information has been extracted from various studies and reports such as the reports of the various Productivity Teams, the Canadian Tariff Board, the Royal Commission on Canada's Economic Prospects, and the Organization for European Economic Co-operation. Finally, some information has been derived from certain journals. Almost all of this evidence relates to the years between 1948 and 1956.

Those sources that seemed likely to be most informed and impartial have been primarily relied upon. All evidence is, of course, subjective to a degree; and no particular claims are made for the evidence presented here on questions that by their nature allow considerable scope for opinion and personal interpretation. It is conceivable, for example, that the reports prepared by the United Kingdom Trade Commissioner's Office in Ottawa may have been coloured by a natural desire to see Anglo-Canadian trade expand; at the same time the desire to provide reliable information and to discourage false hopes has probably also been present. Similarly, the productivity teams and export missions sent to North America may have sought to debunk popular misunderstanding and stimulate interest, but presumably they also sought to learn and to inform. Various other possibilities might be raised along this line. Most of this, however, would be conjecture. In assembling the evidence below the hope has been that by drawing on a broad array of sources a generally accurate impression—even if considerably blurred as to detail—would emerge that could not be put down in large measure either to bias arising from the special interests of the sources or to incompetence on the part of these sources in making comparisons. As far as the writer is aware, no better information is available than that presented here which would necessitate substantial changes in the conclusions summarized on page 49 below.

To begin with the weakest evidence, a certain amount of information exists about the consumer goods industries, and within this category about textile products. This information indicates that British prices of woollen and worsted piece goods sold in Canada in many lines compared favourably with Canadian and United States in the early fifties.[12] There are also indications that the same has been true of certain types of knitwear.[13] On the other hand, the evidence available suggests that prices of many other British textile products were higher than the price at which most products of this type were sold in Canada. This applies to ready-made clothing such as women's wear, children's wear, and rainwear.[14] The retail price of men's ready-made clothing is said to have been considerably higher than that of comparable or slightly inferior North American products, and this factor is thought to have seriously limited demand for the British product.[15] Above-average British prices are also indicated for certain cotton textile products and other household textiles in the period 1950-1.[16] Much the same is apparently true of prices of some types of velveteen, lace, artificial silk, narrow fabrics, drapery, upholstery fabrics, carpets, and rugs.[17] In short, as far as this group of commodities is concerned it would seem (freely granting the serious limitations of the evidence) that the prices of some British textile products sold in Canada during the period covered by the information available (1950-6) were, generally speaking, as high as or slightly higher than the prices at which the majority of Canadian sales were executed, with the major exception of woollen and worsted piece goods.

Another group of consumer goods on which some evidence exists is leather goods. Here the picture is somewhat mixed with British prices rather higher than average for leather hand bags, about average for luggage, and below average for gloves and some kinds of waterproof footwear.[18] Prices of British-made sports goods were generally higher than the price ranges at which most Canadian sales were made.[19] The same is true of household glassware, crystal, china, and pottery.[20] As regards cutlery and flatware, it seems that United Kingdom prices in some lines have compared favourably with those quoted by other sellers.[21]

As for electrical appliances for use in homes, the British product is in some cases so different from that sold in North America as to make a price comparison extremely difficult, if not impossible. This is particularly true for such items as washing machines, refrigerators, and stoves.[22] Information included in several studies (1955-6) of the electrical and electronic industries suggests that since 1949 prices in Canada of British goods have compared favourably in the case of small, standardized appliances such as toasters, irons, and electric shavers, as well as for certain kinds of radio, television, and recording equipment.[23]

In the case of motor cars about all one can say is that British cars are available in Canada at price ranges below those at which the great volume of sales are made but that British-made automobiles account for only a small share of the Canadian automobile market. When account is taken of horse-power, size, weight and certain other factors, it has been suggested that British cars are more expensive than their North American counterparts.[24] This conclusion may, however, be drawn on the basis of biased measurements and may fail to give adequate emphasis to differences in the quality of engineering and durability.

So much for consumer goods. The information relating to producer goods is of somewhat better quality and rather more comprehensive. A brief study in 1953 of the competitive position of British iron and steel prices suggested that the British industry can provide almost all types of primary and semi-fabricated iron and steel products at lower prices than producers of any other country in the world.[25] This survey goes on to affirm that the British price position in the early fifties was stronger than pre-war. In this conclusion the study corroborates the earlier findings of the United Kingdom Productivity Team that visited the United States.[26] The recent report by the Tariff Board on pipes and tubes of iron and steel arrives at the following conclusion:

With regard to United Kingdom competition, Canadian f.o.b. mill prices are about 50 per cent higher than the United Kingdom f.o.b. export port prices. The freight advantage held by Canadian mills, amounting to about 11 per cent (of f.o.b. export price) at Montreal and 4 per cent at Vancouver, plus, in each case, duty under 397 (a) of 15 per cent still permits the United Kingdom product to land at a lower price than the Canadian. However, United Kingdom products normally enter Canadian warehouse and by the time handling, warehouse charges and mark-up are added, the pipe sells for something close to the prevailing Canadian market price.[27]

In another report on basic iron and steel products the Board points out that "North American pricing policy in steel contrasts sharply with that prevailing in the United Kingdom and Europe. Export prices of overseas producers vary greatly, in close sympathy with the level of demand. . . . These wide variations appear to have had little influence on Canadian prices and imports. . . ."[28] Price data collected by the Board suggest that, primarily in the western provinces and Quebec, British iron and steel products have undersold some substitute Canadian and United States products at certain times (for example, 1953-4).[29] Since 1954 this competitive advantage for the United Kingdom has declined and for some products it has apparently been lost (for example, in structural shapes, rolled sheets, and plates). In the case of steel wire rope, another source indicates that British prices have been as much as 15 to 20 per cent below the price of locally made wire rope.[30]

In a report on zinc and its products the Tariff Board found that "imports from overseas are highly competitive, European and United Kingdom price levels being well below North American list prices."[31]

The information at hand seems fairly conclusive for engineering products. A survey of the machine tool industry made in 1954 indicated that Britain's average prices tended to be low relative to those of other countries (including the United States).[32] Furthermore, even prior to World War II, it seems British machine tool prices compared very favourably and in overseas markets were generally cheaper than American products.[33] These conclusions regarding Britain's machine tool industry are further underlined by the *Productivity Team Report* on metalworking machine tools:

. . . the United States machine tool industry is, normally, priced out of its export markets (except for certain special machinery which maybe it alone makes). . . . foreign competitors can, unless controlled by fiscal measures or national preference, force the United States makers of the usual standard machine tools out of their own home market, leaving them to make, principally, only special machines.[34]

Nor is this generally favourable situation confined only to metalworking machinery. A similarly strong British price position is indicated by the Productivity

Team reporting on the woodworking machinery industry in 1951.[35] Also, during the early fifties British prices in Canada for the following types of machinery seem, in the main, to have been as low or lower than the prices of substitutable United States and Canadian products: cranes and hoists; excavators; textile machinery; printing machinery; oil field equipment; laundry and dry cleaning machinery; paper converting machinery; petroleum refining equipment; coal mining machinery; pulp and paper machinery; pumps.[36] Much the same seems to have been true for diesel engines and diesel marine engines as well as for mining machinery and equipment and electric fork lift trucks.[37]

The foregoing picture with respect to industrial machinery is confirmed in a special study prepared for the Royal Commission on Canada's Economic Prospects:

> ... the level of tariffs is ineffective when applied to imports from the United Kingdom, Western Germany and other European sources which are low cost producers. This lack of protection bears hardly on the machine tool section of the industry where it has caused the manufacture of smaller standard machine tools to virtually cease. It leaves the machine tool builders to compete on the larger and special purpose machines where they have found their selling prices to be as much as 25 % above the price of comparable machines imported from the United Kingdom and 40 % above those from Western Germany, even though the imported machines have borne duty and transportation costs. These variations are representative of the maximum spread between the prices of Canadian and European machine tools of the types stated and do not necessarily apply to all machine tools of those types. Nevertheless, it is probably true to say that the Canadian machine tool builder sells his machine on quality, suitability, delivery, service and the willingness of some manufacturers to pay a higher price to buy a Canadian made machine.[38]

In the case of agricultural machinery it appears that British prices were higher than average prior to devaluation but were more favourable afterward. A study in 1948 found that Canadian machines were available in Canada at lower prices than British models although British prices seemed only slightly lower than United States prices.[39] Subsequently, however, British prices vis-à-vis the United States became favourable.[40] Whether this improvement was sufficient to overcome the Canadian price advantage is not clear, but seems probable.[41]

British prices of railway locomotives also apparently have been comparatively low. A study prior to devaluation found British export prices about one-third lower than current (1947) United States and Canadian prices.[42] A later study states that prior to World War II Canadian prices were 50 per cent higher than British prices. By 1948 much of this differential is alleged to have disappeared but devaluation in 1949 provided new relief to British producers.[43]

There seems little doubt that British prices of many kinds of industrial electrical and electronic equipment have compared favourable in the Canadian market.[44] In the field of heavy custom-built apparatus, which tends to be relatively labour intensive, British prices have compared especially favourably with the prices of North American goods:

> ... the devaluation of Sterling—during 1949—together with the recent appreciation of the Canadian dollar has greatly increased the severity of import competition in many lines of heavy apparatus....
>
> ... The decline in Canadian prices of heavy apparatus since 1949 despite rising costs supports the conclusion that the competitive advantage gained by the manufacturers in the United Kingdom has been very large....[45]

Further evidence is provided by the fact that United Kingdom firms have almost consistently underbid United States firms for certain large United States contracts.[46]

As for chemical products, British prices again seem generally to have been somewhat below the average for North American products. The Productivity Team reporting on pharmaceuticals in 1950 stated:

It has been interesting to compare the selling prices in the two countries [Britain and the United States] of some pharmaceutical products of the same composition and supplied in packings of the same size. The prices used were the net prices to wholesalers. This comparison showed that the great majority of those considered are sold in America at higher prices than they are in Britain, when the equivalent prices are calculated at the pre-devaluation rate of exchange as well as at the present rate.[47]

Much the same seems to be true as regards British and United States prices of heavy chemicals. The 1952 *Productivity Team Report* on heavy chemicals presents a price comparison.[48] In the sample considered, British prices range from 70 to 110 per cent of the United States prices and in 9 out of the 10 cases cited British prices are as low as or lower than United States prices.

Another group of products for which British prices in many instances have been below the average for North American products is hand tools, including in this category woodworkers' and engineering hand tools (though German prices have been lower on some of these items).[49] A similar picture is indicated for steel office furniture and equipment (excluding steel desks), sanitary earthenware, laboratory glass, commercial fishing nets (Japanese prices have been lower), industrial valves, and rubber belting.[50]

Some products for which British prices have apparently been higher than those of competing suppliers include roofing felt and paper, steel desks, druggist's rubber sundries, garden stocks and seeds, cotton belting, glazed tiles, and gas and diesel fork lift trucks.[51]

The general impressions yielded by these gleanings on the question of Britain's competitive price position in Canada are broadly supported by several recent studies. The first indicates that in 1948 Canadian prices in fourteen major industries were on average about 4 per cent higher than British prices.[52] The devaluation of 1949 undoubtedly increased this differential significantly. In addition, "A Survey of British Trade Problems and Practices in the Canadian Market" conducted by the Canadian Importers and Traders Association Inc. found British prices generally competitive. According to the report on this survey, almost 80 per cent of those companies reporting indicated that British prices were "good" or "satisfactory."

A third study was made under the auspices of the Organization for European Economic Co-operation by Messrs. Gilbert and Kravis. For present purposes, this study is limited in its usefulness in a number of ways. In the first place, the study compares only American and European (including United Kingdom) prices and does not extend to Canadian prices. Also, some of the data relate to domestic and semi-domestic goods which do not directly enter into international trade. In addition, even where the data relate to international goods, they relate only to the domestic sale of these goods. The comparison, therefore, does not reflect any difference between domestic and export prices nor such factors as transit costs, tariffs, and mark-ups that affect the price at which imported goods sell in Canada. Furthermore, in the present context, comparison based on domestic market prices is limited because of differences in indirect taxes, subsidies, and depreciation allowances in the countries compared. Fortunately, in instances where this is particularly important, figures on a factor cost basis have also been provided.

In spite of these limitations, the study by Messrs. Gilbert and Kravis has some significance for purposes of this essay. For one thing, the study is authoritative and presumably is based on the best information that could be marshalled under the aegis of the Organization for European Economic Co-operation. For another, British exports to Canada compete not only with Canadian products but also with United States products. Further, even though so-called domestic goods do not directly enter into international trade, they do enter indirectly since they are reflected in production costs. In addition, the statistical tables are sufficiently detailed so that one can isolate some of the commodity groups that do play an important role in international trade. Figures relating to some of these groups are reproduced in Table XXIV. It bears mention, finally, that in making the calculations, Messrs. Gilbert and Kravis state that they made an adjustment to take account of measurable differences in quality between British and American goods.

As far as the general level of absolute prices is concerned, Table XXIV indicates that in 1950 British prices, on average, were anywhere from 21 to 68 per cent lower than American prices, given the official rate of exchange between

TABLE XXIV

PURCHASING POWER IN THE UNITED KINGDOM OF THE STERLING EQUIVALENT OF ONE UNITED STATES DOLLAR CONVERTED AT THE OFFICIAL RATE OF EXCHANGE, 1950, 1955
(Valued at market prices; factor costs in brackets)

	U.K. weights			U.S. weights		
	1950		1955	1950		1955
Exchange rate	1.00	(1.00)	1.00	1.00	(1.00)	1.00
Gross national product	1.63	(1.68)	1.48	1.21	(1.32)	1.12
Consumption	1.58		1.44	1.16		1.09
Investment	1.41		1.31	1.26		1.15
Government	2.32		1.95	1.67		1.29
non-alcoholic beverages	2.25	(2.01)		1.83	(1.86)	
sugar & products	1.30	(1.25)		1.28	(1.22)	
alcoholic beverages	.93	(1.67)		.77	(1.44)	
tobacco	.41	(1.06)		.40	(1.09)	
footwear	1.46			1.45		
clothing & household textiles	1.13			1.03		
household goods	.96			.92		
transportation equipment	.66	(.78)		.66	(.78)	
producers' durable goods	1.18			1.04		
non-residential construction goods	1.17			1.21		

SOURCES: M. Gilbert and I. B. Kravis, *An International Comparison of National Products and the Purchasing Power of Currencies* (Paris: O.E.E.C., 1954); M. Gilbert and associates, *Comparative National Products and Price Levels* (Paris: O.E.E.C., 1958). Factor cost figures have been taken from the first of these sources.

the pound and the United States dollar. Put another way, in order for the general level of absolute prices in Britain in 1950 to have been equal to the United States level, the sterling-dollar rate of exchange should have been at some figure between about $3.40 and $4.70 to the pound; in fact, it was about $2.80. Table XXIV also shows that the United Kingdom had lost some of this price advantage relative to the United States by 1955.

At the commodity level, it will be observed that with the exception of household goods and transportation equipment British prices in 1950 compared favourably with those of the United States. The general impression emerging from the figures is roughly in agreement with the other evidence already presented on absolute price differences.[53]

To sum up, the evidence that the writer has been able to collect on Britain's post-war comparative price position, reckoned in absolute terms, suggests the following conclusions:

(a) Generally speaking, British prices since 1949 seem to have been low relative to North American price levels. That is to say, in many lines British goods have been available at prices that were the same as or below the prices at which the majority of sales were made in Canada of functionally substitutable North American goods.

(b) On balance it seems that the sector of the market where Britain's comparative price position since 1949 has been strongest has been producers' goods and equipment. Examples have been cited for this sector where British products seem to have held a very substantial price advantage over United States and Canadian supplies.

(c) In the consumer goods sector, Britain's price position has apparently been quite strong in certain sectors of the market such as woollen and worsted piece goods, certain types of leather goods, and cutlery. For some varieties of consumer goods, however, prices of British products have evidently been higher than the prices at which most sales have been made in Canada.

As has been emphasized, the evidence upon which these generalizations are based is far from perfect; and as indicated at the beginning of this section, there are serious conceptual difficulties in meaningfully interpreting this evidence, assuming the broad impression it creates to be generally correct. None the less, the foregoing conclusions do lead to two further considerations. First, the apparent strength of Britain's competitive price position as attested to by the foregoing evidence seems to indicate that the small share of sales that Britain commands in many commodity lines in the Canadian market cannot be mainly attributed to the prices asked but must be accounted for to a considerable extent by other factors. In other words, the implication is that low prices have been relied upon in many instances to overcome handicaps with respect to various non-price factors. In this connection, it is important to note that if extra costs had been incurred to make British goods more competitive in their non-price characteristics, British prices might have risen considerably. For this reason there is no way of knowing whether, on balance, the price of British goods relative to North American goods is high or low. Secondly, although the foregoing evidence gives the impression that Britain's relative price position has generally been quite strong for producer goods, Britain's share of Canadian sales in these producer goods lines and increases in this share have, in many instances, not been correspondingly impressive. This would seem to suggest that non-price factors have been quite important as far as some of these producer goods lines are concerned and that British suppliers have relied heavily upon favourable prices to overcome non-price impediments to sales of their goods.

3. COMPARATIVE MONEY COSTS

So far in this chapter the trend and level of British prices relative to Canadian and United States prices has been examined on the basis of information pertaining directly to prices. In order to check the impressions gained from this information, it is useful to consider briefly the trend and level of British production costs relative to production costs in Canada and the United States.

Labour

One of the more important components of production cost is, of course, labour cost. Figures on average hourly earnings in Canada, Britain, and the United States since 1938 are shown in Table XXV. Several points are particularly noteworthy. First, in 1957 average hourly earnings (converted at the official rates of exchange) in manufacturing in Britain were about 60 per cent lower than in Canada and 70 per cent lower than in the United States. Average hourly earnings in Britain reached their post-war low point, relative to average hourly earnings in Canada and the United States, about 1952. Since 1952 the differential has narrowed somewhat. Secondly, and more significant, these relationships changed appreciably between 1938 and 1957. In 1938 average hourly earnings in Britain were about 35 per cent lower than in Canada and less than 60 per cent lower than in the United States. From 1938 to 1957 average hourly earnings in Canadian manufacturing increased 152 per cent more than in British manufacturing. Consequently, for labour cost per unit of manufacturing output in Canada to have borne the same relationship to British labour cost in 1957 as in 1938, labour productivity in Canada would have had to increase 152 per cent more than in Britain. On the same reasoning, labour productivity in the United States would have had to increase 82 per cent more than in Britain during these nineteen years. In terms of average rates of increase compounded annually, average hourly earnings from 1938 to 1957 in Canada increased by about 7¼ per cent per year, in Britain by about 4½ per cent, and in the United States by about 6¼ per cent. This means that the increase in labour productivity in Canada and the United States would have had to exceed the British rate of increase by about 2¾ and 1¾ per cent respectively. Available evidence on productivity, as indicated below, suggests that this is implausible and that since 1949 British producers have enjoyed a labour cost advantage in Canada relative to pre-war.

Additional information pertaining to wages in Canada, Britain, and the United States is summarized in Table XXVI. For various reasons, readily apparent from the source material, the data prior to 1938 are less satisfactory than those since 1938. Notwithstanding this qualification, the hourly earnings index numbers suggest that British wage rates increased slightly less from the late twenties to the late thirties than did North American wage rates.

Hourly earnings figures in themselves are, of course, inconclusive. Estimates

TABLE XXV

AVERAGE HOURLY EARNINGS IN MANUFACTURING

	Can.	U.K. (Canadian cents)	U.S.	Comparison	
				U.K./Can. (percentage)	U.K./U.S.
1938	41.7	26.6	63.2	64	42
1947	80.3	48.9	123.7	61	40
1948	91.3	52.4	135.0	57	39
1949	98.6	50.4	144.1	51	35
1950	103.6	42.5	159.3	41	27
1951	116.8	45.2	167.4	39	27
1952	129.2	45.1	163.5	35	28
1953	135.8	48.1	174.1	35	28
1954	140.8	50.5	176.1	36	29
1955	144.5	55.1	185.4	38	30
1956	151.5	59.4	194.9	39	30
1957	160.0	61.7	198.5	39	31
Percentage change					
1948/38	119	97	114		
1957/48	75	18	47		
1957/38	284	132	214		

SOURCES: Dominion Bureau of Statistics, *Canadian Statistical Review*, 1957 Supp. and monthly issues; United Nations, *Monthly Bulletin of Statistics, Statistical Yearbook, 1954.*

of labour cost per unit of output are rather more meaningful in judging the competitive position of different producers. Accordingly, the figures shown in the last three columns of Table XXVI have been computed to indicate changes in the wage cost per unit of output in Canada, Britain, and the United States. These figures have been calculated by dividing hourly earnings index numbers by index numbers relating to output per man-hour. Such a calculation extending over many years is subject to serious qualifications. There are, for example, all the technical problems associated with computing output per man-hour; as already noted, the hourly earnings series for Canada and Britain are somewhat unsatisfactory for years prior to 1938; and the output per man-hour series are sketchy and incomplete for years prior to 1948.

In view of these limitations the figures shown in the last three columns of Table XXVI must be viewed with some scepticism, particularly for the period before 1948. None the less, the figures do suggest rather clearly that from 1948 to 1957 wage cost (in Canadian currency) per unit of manufacturing output in Britain decreased, if anything, whereas in the United States and particularly in Canada labour cost increased.

The general conclusion that British manufacturers have gained a labour cost advantage over their Canadian competitors is generally supported by figures provided in a recent study of British-Canadian productivity in 1948.[54] In the fourteen industries examined it was found that the wage and salary cost per unit of output in 1948 was about 9 per cent higher in Canada than in Britain.[55] The 1949 devaluation undoubtedly increased this differential appreciably.

TABLE XXVI

Labour Cost in Manufacturing
(Index numbers, 1926 = 100)

| | Hourly earnings | | | | | Wage cost per unit(d) | | |
| | Local currency | | | Can. currency | | of output | | |
	Can.(a)	U.K.(b)	U.S.(c)	U.K.	U.S.	Can.(e)	U.K.(f)	U.S.(g)
1913	51	(52)	40	(51)	40	n.a.	67	61
1927	101	100	100	100	100	98	100	98
1928	102	100	103	100	103	96	n.a.	95
1929	103	99	103	100	104	98	n.a.	93
1936	96	97	101	99	101	n.a.	n.a.	77
1937	104	101	114	103	114	n.a.	n.a.	88
1938	107	104	114	105	115	n.a.	89	87
1948	234	250	246	208	246	145	154	154
1949	253	258	256	200	263	159	142	156
1950	266	268	267	168	290	161	114	162
1951	300	294	290	178	305	171	120	170
1952	332	317	305	178	299	182	122	162
1953	348	334	323	190	318	183	125	166
1954	361	354	330	199	321	187	127	160
1955	371	384	343	218	338	198	134	162
1956	389	414	361	235	355	n.a.	n.a.	166

SOURCES:

(a) Index of wage rates in manufacturing 1913-38; average hourly earnings in manufacturing thereafter—Dept. of Labour, *Wage Rates and Hours of Labour in Canada*, 1953; Dominion Bureau of Statistics, *Canadian Statistical Review*, 1957 Supp. and monthly issues.

(b) Index of average weekly wage rates, 1913-38; average hourly earnings in manufacturing thereafter—*Times Review of Industry* (London & Cambridge Economic Bulletin no. 24), Dec. 1957; *United Nations Statistical Yearbook, 1954, Monthly Bulletin of Statistics.*

(c) Average hourly earnings in manufacturing, U.S. Dept. of Commerce, *Historical Statistics of the United States, 1789-1945*, Series D-117, 124; *Statistical Abstract of the United States, 1958*, p. 227.

(d) Index of hourly earnings in Canadian currency divided by an index of output per man-hour obtained from the following sources.

(e) Royal Commission on Canada's Economic Prospects, *Output, Labour and Capital in the Canadian Economy*, prepared by W. C. Hood and Anthony Scott, chapter 5, Appendix F.

(f) 1913-48, *ibid.*, p. 30. Output per man-hour for 1926 and 1927 has been assumed equal to that in 1925; 1948-55, D. MacDougall, *The World Dollar Problem* (London: Macmillan & Co., 1957), p. 131.

(g) Joint Economic Committee, *Productivity, Prices and Incomes*, 85 Cong., 1st Sess. (Washington: G.P.O., 1957), p. 148.

The same general conclusion emerges from a study of comparative money costs made by the National Industrial Conference Board and based on the experience of some American producers with manufacturing establishments producing the same or similar products at home and abroad. The reports of these producers indicate that in 1956-7 British labour costs per unit of output in manufacturing were significantly less than in the United States and Canada.[56]

Two further aspects of labour cost merit mention. First, it is generally true that the wages paid to female workers are less than those paid male workers. Because of this differential British manufacturers may gain some advantage vis-à-vis the Canadian market since women workers appear to make up a larger part of the manufacturing labour force in Britain than in either Canada or the United States. Since 1948 roughly 32 per cent of all manufacturing employees in the United Kingdom have been female; the corresponding figure for Canada is about 24 per cent and for the United States about 26 per cent.[57]

Secondly, there is evidence that the ratio of operatives to total employment is not greatly different in Britain and Canada.[58] At the same time it is clear that British salaries and wages to non-operatives are lower than in Canada when converted at the official rate of exchange. Moreover, this disparity increased sharply with devaluation in 1949. Thus, as regards overhead costs arising from salaries and wages to non-operatives, British producers have had a competitive advantage over their Canadian counterparts.

Raw Material

A second important component of production cost is the cost of raw materials. For a number of reasons it seems unlikely that, in general, the absolute cost of materials is significantly higher in the United Kingdom than in the United States and Canada.

Britain acquires a relatively large proportion of her industrial raw materials on international markets. Abstracting for the moment from transit costs of various kinds and tariffs, raw material costs are probably no higher for British producers than for North American producers in cases where both purchase requirements in third areas. Where British and North American producers rely upon North American materials, it is also unlikely that British producers are at much of a disadvantage, though in some instances they may be affected somewhat by discriminatory pricing between domestic and foreign sales. A third situation is one in which North American producers depend mainly on North American raw material supplies and British producers depend upon raw materials supplied from third areas. In so far as this reliance on different sources reflects ordinary commercial considerations, British producers are again unlikely to be at much of a disadvantage except perhaps because of transit and tariff costs. If, however, British producers are prevented from buying raw materials in the cheapest market because of currency or other restrictions, then they will be at a cost disadvantage. There is some evidence to suggest that on occasion since World War II British buyers have in fact been forced into higher-priced non-dollar markets;[59] but it is unlikely that restrictions of this sort exacted a very heavy toll on Britain's competitive position vis-à-vis the Canadian market.

It seems rather unlikely that this general picture of British imports of raw materials is greatly altered by introducing transit costs and tariffs. Water transport is particularly cheap and well-suited to the shipment of basic raw materials; and in some cases British transport costs may be lower than in North America where higher-cost rail and motor transport must be relied upon. As for tariffs, the adverse competitive effects are probably also small. Many industrial raw materials enter Britain duty free; and where there is a tariff it generally tends to be low. Moreover, the duties levied by Canada and the United States on industrial raw materials may well be as high, on average, as in Britain. All things considered, therefore, it seems unlikely that the cost of industrial raw materials imported into Britain is much higher than the cost of these materials to North American producers.

With respect to raw materials provided from domestic sources in Britain, it is possible that British producers enjoy some advantage over their North American counterparts, if only because of the advantage accruing from the labour component of the price of these domestic supplies. As already indicated, British prices of that basically important commodity, primary iron and steel, compare favourably with North American prices.[60] Another example already referred to is heavy chemicals.

A major exception to this general picture is the cost of fuel which is substantially more costly in Britain than in North America.

In addition to the cost of raw materials and fuel, one must also take account of the effectiveness with which these ingredients are used if one is concerned with the price of the final product. The study of British-Canadian industrial productivity already referred to suggests that in 1948 "the Canadian average use of materials and fuel together was not widely different from the British... and that Canadian fuel use... was generally below the British...."[61] It was also found that the combined cost of fuel and materials per unit of output in the fourteen industries examined was about 13 per cent higher in Britain than in Canada in 1948.[62]

TABLE XXVII

PRICE CHANGES IN INDUSTRIAL MATERIALS AND FUELS
SELECTED YEARS 1926-57, CANADA, UNITED KINGDOM, AND UNITED STATES
(Index numbers expressed in Canadian currency)

	Industrial Materials				Fuel for Manufacturing		
	Can.(a)	U.K.(b)	U.S.(c)		Can.(d)	U.K.(e)	U.S.(f)
1926	100	100	100				
1929	92	91	98				
1932	51	50	62				
1935	63	70	78				
1938	66	74	73				
1948	154	249	182				
1948	100	100	100	1948	100	100*	100
1951	139	123	126	1951	107	82	105
1954	106	85	95	1954	111	92	97
				1956	115	111	105
1957	114	89	101	1957	120	116	108

SOURCES:
(a) 1926-48, industrial materials including food products, Dominion Bureau of Statistics *Canadian Statistical Review*, 1957 Supp. and monthly issues; 1948-57, industrial materials excluding food, Dominion Bureau of Statistics, unpublished.
(b) 1926-50, raw materials, *Statist* index; 1950-7, basic materials, excluding fuels, used in non-food manufacturing, *Times Review of Industry* (London & Cambridge Economic Bulletin no. 24), Dec. 1957.
(c) 1926-48, crude materials for further processing, Joint Economic Committee, *Productivity, Prices and Incomes*, 85 Cong., 1st Sess. (Washington: G.P.O., 1957), p. 123; 1948-57, non-food materials excluding fuels, U.S. Dept. of Commerce, *Statistical Abstract of the United States*, 1958.
(d) Simple average of fuel oil, light industrial, and coal. Dominion Bureau of Statistics, unpublished.
(e) Central Statistical Office, *Annual Abstract of Statistics, Monthly Digest of Statistics*.
(f) U.S. Dept. of Commerce, *Statistical Abstract of the United States, 1958*.
* June 30, 1949.

Table XXVII suggests that much of this differential may have disappeared with devaluation in 1949.[63] These statistics also must be interpreted with caution because of a certain lack of comparability and other statistical problems. Nevertheless, they indicate that since 1948 costs of industrial materials, expressed in Canadian currency, have increased more in the United States than in Britain and more in Canada than in the United States. Apparently, the cost of fuel in the United Kingdom increased more from 1948 to 1957 than in the United States; but British fuel costs if anything seem to have increased somewhat less than in Canada.

The view that British producers recently have enjoyed a cost advantage in materials over Canadian producers is supported by the National Industrial Conference Board study referred to earlier. According to the statistics shown in this study, the direct materials cost per unit of output of firms producing similar products in North America and Britain in 1956-7 was slightly higher in Britain than in the United States; and direct materials cost in Canada was appreciably higher than in either Britain or the United States.[64]

Capital Costs

Three main elements of capital cost will be referred to here: the rate of interest and tax rates on corporation profits; the cost of plant, machinery and equipment; and the amount of capital employed. The conceptual and statistical problems arising with respect to these aspects of capital cost, especially the latter two, are very difficult and complex. Without going into these many problems, the discussion below attempts on the basis of recent work done by others to answer two questions in a general way. First, is it likely that capital costs recently have been higher in Britain than in Canada and the United States? Secondly, is it likely that capital costs have increased more in Britain than in Canada and the United States?

TABLE XXVIII

INTEREST RATES: CANADA, UNITED KINGDOM, UNITED STATES, SELECTED YEARS, 1929-57

	1929	1938	1948	1951	1954	1957
Long-term government bonds						
Canada	4.35	3.09	2.94	3.24	3.14	4.17
U.K.	4.60	3.38	3.21	3.78	3.75	5.01
U.S.	3.60	2.61	2.44	2.57	2.55	3.47
Money market rates						
Canada	n.a.	0.59	0.41	0.80	1.44	3.76
U.K.	5.25	0.61	0.51	0.56	1.80	4.80
U.S.	4.42	0.05	1.04	1.55	0.95	3.26

SOURCES: United Nations, *Statistical Yearbook 1954; Monthly Bulletin of Statistics*. As indicated in these sources, the figures shown above, especially for long-term bonds, do not refer to the same type of security in each country.

Some information on interest rates is summarized in Table XXVIII. From these figures it would seem that interest rates have generally been somewhat higher in the United Kingdom than in Canada and the United States. Moreover, after 1948

TABLE XXIX

PRICES OF PLANT, MACHINERY, AND EQUIPMENT:
CANADA, UNITED KINGDOM, UNITED STATES, SELECTED YEARS, 1926-56

(Index numbers expressed in Canadian currency, 1938 = 100)

	Canada(a)		U.K.(b)		U.S.(c)	
	New machines & equipment	Non-residential construction	Plant & machinery	Fixed capital in manu-facturing	Producers' durable equipment	Non-residential construction
1926	102	103	81	100	102	108
1929	100	108	82	95	105	105
1938	100	100	100	100	100	100
1948	156	166	182	181	154	211
1950	176	182	144	142	191	235
1952	201	219	155	156	188	236
1954	208	227	160	160	189	247
1956	225	246	179	180	209	266
1957	237	254	181	185	216	273

SOURCES:

(a) Business gross fixed capital formation, new machinery and equipment, and new non-residential construction, Dominion Bureau of Statistics, *National Accounts, Income and Expenditure, 1926-1956,* Table 6.

(b) 1926-38, plant and machinery, Philip Redfern, "Net Investment in Fixed Assets in the United Kingdom, 1938-1953," *Journal of the Royal Statistical Society,* Series A (General), vol. 118, part II, 1955, p. 171; general index of price of capital goods, E. H. Phelps Brown and Bernard Weber, "Accumulation, Productivity and Distribution in the British Economy 1870-1938," *Economic Journal,* LXIII (June 1953), Table III, p. 287; 1938-56 derived from Central Statistical Office, *National Income and Expenditure, 1958,* Tables 56 to 59.

(c) 1926-9, producer durable commodities and new non-residential private construction, derived from Simon Kuznets, *National Product since 1869* (New York: National Bureau of Economic Research, Inc., 1946), part I, Tables 6, 7 and 8; 1929-56, gross private domestic investment, producers' durable equipment, and construction other than residential non-farm, U.S. Dept. of Commerce, *Survey of Current Business,* July 1958, Table 8.

British rates apparently rose somewhat more than in Canada and the United States.

This interest rate picture as far as Britain is concerned is not changed very much when consideration is given to the relative level of corporate profit taxes, which also affects the cost and availability of loanable funds. The British tax on corporate profits has, since World War II at least, been considerably lower than in Canada and the United States. However, to make a comparison one must look at the total tax paid by corporations and their shareholders. If one takes into account the standard rate of corporation income tax and the profits tax, it seems that since World War II the amount that British companies could retain for reinvestment after tax was not significantly greater than in Canada and the United States.[65]

Secondly, there is the question of the relative cost of plant and equipment in Britain and North America. Figures pertaining to the cost of these capital assets are summarized in Table XXIX. From 1926 to 1938 the cost of capital assets, on average, may have increased somewhat more in Britain than in either of the other two countries. Since 1948, however, it is evident that the cost of plant and equipment in Britain has fallen substantially relative to the cost in Canada and the United States.

A third aspect of capital cost relates to the amount of capital used in conjunction with other inputs in the productive process. Reliable data bearing on this question are, unfortunately, rather scarce. Such evidence as is available indicates that in 1938 the capital stock of plant and equipment per employee in Canada was substantially higher than in Britain.[66] Table XXX shows that the amount of capital per worker has increased significantly less in Britain since

TABLE XXX

CAPITAL PER WORKER

(Index numbers expressed in local currency, 1929 = 100)

	Canada		U.K.	U.S.	
	Industrial gross stock			Reproducible capital per member of labour force	Same, adj. for hours of work
	per worker	per hour	Capital stock per worker		
1925	n.a.	n.a.	98	94	90
1926	107	106	98	n.a.	n.a.
1929	100	100	100	100	100
1938	100	n.a.	105	n.a.	n.a.
1940	97	n.a.	n.a.	87	92
1953	122	150	105	n.a.	n.a.
1955	133	165	n.a.	140	154

SOURCE: Royal Commission on Canada's Economic Prospects, *Output, Labour and Capital in the Canadian Economy*, Table 2.18, p. 49.

1938 than in Canada and the United States. This disparity is even greater when adjustment is made for the hours worked. Consequently, it would seem that British industry generally has used proportionately less capital than North American industry and that this disparity has increased.[67]

The Size of the Market

It remains to consider the influence of market size on Britain's competitive cost position. Although this is a complex question, there seem to be two principal ways in which the size of the market can affect costs. The first is through its effect on the size of the firm. A market may be too small to accommodate plants of the most efficient size, though the plants may be perfectly efficient given the size of the market. If the market were to grow larger, more efficient plants would be feasible and as a consequence costs would be lower. It must be remembered, however, that costs do not decline continuously, and eventually, if the market remains competitive, diseconomies of scale appear which more than offset the economies of scale arising from further expansion.

Aside from economies arising within the firm, the size of the market can also influence costs through economies external to the firm. These are more difficult to comprehend and to identify and have been the subject of long discussion in the history of economics. Very briefly, one can say that as a market expands certain external economies of both a "horizontal" and a "vertical" nature may be expected to manifest themselves.[68] These result largely from the possibility of greater specialization. To provide the full range and variety of commodities to a small market each firm tends to produce a number of products and product varieties. To supply the same over-all range of products in a larger market, each firm tends to specialize more fully, thereby probably reducing production costs in a number of ways. This would be an example of "horizontal" economies. "Vertical" economies, on the other hand, can be thought of in relation to greater specialization in the various stages of production between the raw materials and final product stage, that is, a vertical disintegration of production. This in turn may bring economies of various sorts in its wake which are also external to the firm. In both instances it is large production rather than simply large-scale production which results in a lowering of costs. All this, of course, is little more than an extension of Adam Smith's classic argument for international trade emphasizing specialization, the division of labour, and the size of the market.[69]

How then do these two considerations affect the picture of Britain's competitive cost position? To answer this adequately would require an intensive study of individual industries and the general industrial structure of the three countries primarily concerned. None the less, a few general considerations might be mentioned. On an aggregative basis, Canadian production seems to be about half as large as British output; and British output, in turn, is roughly one-eighth as large as total United States output. Hence, in so far as the size of production affects costs it is conceivable that United Kingdom producers may on balance be at some cost disadvantage vis-à-vis United States producers but may hold some cost advantage over Canadian producers.[70] The evidence is also inconclusive so far as plant size is concerned. A number of studies have been made which indicate that the average size of the factory may be roughly the same in the three countries.[71] This result, however, seems to depend partly on how plant size is measured.[72] Moreover, none of these studies sheds much light on the question of the degree of specialization in the three countries. It is conceivable that factory size might be about the same, on average, but that there might be marked differences in the degree of specialization within each factory's output.

Also relevant in this context is the question of changes in the amount of output in the three countries during the past three decades. From 1926 to 1957 manufacturing output in Britain, as indicated by indexes of industrial production, expanded less than in Canada and the United States.[73] Because of this disparity in the rate of growth in manufacturing output, British producers may have lost certain cost advantages since 1926. However, against this disparity in the rate of growth in British and North American manufacturing output must be set the devaluation of sterling during this period.

The influence of market size, of course, varies considerably from product to product and generalization is extremely difficult. It is noteworthy, however, that a recent Royal Commission study of Canada's secondary manufacturing industries has laid considerable stress on the handicap under which these industries operate because of the relatively small size of the Canadian market.[74] This theme is reiterated in other investigations such as those relating to the Canadian electrical industry and the Canadian industrial machinery industry.[75]

So much then for various factors influencing production costs generally. Much of the foregoing discussion has been rather speculative in nature with little direct evidence to support it. In recent years a number of empirical studies have been made of comparative costs in Britain and North America which generally support the impressions suggested by the foregoing review. First, there are the Royal Commission studies on the electrical and industrial machinery industries already referred to. Secondly, there is the study by Mr. J. B. Heath also referred to above. According to Mr. Heath's estimates, total variable cost per unit of output in the fourteen industries studied were about 7 per cent lower in Canada than in Britain in 1948, the gross margin per unit of output was 51 per cent higher in Canada, and final prices were about 4 per cent higher in Canada. The devaluation of 1949 and subsequent years undoubtedly raised Canadian costs and prices substantially above these levels relative to British costs and prices. Thirdly, the National Industrial Conference Board in 1954 and again in 1958 published a study on production costs in various countries as reported by certain producers manufacturing similar products in these countries.[76] The first study, referring to the period 1952-3, contains the following comment.

Costs of production in general are lower in the United Kingdom than in the United States. Of the twenty-two cases for which information has been collected, the majority stated that production costs were about the same or lower in the United Kingdom than in the United States for the same product. Only two of the replies definitely stated that they were higher. Five maintained that costs were about the same in the two countries. The fifteen remaining replied that United Kingdom costs were lower.
    In the few instances where quantitative data are available, United Kingdom costs are shown to be considerably below those in the United States. In some cases, costs were reported to be 46 %, 50 %, and 57 % of United States costs. (pp. 91-2)

The report goes on to note the substantial cost advantage to the United Kingdom gained through cheaper labour. In some industries, however, this advantage was more than offset by the use of more capital-intensive techniques in the United States, lower raw materials costs, or both (pp. 92 ff). As to costs in Canada, the 1954 survey concludes that "costs of production appear to be about the same or perhaps even above the United States" (p. 96).[77] The second study, referring to the years 1956-7, notes that Canada "appears as a comparatively high-cost production area" (p. 21). The statistics presented indicate that unit costs of production for the firms included in the sample were, on average, some 12 per cent less in Britain than in the United States and about 7 per cent more in Canada than in the United States (p. 37).
    Another study made by John H. Dunning arrives at a similar conclusion.[78] In this case also the production costs of American firms having plants in the United States and Britain are considered. Out of a sample of 140 firms, 21 indicated that over-all costs of production were higher in Britain than in

the United States, 36 that costs were about the same, and 83 that costs were less in Britain—in some cases very much less. The British subsidiary came out best where (*a*) value added by labour (in relation to gross output) was the highest and (*b*) the relative efficiency was the most favourable.

In the course of this chapter an attempt has been made to assess the strength of Britain's price position since 1926 relative to that of her major competitors in the Canadian market, and to relate these findings to Britain's success in selling her goods in Canada during these years. Unfortunately the quality of some of the evidence that has been presented leaves much to be desired and is open to criticism or qualification when considered in isolation. Yet if all the evidence is taken into account, the net effect is to demonstrate, rather conclusively in the writer's view, that there has been comparatively little response in the flow of trade to the changing incentives created by the relative trend in prices. Nor can it be argued, when Britain's price position is shown to be favourable by a comparison of price indexes, that the impression thus created is misleading in the sense of merely reflecting insignificantly small changes in absolute prices or, alternatively, reflecting only a narrowing of an absolute price disadvantage. As suggested above, since 1949 Britain's goods have been available in many commodity lines at prices that were no higher, and in some cases that were lower, than the price at which the majority of sales of functionally substitutable products were made. This is not to say, of course, that lower prices would not have enabled British suppliers to capture a larger portion of the Canadian market. At the same time, it is possible that higher British prices accompanied by increased expenditure on non-price market variables such as selling might also have increased Britain's share of Canadian sales. In any event, it seems that it has not been high prices as such that have primarily limited sales of British goods. The situation appears rather to be that British suppliers have tended to rely upon relatively favourable prices to overcome various non-price disadvantages.

CHAPTER FOUR

NON-PRICE COMPETITION AND MARKET IMPERFECTIONS

1. GENERAL CONSIDERATIONS

TWO MAIN QUESTIONS arise regarding Britain's competitive position in the Canadian market in terms of the many non-price variables that influence sales. First, to what extent can changes in Britain's share of the Canadian market be explained by an increasing inability to compete successfully with other suppliers in such matters as advertising, the quality, style, and variety of products offered, ancilliary services of various kinds, delivery dates—in fact, all the innumerable ways of competing in the market place, excepting price? Second, to what extent can the decrease in Britain's share of the Canadian market be explained by changing market imperfections?

In considering these questions, it is useful to distinguish two ways in which Britain's non-price position might conceivably have been undermined. The more obvious possibility perhaps is that the ability of British suppliers to compete in non-price terms has for one reason or another generally diminished relative to that of other suppliers over a wide range of goods. The second possibility is that those commodity lines in which Britain has been least able to compete in non-price terms have become more important as a proportion of total trade. Britain's market share could thus have been impaired even if within each individual commodity market Britain's non-price competitive ability had remained unchanged. The discussion in chapter II indicated, for example, that producer's goods have become relatively more important in relation to total Canadian demand and also in relation to that portion of total demand satisfied by imports. It is therefore necessary to enquire how this and other shifts in the structure of Canadian demand may have reacted upon Britain's non-price competitive position.

It is also necessary to consider whether a lack of supplies and distribution facilities may have largely forestalled the adverse effects that potentially might have arisen from one or both of the foregoing possibilities, thereby rendering them less significant in explaining the phenomenon under consideration. Before one could conclude that inability to cope with non-price competition had restricted British sales, one would have to be confident that these factors had not been precluded from exercising their adverse influence by the failure of British suppliers to expose their goods to Canadian buyers. To the extent that British goods are just not available in the Canadian market, the fact that British products may not be competitive becomes irrelevant.

In spite of the attention that economists have given to the problems of imperfect and monopolistic competition—in effect the problems at issue here—since the early thirties, there exist few tools for practical analysis of these problems. This lack is fully reflected in the following discussion.

Canada's geographic location and Canadian industrial development since the early twenties have been two fundamental factors influencing the pattern of Canadian trade. It is, therefore, important to try to assess the impact of these two factors upon Britain's export trade with Canada during the past thirty-five years. Obviously, the geographic location of the major trading nations of the world has not changed since 1926. Significant shifts have, however, occurred in the location of suppliers and buyers on the North American continent. The most important of these perhaps have resulted from the continued industrial development in all regions of Canada and the United States, filling in, as it were, more and more of the empty spaces and reducing distances between buyers and sellers. This tendency has been strengthened by the moderate westward movement of economic activity in the United States since World War I. Moreover, Canada's population is heavily concentrated in the industrial areas of Ontario and Quebec; and the degree of concentration in these areas and the west coast has increased over the years.[1] The net effect of these and other developments has been that the line of supply between producers (domestic and American) and the Canadian consumer has, on average, decreased appreciably. The distance between British producers and Canadian consumers, on the other hand, has remained virtually unchanged. This, together with evidence indicating that the volume of trade is inversely correlated with the distance between producer and consumer, suggests that locational changes since World War I have probably reacted adversely on Britain's share of the Canadian market.[2]

Locational developments favouring United States and domestic suppliers over their British counterparts have been strongly reinforced by technological improvements in transportation facilities since 1926. The most important technological change has been the tremendous growth of motor transport from almost nothing in 1926 to its present imposing status. Its flexibility, speed, and general convenience have probably added a considerable premium to production facilities within reach by truck of the consumer. In addition, the competition arising from road transport has acted as a spur to improvements in the service provided by the railways. By comparison with these changes, improvements in water transport have been minor. Nor can it be argued that the advent of air transportation has reinstated the 1926 balance since air transport continues to be at a considerable disadvantage in the shipment of goods.[3] It is unlikely that these adverse repercussions have been allayed to any significant extent by the shift in Canadian demand to producer goods; they may in fact have become more serious because of this shift.

In addition, government measures in Canada subsidizing transportation costs have probably had adverse effects on some British suppliers. The same is true of private special agreements that have been made between suppliers and carriers and the basing-point method of pricing, where these practices have arisen.[4]

Granting these conclusions with respect to location, technological developments, government measures, and special arrangements, one still is in doubt about their importance. Not only does transportation cost comprise a relatively small part of the cost to the final purchaser of many categories of goods, but also sea transport continues to be appreciably less expensive than land transport. It is interesting to note, by way of illustration, that certain types of British products can be shipped to Montreal or Vancouver (via Panama) as cheaply as United

States goods can be shipped from Detroit to either of these two centres.[5] For many products it would seem that transportation costs *per se* are less important than such factors as speed, regularity, and convenience. In these terms there can be little doubt that United States and Canadian producers have reaped a substantial advantage, not only because of the advantages of land transport compared with sea transport, but also because the Canadian market, because of its high level of economic activity and growing mechanization, has probably increased the premium it places upon such factors as speed, regularity, and convenience.

This said, it must be recognized that the advantage gained in these respects by North American suppliers can be overrated. First, since surface craft transportation from Britain to Eastern Canada requires only a week or two, there is limited scope for improvement. Moreover, the importance of liner traffic on the North Atlantic makes shipments over this route fairly regular. Admittedly, the situation is less favourable as far as West Coast trade is concerned since about one month's shipping time is necessary and liner trade is less important. Secondly, some of the time required to import goods is taken up in clearing customs which, though not lengthy, may be important for some kinds of goods. As this applies to imports from all sources, it does not afford an advantage to one country over another but some advantage does accrue to domestic suppliers. Thirdly, the development of air freight facilities has probably added to Britain's competitive position since it has shortened the time necessary to supply certain categories of goods, such as spare parts, where the emphasis on speed and regularity is greatest.[6] Fourthly, in many though not in all instances British suppliers can overcome the competitive disadvantages arising from their location by setting up warehousing facilities in North America. Indeed, the experience of many British business men suggests that this is almost an indispensable condition of selling certain lines of goods in North America.[7] Both of these hedges against time and distance—air transport and local warehousing—when employed involve increased costs, of course, and these have had to be taken into account. Finally, improvements in transatlantic communication facilities such as telephone cables, air mail, and passenger travel have probably been more important as a stimulus to Anglo-Canadian trade than to United States-Canadian trade. In summary, it would appear that the changes in locational relationships discussed above have not favoured British suppliers as much as North American suppliers; but there is some reason to doubt that these adverse developments have been of primary importance in accounting for the decrease in Britain's share of the Canadian market.

So much for some of the narrower aspects of two frequently alleged causes of the decrease in Britain's share of the market—Canada's location and her industrial development. A rather broader aspect of these two factors relates to their influence upon Canadian demand. When Canada's location close to the United States is mentioned as a major factor shaping the pattern of Canadian imports, much emphasis is usually laid upon the fact that Canadians tend to follow United States preferences in such matters as style, quality, packaging, and selling practices. This has clearly been important. What is more, available evidence suggests that the channels through which American influences affect Canadian demand have probably been extended since the twenties. This is true, for example, of foreign travel as indicated by Table XXXI. Not only have the absolute amounts spent by Canadians and Americans in each other's country been overwhelmingly greater than that spent by Britons and Canadians, but also United States-Canadian expenditure has increased considerably more since 1926 than Anglo-Canadian expenditure. As also shown in Table XXXI a somewhat similar situation exists as far as imports of foreign publications are concerned. An informed examination of the influence exercised by the United States

TABLE XXXI

SOME FACTORS AFFECTING CANADIAN IMPORT DEMAND
($ million)

	1926	1932	1938	1948	1957
A. *Foreign travel*					
Can. expenditure in U.S.	70	30	66	113	403
Can. expenditure in U.K.	21	14	15	12	47
U.S. expenditure in Can.	140	103	134	267	325
U.K. expenditure in Can.	8	7	8	9	18
B. *Trade in books and printed matter*					
Can. imports from U.S.	10	10	12	29	75
Can. imports from U.K.	2	2	2	2	4

SOURCES: Dominion Bureau of Statistics, *Canada Year Book,* various issues; *The Canadian Balance of International Payments,* 1926 to 1948, 1957.

on Canada through the various mass communications is to be found in the *Report of the Royal Commission on National Development in the Arts, Letters and Sciences, 1949-1951* (Massey Commission), section II. This report leaves little doubt that developments in the field of mass communications since the early twenties have considerably extended the influence of the United States over Canadian habits and preferences.

More remains to be said, however, about the impact of this influence on Britain's share of the Canadian market. It is possible that a seller providing different products in a different way may gain certain advantages simply because of these differences; and the advantages of "being different" have perhaps become somewhat more important because of some tendency among Canadians to seek ways and means of distinguishing themselves from Americans and of freeing themselves somewhat from United States influence. The evidence available is almost unanimous in acclaiming "no lack of Canadian good-will" for British merchandise.[8]

Then, too, as Canada's manufacturing industries have developed they have tended to imitate United States products in such matters as design and style, packaging, sales promotion, and business methods. Two of the more obvious examples of this are the automobile and household appliance industries. This similarity between Canadian and American industry has been the result of various factors, including particularly the influence of United States technology and capital and the response of Canadian producers to Canadian demand, which has been increasingly exposed to United States influence. Because of this similarity Canadian production has frequently been a closer substitute for United States production than British production. The possible importance of this factor has, however, been considerably limited because many of these developing Canadian industries have continued to rely heavily upon United States parts and components. As already indicated, something like an eighth of Canadian imports in recent years have consisted of parts and components, mainly of United States origin. Development of Canadian industries producing American type products has thus implied some substitution of one kind of import from the United States for another. Nevertheless, in so far as the development of Canadian industry during the past thirty years has displaced imports, the incidence of this displacement may have tended to fall rather more heavily, in relative terms, upon the United States than Britain.

The heterogeneous nature of the Canadian market is another factor detracting from the importance of United States influence on Canadian demand as an explanation of the decrease in Britain's share of the Canadian market. Not only are there distinct differences between the four main regions of Canada as regards consumer demand, but also each province consists of various regional sectors. In past investigations of this subject it has been stated that for some products British manufacturers would be better advised to concentrate their expenditure in particular areas rather than to spread it thinly over the entire country, and that a selling campaign concentrated in one particular region can be quite successful. For some products local press and radio may be effective for advertising purposes.[9] Moreover, it is easy to note the similarities between Canadian and United States markets without noticing the differences. It is noteworthy that business men who have been active in both markets have in some cases been impressed by the differences as well as by the similarities.[10]

Also, it might be recalled that Britain's market share in many other countries besides Canada has been shrinking. Further, in some respects the trend of British exports to the United States in recent years has been somewhat more favourable than the trend of British exports to Canada.[11] In addition, although they still command only a very small share of Canadian markets, certain other foreign suppliers, such as Germany, have increased their relative share of the Canadian market in recent years.

In examining further the importance of Canada's location and Canadian industrial development in accounting for the decrease in Britain's share of the Canadian market, it is necessary to take into account the shifts in Canadian demand noted in chapter II. Sometimes when the inability of British products to compete in non-price terms with North American products is mentioned, it is implied that this inability reflects largely the "irrational" preferences of Canadian consumers and the emphasis on selling costs in North America. It is also suggested that British suppliers are less adept at providing the various "frills" of one kind or another necessary for success in the Canadian market. As far as the evidence goes, it tends to support the view that these "irrational" aspects of demand are more important in the sale of consumer goods than producer goods.[12] It follows that the increase in the relative importance of producer goods imports has been a factor favouring Britain's trade with Canada. Furthermore, the more strongly one holds that British suppliers are at a disadvantage vis-à-vis North American suppliers in catering to these "irrational" preferences, the more important must one regard the benefit that has been reaped by Britain from the relative shift away from consumer goods imports.

As for the more "rational" aspects of demand, it is widely affirmed that British products stand high in respect to quality and it is possible that this is more important in selling producer goods than consumer goods. At the same time, technical problems of various kinds have impeded the sale of British producer goods. For example, problems have arisen because of the difficulty of meeting the requirements of the Canadian Standards Association in the case of electrical equipment, because of differences in the type of screw threads used in North America and in Britain, and because of various technical difficulties encountered for such goods as coal mining machinery, trucks, and tractors.[13] In some instances these obstacles have been overcome, although usually rather belatedly. In the case of electrical equipment, for instance, facilities have been made available in London through which British equipment can be certified as meeting Canadian standards, but this service was not inaugurated until mid 1952.[14] In other cases, very little progress has been made.[15] Consequently, it is apparent that although the change to producer goods demand in the Canadian market may have favoured British sales in some respects, this advantage has been at least partially lost in some important commodity lines because certain technical problems have been solved only belatedly, if at all.

An additional feature of the demand for commodities relates to various ancillary services and benefits. On this question it seems clear that British producers have been at a growing competitive disadvantage. Not only are these ancillary services, such as engineering advice, repair and maintenance services, and spare part facilities, more important to the sale of producer goods but also the evidence plainly suggests that British suppliers have not kept pace with North American suppliers in providing these subsidiary services.[16]

Among other important non-price factors which have impaired Britain's share of the Canadian market is the impact of World War II and its aftermath. With the advent of war many Canadian consumers were forced to switch to North American suppliers and since 1945 these consumers have not been under any corresponding compulsion to return to British suppliers. More harmful perhaps, especially in the longer run, was the loss of many able manufacturer's agents and representatives in Canada to North American producers. A further deterrent to British trade has been the increase in uncertainty that a Canadian business man assumed if he decided to turn his allegiance from a Canadian and United States supplier to a British supplier. The high tension of international relations since the thirties, and indeed since 1900, has held out the constant threat that supplies and spare parts might be cut off.[17] Also, the exchange rate risk has been greater between Canada and Britain than between Canada and the United States, and the disparity in the degree of this risk has probably grown to greater proportions since pre-war. In addition, the dollar shortage itself to some degree may have impaired British exports, in spite of official pressure to sell more in dollar countries. For one thing, the machinery of quotas and foreign exchange controls may have made the problems of selling in the dollar area appear inordinately involved and cumbersome. Moreover, because dollars were in short supply they may not always have been spent as freely on such matters as advertising and promotion as might have been warranted in order to increase dollar sales. Furthermore, some Canadian buyers have apparently been reluctant to buy United Kingdom products since they have not been convinced of the long-term continuity of United Kingdom supplies; United Kingdom efforts to re-enter the Canadian market have sometimes been regarded simply as a "flash in the pan." [18] In part this attitude toward United Kingdom sellers is probably the one usually met by a newcomer; in part, also, it possibly is a result of associating Britain's attempts to increase her exports to Canada during the early post-war period with the dollar crises.

In appraising the importance of these considerations, one might contend that the adverse repercussions of World War II were probably eased considerably by the high level of demand that prevailed in Canada after 1946. For many products this clearly is true. Paradoxically enough, however, the rapid growth of the Canadian market since 1939 in some ways may also have had the opposite effect. There are two principal reasons for this. First, the pattern of Canada's import demand has been such that an increase in demand generally results in a decrease in Britain's share of the market. This reflects the fact, already mentioned, that British exports to Canada have been relatively heavily concentrated in those lines such as textiles and whisky where demand tends to be comparatively stable. A relatively larger share of United States exports to Canada, on the other hand, has consisted of products the demand for which responds more readily to increased business activity.[19]

Secondly, largely because of Canada's rapid economic growth since 1939, accompanied by far-reaching changes in many aspects of production and distribution, some British business men have found North America a country of "horribly rapid progress." [20] This has meant, for example, that one outstanding feature of British products, namely their quality and durability, has been of less importance than might have been expected since the premium on durability is likely to be lower the more the economy is given to change.[21] The changeable economic environment in North America is reflected in the comparatively greater emphasis on such matters as model changes, industrial research, new products, and variants of products. It is also reflected in the comparatively high rate of business turnover and the relative lack of emphasis on such matters as traditions. On the demand side, this environment is enhanced by the heavy emphasis on advertising and selling activities which promote not only new products and methods as they appear but also the very idea of change and newness. Continually changing conditions arising for these and other reasons create a continuing burden of adjustment for would-be suppliers. In the case of North American suppliers, these adjustments have probably come about more readily, if not more easily, simply because the suppliers have been an integral part of the changing conditions. Most British suppliers, on the other hand, have sold only a small portion of their output in North America and, as a consequence, necessary adjustments may perhaps have been made more grudgingly and after substantial damage had been sustained, for example, from the technical difficulties referred to earlier. More important, the individual British producer having the option of selling his output in markets less given to changes of various kinds may in many instances simply have been trying to maximize his profits, as he reckoned them, by eschewing some at least of the extra costs of adjustment arising from the more fickle economic environment in North America.

Finally there is the question of the easy availability of supplies. As suggested at the beginning of this chapter, before it can be said that adverse developments in regard to these non-price variables have contributed to Britain's declining share of the Canadian market, it must be demonstrated that these factors have in fact been operative and have not been forestalled by factors operating on the side of supply. In other words, British goods must have been exposed to the Canadian consumer for him to reject or accept them. The evidence indicates that this necessary prerequisite has, in fact, not always been met. Failure on the part of British producers to supply the Canadian market was most apparent during the immediate post-war years when there was a lack of productive capacity. Comments voiced on both sides of the Atlantic in the late forties and early fifties constantly reiterated the theme of inadequate supply. Statements by Canadians from cabinet ministers to department store executives run in the vein of "we are absolutely starving for British goods."[22] Official and unofficial British comment agrees: "Canadian demand for our goods, within the ruling market conditions, has been beyond our capacity to supply."[23] One senses considerable frustration in the reports of the British trade officials resident in Canada during this period as they refer to the unequalled opportunity for dollar sales and then report a lack of goods, inadequate distribution facilities, and impossible delivery dates.[24] In more recent years, of course, productive capacity has been less strained. The question of Britain's capacity to supply goods to Canada during the post-war period is more fully considered in chapter VI below.

It appears, however, that the difficulty in providing adequate supplies to the Canadian market is not simply a post-war phenomenon that can be attributed mainly to inadequate productive capacity. There is some evidence to suggest that even during the thirties, when productive capacity in the United Kingdom existed in excess, the gap between the British producer and the Canadian consumer was not bridged very successfully.[25] In part, this is explained, as indicated in chapter V, by the existence of various arbitrary public and private restrictions that frustrated the normal market mechanism. In part, also, the problem of supplying the Canadian market has arisen out of the growing inadequacy since the twenties of the distribution system open to British goods; and it is this aspect of the problem that now calls for some consideration.

Two general characteristics of distribution in Canada are especially significant as far as Britain's export trade is concerned. The first is the high cost of distribution; the second is the increasing tendency of manufacturers themselves to take over the task of distribution.

Distribution costs naturally vary greatly according to product, time, place, and special circumstance. An example, said to be extreme, of distribution and other post-production charges is reproduced in Table XXXII. In this case, the price to the final Canadian consumer apparently was over three and a half times more than the f.o.b. price London. Some additional information on distribution charges is summarized in Table XXXIII. From this it seems that distribution charges are less for capital goods than for consumer goods, but according to one source usually account for about 35 per cent of final price.[26]

TABLE XXXII

EXTREME EXAMPLE OF DISTRIBUTION COSTS
AN ASSEMBLY OF COMPONENTS IN THE FORM OF AN AMPLIFIER

Invoiced price, f.o.b. London	$83.82
Freight and insurance	8.56
Customs duty, 15 %	12.57
Excise duty, 15 %	14.46
Sales tax, 10 %	9.64
Brokerage, Canadian inland frt., share of C.S.A. fee, advertising allowance	2.52
Cost to agent	131.57
Agent's addition, 15 %	19.73
Price to jobber	151.30
Jobber's addition, 45 %	68.08
Dealer's "net price"	219.38
Dealer's addition, 40 %*	87.75
Price to consumer	307.13

SOURCE: *Special Register Information Service*, Market Digest on Radio and Television Components, July 18, 1958.

* Assumed.

No satisfactory evidence has been found to indicate what difference, if any, there might be in the distribution costs borne by British, American, and Canadian suppliers. In the absence of evidence it is unclear whether British costs are more likely to have been more or less than those of other suppliers since British producers seem to be at a disadvantage in some respects and an advantage in others. One factor possibly tending to make British distribution costs higher is that sellers of North American goods probably have enjoyed some economies of scale in marketing their goods. Also, British producers not already in the Canadian market, or having only a meagre toe-hold, in most cases have faced heavy initial costs of entry.

During the past three decades sales promotion and distribution costs have become a significantly more important factor in the Canadian market. Partly as a reflection of this, manufacturers themselves have to an ever increasing extent taken over the distribution of their products. This has given the manufacturer tighter control over the distribution of his products, has permitted him to launch more intensive and specialized selling efforts, and has earned certain economies in selling.[27]

British products can enter the Canadian market through a number of distribution channels.[28] First, there is the traditional channel in international trade, the export merchant in Britain and the import merchant in Canada. It is apparent that these traditional traders have become less important as distributors, even in those sectors of trade in which they continue most of their operations—the distribution of consumer goods such as textiles, pottery, and leather goods.[29] This decline in importance is mainly due to the emphasis on distribution in North America and the importance manufacturers attach to "following the goods through" to the final consumer with skilled and costly promotional programmes.[30]

TABLE XXXIII

DISTRIBUTION COSTS: TYPICAL PERCENTAGE MARK-UPS AND COMMISSIONS FOR SELECTED PRODUCTS

	Agent	Jobber	Wholesale	Retail
Women's ready-made clothing	10-15			60-100
Ladies' nylon hosiery			15-20	50-66⅔
Children's ready-made clothing	10			50-80
Men's ready-made clothing	10			60-80
Men's furnishings	6-10		30-40	54-66⅔
Men's underwear & socks			33⅓	60
Men's neckwear			40	60-66⅔
Men's accessories			40	60-66⅔
Lace & embroidery	33⅓			100-150
Narrow fabrics	5		50+	
Corduroys & velveteens	3-5		25-30	50-75
Woven synthetic fabric	5	25-33⅓		66⅔
Blankets & travel rugs	5-20		20-25	40-75
Leather footwear			33⅓	40-50
Luggage			25	50-66⅔
Pottery	7½-10		50	75-100
Glass & crystal tableware	5-10		33⅓	60-100
Cutlery & flatware	10	33⅓		60
Jewellery	10		50	100-150
Garden tools	10		33⅓	50-66⅔
Garden stock and seeds				100
Clay sewer pipe	3½-5		15	
Firebricks			20-25	
Glazed tiles	5-7½	20-33⅓		50
Sanitary ware	5	33⅓-66⅔		
Gas appliances	10-25			33⅓-50
Radio & television components	5-25	40-60		
Veterinary pharmaceutical & biological products			25-100	
Surgical dressings			20-25	40-60
Druggists' rubber sundries	10		33⅓	40-60
Pyrometers	33⅓-42		25	
Packaging machinery	10-33⅓			
Laundry & dry cleaning machinery	20-30			33⅓
Industrial woodworking machinery	15			
Textile machinery	5-20			
Hydraulic presses	10-20			
Woodworker's hand tools	10		33⅓	50
Engineer's hand tools			33⅓	50-66⅔
Paint machinery	15			
Office furniture & accessories				40
Metal furniture	3½-9			40-100

SOURCE: *Special Register Information Service*, market digests for the various products noted 1956-8. These figures must be interpreted with considerable caution. The stages of distribution indicated are imprecise and differences in mark-ups may reflect substantial differences in the services provided by the stage in question. Also, it was not always clear whether the mark-up was based on cost price or selling price, though most of the mark-ups given above are thought to relate to cost price. Blank spaces denote no information.

In many product lines the business of distribution has grown to such importance and is so exacting and costly as to be beyond the capacity of the traditional export-import merchant. A further incentive for the producer to take an active part in the distribution of his products is that he becomes more familiar with the wants and desires of consumers and can cater to them more satisfactorily than would otherwise be the case.

A second channel of distribution is through the London buying offices of Canadian firms. The scope afforded by this channel is considerably limited for at least three reasons. It is restricted largely to consumer goods; it extends to only a relatively few retail outlets in limited areas of Canada; and many department stores strive to buy on an exclusive basis—that is, to be the only outlet for the goods in question.

Thirdly, there is the agency method of distribution which is the most widely used and is found in most commodity lines.[31] The agent has been particularly relied upon for full coverage of the market where consumer goods are concerned. The degree of direct control exercised over agents by manufacturers varies greatly, ranging from very loose and haphazard control to very close supervision. The distributive functions performed by agents also differ greatly. Some agents are simply salesmen who rely on the manufacturer to provide most or all of the accoutrements of selling, such as catalogues, samples, spare parts, and service. Other agents play a much larger role in the distributive process, acting in fact as wholesale merchants. As such they take possession of the goods and take full responsibility for their sale and delivery as well as for stocks, spares, and service.[32]

The agency method of distribution, though successful in some lines, has in general not been able to compete effectively with the integrated production-through-to-marketing arrangements that have become increasingly important. Among other reasons, this can be attributed to the fact that agents carry a variety of non-competing products and usually do not promote and sell any one product as effectively as the manufacturer himself. Moreover, agents naturally tend to concentrate their energies on those lines yielding the highest net return. Accordingly, the agent may pursue sales less agressively in product lines where, for one reason or another, profits are less; at the same time, the distribution charge for these less profitable lines can be high in comparison with the cost of distribution when done by the manufacturer himself. Also, there is the problem of ensuring that competent agents are chosen and that they are not carrying competing commodity lines. In addition, the agency method of distribution gives rise to more uncertainty than an integrated production-distribution arrangement. For example, the prospective buyer as well as the producer of a product must face the prospect that an agent may cease operations entirely or may take on another line of goods after a time. From the agent's standpoint there is the possibility that if he really pushes sales of a product he may work himself out of a job; if sales increase sharply and become sufficiently large the producing firm may decide that the time has come to set up its own distribution facilities.

The fourth major distribution channel open to British goods is the subsidiary company and branch office. Under such an arrangement the producer assumes complete control over distribution. It is generally agreed that as the need to provide technical service and advice increases, it is more and more essential for the manufacturer to engage directly and actively in the distribution of his products if sales are to be made. The Dollar Exports Board has suggested that in general the ideal form of representation for capital goods is the subsidiary or branch office.

The changing importance of these various distribution facilities as effective outlets for British goods is significant in explaining Britain's difficulties in Canada. First, the greater emphasis on producers' goods in the Canadian market has increased the importance of distribution facilities in which the manufacturer is an active, if not the sole, participant. It is in this sector of the market where the distribution outlets open to British suppliers have probably been most inferior to the facilities open to North American products. The inadequate provision of various ancillary services has already been mentioned and to some extent this can be attributed to inadequate distribution facilities; other ways in which trade has been impaired through this source could be elaborated. Secondly, in the distribution of consumer goods in North America wholesale merchants and agents have in many cases become less and less effective. Increasingly the costly business of distribution has been taken over by the manufacturer himself. Thirdly, those areas (textiles, for example) where the traditional channels of distribution have remained important include many of the more static sectors of the Canadian market.

The general conclusions to be drawn from these considerations seem quite clear. Changes in distribution methods within the Canadian market and shifts in Canadian demand combined with a legacy of relatively heavy dependence by Britain on traditional products and traditional distribution methods have tended over the years to make the distribution channels connecting British production and the Canadian market more constrained and ineffective. Much of this comes down to a question of investment in distribution and suggests that, for one reason or another, British producers have not been prepared to commit themselves in the Canadian market to a sufficient degree to put themselves on a more equal footing with their North American competitors.

This leads to consideration of another significant aspect of the Canadian market and a notable consequence of United States influence and Canada's industrial growth. It seems to be generally agreed that the Canadian market, because of its level of industrial development and the easy access afforded foreign goods, is one of the more highly competitive markets in the world and that, in this characteristic, it resembles the American market more closely than the British.[33] Moreover, if only because of the longer period during which a sellers' market prevailed in Britain after the war and because of the post-war restrictions on dollar imports, this disparity in the degree of competition between North America and Britain may have been somewhat greater during the years after World War II. In so far as any disparity between the pace of competition in the Canadian market and the British market may have increased it seems likely that the possibilities for trade between British suppliers and Canadian consumers were diminished.[34]

With regard to all these factors, as well as prices, trade restrictions, and supply problems, it must be recognized that inertia will always find an excuse for itself if it can. Thus, complaints about prices, deliveries, promotion, supply problems, and all the other possibilities that might be mentioned may simply be an excuse offered to cover up a lack of initiative and to rationalize the convenience of adhering to current practices. This inertia may exist on the buyer's side of the market as well as the seller's. For instance, one might ask, in view of the evidence presented in chapter III, why Canadian buyers have not made more effort to buy British goods in those instances where British prices have been favourable. Partly, this may be attributable to such non-price factors as design, delivery, distribution, and the fact of Canadian buyers becoming accustomed to being "sold" a product, partly to trade restrictions of various kinds, and partly to supply problems. An additional possibility, however, is simply habit and inertia which may have been justified in terms of these other considerations. Unfortunately there seems to be no satisfactory way of determining the relative importance of this possibility.

2. SOME ILLUSTRATIVE EXAMPLES

The following brief "digests" have been compiled from a number of special studies and from the Special Register Information Service reports prepared by the United Kingdom Trade Commissioner Service in Canada. No particular claim is made for the competence and objectivity of the authors of these studies and reports, though, as far as the writer can judge, the sources used warrant at least as much confidence as any other information available on the questions at issue here. For several reasons it seems likely that they give an overly pessimistic impression of British difficulties in the Canadian market if one is thinking of British exports as a whole. In the first place, a bias arises from the natural tendency to give more attention in these studies and reports to instances where Britain's situation in terms of some non-price variable has compared unfavourably with that of North American suppliers; where the comparison has been favourable there has been less reason for pointing to it. In the case of trade missions, this tendency has reflected one of the main purposes of the missions, namely, to examine the main impediments to trade with a view to increasing its flow. Much the same is true of the Special Register Information Service reports. These apparently are prepared for the information of actual or potential British exporters to Canada. The objective seems to be to provide a brief, straightforward market survey for various goods, giving some idea of the prospect that the market holds for British suppliers, an indication of the main problems to be met in the market, and a criticism of some of the methods used by British suppliers in the past along with an indication of how these might be improved. All this presumably is a part of the Trade Commissioner Service's normal job of providing information to the British business community about the Canadian market and of trying to encourage British sales in Canada.

Comments from the various studies and reports have been selected for inclusion here in order to illustrate by specific example some of the problems encountered by British sellers to Canada. Selection on this basis has no doubt reinforced the tendency already noted for these summaries to give an exaggerated impression of British difficulties in the Canadian market.

It should not be inferred that the specific non-price variable mentioned in a summary is the most important or only factor influencing sales; nor is it intended to suggest that a significant change in any market variable should be undertaken or would of itself appreciably alter sales if it were undertaken. No attempt has been made to indicate all the product lines in which any particular variable may have been important or unimportant in impairing sales. Also, these summaries should not be construed as summaries of all that the authors of a study say about the particular products in question; the summaries here merely relate to isolated comments in these sources. Finally, it should be noted that the points summarized below relate to the periods when the comments appeared (indicated by the dates cited) and that the importance of any factor mentioned may have varied considerably from period to period depending upon changes in the economic climate in North America and Britain. The comments below should therefore be interpreted with care; they are intended merely to be illustrative. The classification has no analytical significance.

(a) Promotion and Distribution

1. Cotton sheets and pillowcases. One of the principal complaints against United Kingdom suppliers is lack of attention to suitable packaging. (*S.R.I.S.*, Oct. 27, 1950.)

2. Leather footwear. Criticisms of packaging have been made. Shoe boxes sometimes arrive from the United Kingdom so damaged that they are unsuitable for storing. (*S.R.I.S.*, April 11, 1958.)

3. Pottery. In view of increased competition, more advertising should be undertaken by United Kingdom pottery interests. (*S.R.I.S.*, Oct. 5, 1956.)

4. Linen textiles. There is nothing sold in Canada that can compare with the quality, beauty, and durability of "Irish linens" but buyers claim that United Kingdom manufacturers are slow in changing their designs and in providing the colours needed in Canada. Consequently, colourful rayon and rayon/cotton mixtures are capturing a great deal of the linen trade. More imaginative designing, a more spirited advertising programme, and improved packing are needed to increase the sales in Canada. Prompt and reliable deliveries would do much to induce buyers to place larger orders. (*S.R.I.S.*, Jan. 2, 1951.)

5. Industrial protective clothing. The small share of the market which British firms command is partially due to a lack of serious selling effort. (*S.R.I.S.*, Feb. 27, 1956.)

6. Pumps. Aggressive advertising and promotion are necessary. United Kingdom firms tend to be more conservative than North American manufacturers in quoting efficiency ratings. (*S.R.I.S.*, April 22, 1955.)

7. Excavators. The United Kingdom has mainly "second-choice" distributors. Servicing and availability of spare parts is a major hurdle to selling in Canada. Promotional activities such as visits by technical representatives, sales conventions, etc., tend to keep the United States firms supplied with enthusiastic distributors. (*S.R.I.S.*, Oct. 29, 1954.)

8. Drugs and medicines. In general, drugs, and medicines from the United Kingdom are competitive in price and quality; presentation and packaging are adequate, but United Kingdom products are not known to the public because of insufficient promotion and advertising. (*S.R.I.S.*, April 29, 1954.)

9. Pulp and paper machinery. An adequate sales and technical staff (including engineers) is necessary not only to consult with consulting engineers over installation, but also to service the machinery. Trade literature would be improved if it contained more detailed technical information. (*S.R.I.S.*, July 25, 1952.) Lack of knowledge in Canada regarding British products is partly a reflection of the lack of sales promotion on the part of British manufacurers. (*Report of the Members of a Pulp and Paper Trade Mission to the United Kingdom*, Oct.-Nov. 1954.)

10. Diesel engines. Engines of United Kingdom manufacture can compete with most American and Canadian products in design, weight per horsepower, efficiency of operation, cheapness of maintenance, and price, which in many cases is lower than that of the American product. There is therefore no reason why British manufacturers should not enter the market, but if they decide to do so they must do so whole-heartedly and establish an efficient organization with fully qualified staff for spares and servicing, preferably in the form of a Canadian subsidiary company. Delivery of parts must be from stock since no operator can afford the risk of having his equipment tied up during his working season while parts are being shipped from the United Kingdom. (*S.R.I.S.*, Feb. 29, 1952; April 12, 1954.)

11. Steel office furniture and equipment. Better packaging would help to ensure that goods arrive unmarred. (*S.R.I.S.*, Feb. 27, 1951.)

12. Sanitary earthenware. Advertising by United Kingdom manufacturers is said to have been generally inadequate or entirely lacking. (*S.R.I.S.*, Feb. 22, 1952.)

13. Woodworking and sawmilling machinery. Both reports state that the indifference of United Kingdom manufacturers combined with extended delivery, insufficient promotion, and inadequate technical service have kept the United Kingdom portion of the market small. (*S.R.I.S.*, May 13, 1950; March 14, 1952.)

14. Oil refinery equipment. Some firms are well informed about Canadian conditions and have their own representatives or plants in Canada. Others are represented by agents, some of whom are unqualified. Still others are attempting to do business from the United Kingdom. Technical sales representation, information, and service facilities comparable to those offered by Canadian and United States suppliers, more appreciation of Canada's geography, and the need for greater contact with the engineering and contracting firms who do work for the oil companies are requisites to an increase in business with the oil industry in Canada. (*Report of Visit to the United Kingdom, 1955*, The Petroleum Industry, p. 9.)

15. Metal mining machinery. Although most firms are represented in Canada, too many are represented only by manufacturers' agents. Firms should have their own permanent representation in Canada and senior executives should keep in close personal touch with the Canadian mining industry. (*Report to the Directors of the Canadian Metal Mining Association on the Mission to the United Kingdom*, Nov. 1955.)

16. Agricultural machinery. It was surprising to discover that the importer-wholesaler of the kind to be found in other countries hardly exists in Canada. The Canadian firm handling American agricultural machinery expects and receives attention from the manufacturer direct. (Board of Trade, *Report of the British Agricultural Machinery Mission to Canada, 1949*, p. 36.)

17. Packaging. There was quite clearly general satisfaction with packaging in the industrial and commercial fields, but consumer packaging was very heavily criticized. (Canadian Importers and Traders Association Inc., *A Survey of British Trade Problems and Practices in the Canadian Market*, 1957, p. 10.)

18. Advertising. To encourage "advertising and sales promotion" in the United States, Canada, and other dollar account countries, the Export Credits Guarantee Department has a special policy which insures the exporter against up to 50 per cent of possible losses through the cost of his promotion activities not being covered by an agreed proportion of total sales made by him over an agreed period. The very limited use made of the scheme is partly a result of ignorance, partly a reflection of the fact that very large companies do not always require it, but it is also a sign of distressingly low level of sales promotion activity in the dollar area. (*Financial Times*, "Advertising for Export," Feb. 27, 1956.)

19. Engineering goods. It is particularly difficult to locate good agents for engineering equipment in Canada because, when United Kingdom manufacturers were excluded from the market in the war years, most agents transferred their allegiance to United States suppliers and are no longer available. (Board of Trade, *Report of the United Kingdom Engineering Mission, 1949*, p. 38.)

20. Methods of distribution. There is a decided trend in Canada for manufacturers to sell directly to the retail trade, and to perform functions formerly undertaken by wholesalers. To a very large extent the tendency has been for the wholesaler to be replaced by the marketing organization of the manufacturers. In import trade, the wholesaler, although there is a tendency for him to be supplanted by the specialized distributor, plays a more prominent part than he does in domestic trade. Wholesale firms in Canada, unless they have exclusive distribution, are not inclined to stress the claims of a particular manufacturer, but handle lines for which there is a demand. It is therefore usually necessary for the demand to be created either by advertising or detail work, or both, by the United Kingdom firm's representatives. Nevertheless, the method of selling direct to the retailer by the manufacturer's own local organization is worth consideration by all United Kingdom firms hoping to achieve volume sales in Canada. Direct selling to retailers is, however, extensively practised in Canada by Canadian and United States manufacturers, and has been successfully adopted by some United Kingdom manufacturers. (Board of Trade, *Exporting to Canada*, p. 15.)

21. British prices, style, design and quality. These are generally satisfactory. The causes of failure were confined to a basic lack of knowledge of the Canadian market, distribution and general sales organizational methods and conditions in Canada. (Canadian Importers & Traders Association Inc., *A Survey of British Trade Problems and Practices in the Canadian Market*, pp. 3-4.)

A recurring theme in the source material is the lack of an adequate bridge, as it were, between the Canadian customer and the British producer. Canadian customers in some cases seem to be unfamiliar with British products and would apparently not know where to buy them if they wanted to. British producers on their side are sometimes equally unfamiliar with the Canadian market. This point emerges from the report of the United Kingdom engineering, clothing, and agricultural missions to Canada. It is also indicated in the report of the Machine

Tool Trades Association on the International Trade Fair held in Toronto, 1950, and the Report of the Fisheries Association of British Columbia made in 1953. A typical statement relating to this problem is the following which appears in the Engineering Mission report in connection with meat-packing machinery: "With one exception United Kingdom manufacturers of suitable equipment are neither known nor represented in Canada and there would appear to be prospects for the sale of a variety of specialized items which offer advantages over or are equal to United States equivalents."[35]

(b) Business Methods

22. *Hosiery and knitwear.* Serious competition to the United Kingdom comes from the Canadian supplier who is very attentive to the retailer. (S.R.I.S., May 6, 1954.)

23. *Drapery and upholstery fabrics.* Buyers sometimes complain of supercilious treatment by London firms. This compares unfavourably with the friendly American treatment. Furthermore, the disinclination to agree to modifications may lose sales. (S.R.I.S., March 28, 1955.)

24. *Women's ready-made clothing.* The United Kingdom will not gain significantly more sales in Canada until they recognize that Canada is a separate problem from the British market. Visits to Canada by designers and manufacturers would be helpful. (S.R.I.S., June 25, 1952; April 13, 1956.)

25. *Children's ready-made clothing.* The adoption of the Canadian practice of grouping sizes under a single price quotation is desirable. For some lines it would be advantageous to supply retailers with size conversion charts, particularly if small retailers in eastern Canada are to be attracted to United Kingdom products. (S.R.I.S., July 4, 1952; March 13, 1956.)

26. *Power-operated hand tools.* Personal visits to Canada by United Kingdom manufacturers enables them to personally assess the market and ensure that the best possible type of representation is obtained. (S.R.I.S., March 30, 1954.)

27. *Metal mining machinery.* British manufacturers must realize that the Canadian mining industry may purchase its supplies anywhere in the world and that it lacks for nothing. (*Report to the Directors of the Canadian Metal Mining Association on the Mission to the United Kingdom,* Nov. 1955.)

28. *Glazed tiles.* Business is mainly done in western Canada through contractors, in the east either through jobbers or contractors. The Canadian and American manufacturers allow jobbers a 20–33¹/₃ per cent discount, but since the British sell to jobbers and contracts at the same price, it is difficult for them to sell to jobbers. (S.R.I.S., Jan. 25, 1956.)

29. *Musical instruments.* The inconvenience of converting sterling prices, adding duty charges, sales tax, freight rates, etc., has meant many smaller dealers do not carry United Kingdom products. (S.R.I.S., April 25, 1958.)

30. *General exports.* Catalogues and technical advertisements should be complete in their descriptions and specifications. (Board of Trade, *Report of the United Kingdom Engineering Mission, 1948,* p. 39.)

31. *"Buy British" slogans.* "...the 'Buy British' campaign has been overdone and reliance should be placed on ordinary business methods of selling rather than upon what is regarded as the objectionable type of slogan such as 'Britain

Delivers the Goods' . . ." (*Report on the British Tool, Machine Tool and Scientific Instrument Section Exhibition at the Canadian Industrial Trade Fair, Toronto. 1950, p. 36.*)

32. *Market evaluation.* Out of 268 answers to this particular question, 178 indicated that British business men do not readily accept advice on Canadian market and marketing problems. (Canadian Importers and Traders Association Inc., *A Survey of British Trade Problems and Practices in the Canadian Market,* p. 5.)

33. *Selling policy.* In formulating their selling policy for Canada, United Kingdom manufacturers must take account of the sale approach and services which Canadian buyers have come to expect, for competition has set standards that have rarely been equalled. Not only is the presentation and detail of information given in catalogues and other sales literature excellent and the response to and "follow-up" of enquiries and tenders prompt, energetic, and competent, but a very high standard is evident in the whole field of consulting engineer services. This standard is maintained both by technical sales engineers and by erecting engineers. The time factor is also of extreme importance. The Mission found that many orders had been lost owing to delay in submitting quotations, and sometimes simply because these had been sent by sea instead of by air mail. (Board of Trade, *Report of the United Kingdom Engineering Mission, 1948,* p. 37.)

(c) Sales Service

34. *Oil field equipment.* It seems desirable for a key technical staff of United Kingdom men to operate in Canada with a Canadian sales force. (*S.R.I.S.,* Oct. 29, 1951.) Canadian firms must have full confidence in British after-sales service. (*S.R.I.S.,* July 26, 1955.)

35. *Textile machinery.* To gain a greater share of the Canadian market, United Kingdom manufacturers should give particular attention to: improved delivery schedules; development of machinery of high speed and output; advertising; special characteristics and requirements of the Canadian textile industry; maximum co-operation through all stages of selling, installation, and operation of machinery. (*S.R.I.S.,* June 20, 1951.)

36. *Power and gang lawn mowers.* United Kingdom manufacturers lose sales because of inadequate stockholding by distributors as well as a lack of servicing facilities. Unfamiliarity with United Kingdom models also causes sales difficulties. (*S.R.I.S.,* Sept. 14, 1951.)

37. *Gas meters.* Three United Kingdom firms who supply good service in spare parts, etc., have captured some of the market, but lack of servicing is still an obstacle to United Kingdom sales. (*S.R.I.S.,* May 15, 1956.)

38. *Industrial woodworking machinery.* Poor after-sales service has been indicated as a primary obstacle to the sale of some United Kingdom machines. (*S.R.I.S.,* Nov. 15, 1957.)

39. *Diesel engines.* American engine manufacturers, whether they maintain a Canadian subsidiary company or not, arrange for their service representatives to call about once a month on every owner of a truck or bus in which one of their engines is installed. To this end, they insist that the truck or bus manu-

facturer notifies them whenever a sale is made to a new customer. The guarantees given by American manufacturers are usually very generous; twelve months, or 100,000 miles, is not unusual. (*S.R.I.S.*, Feb. 29, 1952; April 12, 1954.)

40. Metal mining machinery. Those British firms which have been successful in Canada maintain reliable and adequate service. Many British firms, however, have attempted to sell in Canada without adequate service facilities. (*Report to the Directors of the Canadian Metal Mining Association on the Mission to the United Kingdom,* Nov. 1955.)

(d) Delivery

41. Woollen and worsted piece goods. Late delivery, which is considered a valid reason for cancelling orders, is the most frequently mentioned deterrent to British sales. (*S.R.I.S.*, Sept. 2, 1953.)

42. Cotton sheets and pillowcases. A principal complaint against United Kingdom suppliers is failure to deliver on time. (*S.R.I.S.*, Oct. 27, 1950.)

43. Pumps. Prompt deliveries are vital. For this reason a complete range of pumps must be adequately stocked. Deliveries from North American suppliers usually are very short indeed and in many cases immediate. (*S.R.I.S.*, April 22, 1955.)

44. Pulp and paper machinery. Early delivery is probably even more important than a favoured price and it seems certain that orders have been lost because protracted delivery dates have been quoted. (*S.R.I.S.*, July 25, 1952.)

45. Glazed tiles. Perhaps the biggest obstacle to increased British sales to Canada is delivery delays. German and Japanese firms quote delivery dates of three months. British deliveries of nine months are not uncommon and in one case a delivery date of eighteen months was given. (*S.R.I.S.*, Jan. 25, 1956.)

46. Diesel engines. Short delivery periods on the larger engines are essential. (*S.R.I.S.*, April 12, 1954.)

47. Packaging machinery. Possibly the greatest obstacle to the sale of United Kingdom packaging machinery is lengthy deliveries and broken delivery promises. (*S.R.I.S.*, Aug. 17, 1955.)

48. Sanitary earthenware. Delivery delays result in jobbers turning to other suppliers. (*S.R.I.S.*, Feb. 22, 1952.)

49. Woodworking and sawmilling machinery. A main purpose of the second survey is to stress a fact mentioned in the first—extended delivery dates are impeding sales in the field. (*S.R.I.S.*, May 13, 1950; March 14, 1952.)

50. Ready-made rainwear. To overcome delays in deliveries and to service smaller stores that lack direct importing facilities, stockholding is desirable. (*S.R.I.S.*, Feb. 10, 1953.)

51. Hosiery and knitwear. If supply difficulties could be overcome and delivery speeded up, United Kingdom sales should be considerably increased. (*S.R.I.S.*, May 6, 1954.)

52. Oil field equipment. The problem of delivery dates and adequate servicing are two major problems United Kingdom firms must face. (*S.R.I.S.*, Oct. 29, 1951.)

53. Textile machinery. Delayed deliveries and uncertainty of delivery are the largest problems confronting United Kingdom firms. These problems have already caused considerable unfavourable publicity. (*S.R.I.S.*, June 20, 1951; July 5, 1957.)

54. *Coal mining equipment.* The performance of United Kingdom exporters in the matter of deliveries and servicing is widely regarded as falling below the standard set by United States manufacturers. (*S.R.I.S.*, Oct. 5, 1953.)

55. *Printing machinery.* United Kingdom delivery is now characterized as "generally good but still requiring reminders." (*S.R.I.S.*, June 9, 1954.)

56. *Hydraulic presses.* In one instance a United Kingdom manufacturer who quoted a delivery date of 8–9 months lost out to an American manufacturer who quoted 12–14 weeks delivery date. A normal United States delivery for this type of press might be around 5–6 months. (*S.R.I.S.*, June 3, 1958.)

57. *Builders' hardware.* The United Kingdom would participate in a larger share of the market if stock supplies were held in Canada to ensure speedy delivery, and efficient, well-supported local representatives were appointed. (*S.R.I.S.*, Feb. 22, 1952.)

58. *Men's leather gloves.* Improved delivery service would be a practical way to encourage Canadians to buy more from the United Kingdom. (*S.R.I.S.*, Jan. 21, 1955.)

59. *Cutlery and flatware.* RELATIVE ADVANTAGES OF UNITED KINGDOM CUTLERY: United Kingdom cutlery is acknowledged by most Canadians to be of excellent quality; there is a considerable tariff preference in favour of most United Kingdom cutlery items; a small number of leading Sheffield cutlers have built up a personal reputation by many years' trading in Canada; cheap United Kingdom cutlery is usually preferred to other imported lines, if prices and deliveries are comparable. DISADVANTAGES: It is extremely difficult for United Kingdom manufacturers of domestic tableware to compete in Canada owing to the extensive advertising and promotion carried out by North American manufacturers; in a few cases Canadians prefer the design of United States cutlery to the standard United Kingdom product; delivery dates for United Kingdom cutlery, although better than formerly, are lengthy in comparison with United States and Canadian products. The conservative attitude towards the Canadian market with which many Sheffield manufacturers are credited in Canada results in a loss of trade as Canadians are accustomed to buying from North American manufacturers whose selling methods are both intensive and progressive. (*S.R.I.S.*, March 15, 1955.)

60. *Clothing.* Delivery must be prompt because of the seasonality of sales. (Board of Trade, *Report by the United Kingdom Clothing Mission to Canada, March, 1949*, pp. 7-8.)

61. *Oil refinery equipment.* Delivery dates tend to be inordinately long especially for custom-made items. In the matter of delivery promises, despite some notable exceptions and some improvement in recent years, United Kingdom suppliers have over the past six years the poorest record of promises kept in comparison with suppliers from North America and continental Europe. Realistic delivery promises are essential. (*Report of Visit to the United Kingdom*, Petroleum Industry, 1955, p. 4.)

62. *Pulp and paper industry equipment.* Delivery times had been cut in half from 1952 but still averaged 12–15 months. (*Report of the Members of a Pulp and Paper Trade Mission to the United Kingdom*, Oct.-Nov. 1954.)

63. *Metal mining machinery.* Many British firms have failed to trade in Canada because of slow deliveries. Although there has been substantial improvement recently, the situation is still not entirely satisfactory. (*Report to the Directors of the Canadian Metal Mining Association on the Mission to the United Kingdom*, Nov. 1955.)

Available Special Register Information Survey reports suggest that slow and unreliable delivery has also deterred British sales in Canada of the following products: women's and children's ready-made clothing (Aug. 13, March 13, 1956), laces and embroidery (Oct. 5, 1955), narrow fabrics (Aug. 31, 1955), pottery (Oct. 5, 1956), pianos (July 20, 1955), druggist's rubber sundries (May 10, 1957), builder's hardware (June 15, 1955), mechanical belting (Jan. 17, 1955), and industrial valves (Aug. 26, 1955), among others.

64. *General.* Over past years delivery periods have been heavily criticized. This condition was supported by approximately 50 per cent of respondents, the bulk of whom were in capital goods or industrial product lines. (Canadian Importers and Traders Association, Inc., *A Survey of British Trade Problems and Practices in the Canadian Market*, p. 3.)

(e) Stocks

65. *Leather footwear.* In the over-all picture the United Kingdom manufacturer is perhaps most handicapped in attempting to compete with the near immediate delivery and service which the Canadian industry is able to provide. (Leather Footwear, *S.R.I.S.*, April 11, 1958.)

66. *Woollen and worsted piece goods.* Local stockholding is essential for the bespoke tailoring trade. (*S.R.I.S.*, Sept. 2, 1953.)

67. *Linen textiles.* Stockholding by resident agents is an aid to sales. (*S.R.I.S.*, Jan. 2, 1951.)

68. *Diesel engines.* Stockholding of small and medium-sized engines as well as spare parts is vital. (*S.R.I.S.*, Feb. 29, 1952; April 12, 1954.)

69. *Paper converting machinery.* In the past British equipment was often not considered because of the difficulty of obtaining spare parts. (*S.R.I.S.*, Dec. 9, 1957.)

70. *Textile machinery.* Arrangements for stockholding of parts needing frequent replacement should be made. (*S.R.I.S.*, June 20, 1951.)

71. *Builders' hardware.* Stock supplies are essential to meet market demand. (*S.R.I.S.*, Feb. 22, 1952.)

72. *Children's ready-made clothing.* Children's clothing made in the United Kingdom is unlikely to be sold by more than a small number of Canadian retailers unless stocks are made available in Canada. (*S.R.I.S.*, July 4, 1952.)

73. *Engineers' hand tools and woodworking hand tools.* Although it is feasible to sell many lines of tools without maintaining local stocks, there is a strong tendency for Canadian accounts to expect small replacement orders to be available from local sources. (*S.R.I.S.*, Nov. 30, 1954; Nov. 26, 1954; Sept. 19, 1952.)

74. *Cranes and hoists.* Distributors must stock small hand hoists, small mobile cranes, as well as certain other items. (*S.R.I.S.*, Feb. 24, 1951.)

75. *Drapery and upholstery fabrics.* North American manufacturers sell from

stock to a greater degree than United Kingdom firms. As a result United Kingdom deliveries compare most unfavourably with North American performance. (*S.R.I.S.*, March 21, 1955.)

76. *Hosiery and knitwear.* To reach medium-priced fields the United Kingdom will have to meet the important problem of holding stocks in Canada to immediately fill repeat orders. (*S.R.I.S.*, May 6, 1956.)

(f) Design and Styling

77. *Men's ready-made clothing.* Standard measurements are said to differ in Canada from those of the United Kingdom. The design of suit coat jackets is frequently not what the Canadian consumer desires. However, in the field of men's trousers, proportionate styling and better fitting have led to considerable success. (*S.R.I.S.*, Oct. 3, 1955.)

78. *Children's ready-made clothing.* Although there is some demand for smocked and party dresses for younger girls, current United Kingdom dress designs and colours are unsuitable for Canada. (*S.R.I.S.*, July 4, 1952.)

79. *Men's shirts.* One reason British shirts are not bought in Canada is because Canadian men generally prefer attached collars. (Board of Trade, *Report of the United Kingdom Clothing Mission to Canada, 1949.*)

80. *Petroleum refinery equipment and oil field equipment.* All refinery and absorption plant equipment used in Canada conforms to the American Petroleum Institute standards. (*S.R.I.S.*, May 21, 1952; July 26, 1955.)

81. *Radio equipment and components.* American design standards are practically universal in Canada. The greatest aid to sales of British components is interchangeability with United States and Canadian parts. (*S.R.I.S.*, Dec. 4, 1951; July 18, 1958.)

82. *Roofing felt and paper.* United Kingdom paper and roll roofings do not comply with Canadian Standard Weights. (May 10, 1957.)

83. *Paint and varnish materials.* Trade specifications exist for various chemicals and British standards are sometimes regarded as indefinite. (*S.R.I.S.*, May 21, 1953.)

84. *Domestic hardware.* United Kingdom goods are at a disadvantage in terms of colour, style, and design. (*S.R.I.S.*, Jan. 2, 1950; April 13, 1956.)

85. *Glass and crystal.* British manufacturers have fallen behind in the field of contemporary design through their concentration on products of traditional designs. (*S.R.I.S.*, Jan. 17, 1958.)

86. *Pottery.* By the speedy action of British potters in producing contemporary design and shapes, United Kingdom contemporary pottery enjoys a marked success in Canada. (*S.R.I.S.*, Oct. 5, 1956.)

87. *Pianos.* By catering to Canadian wishes in taste and style, one piano firm has achieved a fairly successful record of sales. (*S.R.I.S.*, July 20, 1955.)

88. *Engineers' hand tools.* Complaints are received from Canadian dealers about the quality and design of the packaging of United Kingdom tools. In addition, the products offered must be similar in design and styling to American products. (*S.R.I.S.*, Sept. 19, 1952; Nov. 30, 1954.) In a later report it is stated that United Kingdom suppliers are now packing their products attractively. (April 14, 1958.)

89. *Ladies' handbags.* Style is an important factor influencing sales and a large variety of styles are required for each season of the year. (*S.R.I.S.*, Nov. 22, 1954.)

90. *Luggage.* United Kingdom leather luggage enjoys a high reputation in Canada. (*S.R.I.S.*, March 8, 1954.)

91. *Drapery and upholstery fabrics.* Although it is considered impractical and inadvisable for United Kingdom manufacturers to attempt to copy the design of the North American products, they are unlikely to enjoy a brisk demand for their more traditional lines unless these can be offered in the lively colour combinations demanded by the Canadian customer. (*S.R.I.S.*, March 21, 1955.)

92. *Air conditioning equipment.* Some designs from the United Kingdom require special tools for servicing because of a different screw thread. (*S.R.I.S.*, Feb. 2, 1951.)

93. *Sanitary earthenware.* There is a fundamental difference between the British and North American product: British manufacturers mainly use glazed earthenware, North American manufacturers use mainly vitreous china. Technically there are advantages and disadvantages with both materials. Irrespective of the technical merits of each material, there is the indisputable fact that the Canadian plumbing trade generally is sold on vitreous china as a result of effective promotion by Canadian and United States manufacturers over a considerable period. (*S.R.I.S.*, Feb. 22, 1952.)

94. *Woollen and worsted piece goods.* Many products suitable for the British market are not salable in Canada. The Canadian market generally requires lightweight medium to low grade clothes, of light or bright colour. (*S.R.I.S.*, Sept. 21, 1953.)

95. *Cotton towels.* United Kingdom firms are sometimes criticized for lack of a wide range of good colours. (*S.R.I.S.*, Oct. 30, 1950.)

96. *Children's ready-made clothing.* Outfits for teenage girls need to be brighter and more stylish and boys' outer garments are in general much more casual than is usual in Great Britain. Sales of girls' sportswear are restricted because of poor styling and fitting. (*S.R.I.S.*, July 4, 1952; March 13, 1956.)

97. *Industrial protective clothing.* The apparent formidable difference in standards may have tended to intimidate British firms in the past. (*S.R.I.S.*, Feb. 27, 1956.)

98. *Pumps.* Generally pumps of United Kingdom design are acceptable in Canada. There are, however, some differences from North American design which the Canadian will not accept. Canadian requirements correspond very closely with United States standards. Also new equipment must fit in with existing equipment, most of which is from the United States. For example, it is important that flange dimensions, bolt nuts, studs, screw threads, etc., conform to American standards. For use in Canada equipment must be rugged. (*S.R.I.S.*, April 22, 1955.)

99. *Lawn mowers.* Some United Kingdom lawn mowers, it is alleged, are designed for very smooth lawns and are frequently unsatisfactory for the rougher lawns in Canada requiring a more rugged machine. (*S.R.I.S.*, Sept. 14, 1951.)

100. *Cranes and hoists.* Machinery likely to be used in the open air should be winterized; and cabs should be adequately heated. (*S.R.I.S.*, Feb. 24, 1951.)

101. *Fork lift trucks.* The more frequent and more serious complaints re-

gistered against British equipment concern servicing problems and differences from North American standards. (*S.R.I.S.*, March 4, 1956.)

102. Paper converting machinery. Many Canadian buyers state that they would sooner buy from Britain than the United States provided . . . that British machines have been brought into line with their requirements. (*S.R.I.S.*, Dec. 9, 1957.)

103. Bakery machinery. While the comments of many representatives of the bakery trade in Canada were almost unanimously favourable in respect to the durability and reliability of United Kingdom machinery, it was suggested in general terms that recent technical advances in American equipment design had tended to outdate comparable United Kingdom machinery. (*S.R.I.S.*, Jan. 2, 1951.)

104. Diesel engines. In many applications, although perhaps not in marine, diesels of higher speed and lighter weight than are available from United Kingdom firms are now becoming popular, following American practice. (*S.R.I.S.*, April 12, 1954.)

105. Marine diesels. There is some feeling that United Kingdom engines are built for a quality of fuel oil not available in Canada. (*S.R.I.S.*, Feb. 29, 1952.)

106. Printing machinery. The Canadian buyer's impression of British machines is that there is insufficient emphasis on speed and the reduction of both set-up time and floor space. Also on some machines there is not enough simplification and streamlining. (*S.R.I.S.*, June 9, 1954.)

107. Metal mining equipment. The quality of British products certainly matches that of Canadian and American goods. Good engineering design is foremost in the mind of the British manufacturer to such an extent that at times he can be accused of "over-designing." This would prove an asset in the case of equipment designed to meet rigid specifications, but otherwise holds up production and delivery. (*Report to the Directors of the Canadian Metal Mining Association on the Mission to the United Kingdom*, Nov. 1955.)

108. Engineering goods. Quality is generally quite good. (Board of Trade, *Report of the United Kingdom Engineering Mission, 1948*, p. 35.)

109. Trucks, tractors, mining equipment. Physical differences between the United Kingdom and Canada mean that United Kingdom products must be modified before they can be sold in Canada. (*Planning*, XVI (Feb. 1949); XVII (Aug. 1949); Board of Trade, *Report of the British Agricultural Machinery Mission to Canada, 1948, passim.*)

110. Rubber-proofed clothing. Exports to Canada which used to be considerable fell away because of a change in consumer habits; there remained a limited demand in the agricultural districts, but the general public as a whole turned to chemically proofed raincoats, leaving rubber-proofed clothing for the special requirements of miners and other industrial workers. (Working Party Report, *Rubber Proofed Clothing*, 1947.)

(g) Credit

111. Terms of payment. The terms on which the majority of Canadian buyers endeavour to do business are more extended than United Kingdom manufacturers sometimes desire to recognize. (Board of Trade, *Exporting to Canada*, p. 29.)

112. Excavators. The "tight money policy" of 1957 cut straight sales. "Trade-ins" as down payment would leave distributor without cash and "rental-purchase" system gave the renter an agreed period (one year) to decide before buying. If he buys, he receives at least 90 per cent credit for his rent (generally 5 to 10 per cent of selling price). Thus, financing the distributors becomes a major problem for United Kingdom firms. (S.R.I.S., May 15, 1958; Oct. 29, 1954.)

113. Hosiery and knitwear. The Canadian manufacturer normally grants 30 days' credit from date of invoice. This is roughly equivalent to 60 days' credit from a United Kingdom manufacturer and is clearly the yardstick for a United Kingdom manufacturer considering the problem. (S.R.I.S., May 6, 1954.)

114. Pipe and other organs. The necessity of paying up to 80 per cent of the value with the order—a practice customary in the United Kingdom—is disliked in Canada. (S.R.I.S., Aug. 1, 1957.)

115. Textile machinery. There is need for liberal financing terms when competing with the United States. The customary 25 per cent down payment required by British sellers is said to be disliked by many. (S.R.I.S., July 2, 1951.)

116. Diesel engines. There have been reports of discrimination by acceptance companies against United Kingdom diesels but it seems that the discrimination is against the dealers who handle them and not against the engines. (S.R.I.S., April 12, 1954.)

(h) Engineering Equipment and Education

117. Excavators. The part played in Canadian operations by the large United States contractors is significant for they are invariably wedded to United States equipment. (S.R.I.S., Oct. 29, 1954.)

118. Oil field equipment. Company purchasing is strongly influenced by what the men in the field prefer. Having trained with American equipment and having grown accustomed to it through long use, the men in the field are likely to prove the toughest obstacle to the introduction of British equipment. (S.R.I.S., Oct. 29, 1951.)

119. Coal mining equipment. Many Canadian mining engineers have been trained to American methods and are unfamiliar with British machinery. (S.R.I.S., Oct. 5, 1953.)

120. Petroleum refinery equipment. The reluctance of construction firms and oil companies to favour British equipment springs largely from a lack of confidence regarding deliveries and after-sales service. (S.R.I.S., May 21, 1952.)

The foregoing information relates to the post-war period, a fact which might suggest that these problems were merely the result of World War II and its aftermath. This inference would be incorrect. Although problems of the sort noted above probably were enhanced by the war and its repercussions, it is evident that many of these difficulties were apparent before the advent of war. This is indicated by various portions of the reports of the Balfour Commission which examined British industry and trade in the late twenties. Some of the remarks made in these reports are in much the same vein as those made during the post-war period.

... if Britain is to increase her exports to Canada, certain adaptations are necessary. Canada will not buy from Britain on the score of quality only—it must be quality plus suitability and reasonably prompt availability.... Quality alone, no matter how strong the sentiment may be, will not overcome an unsuitable style, bad packing or delay in delivery....

Importers in the Dominion expect a manufacturer or exporter desiring a share of their orders to make business free from irritation and to offer a service at least comparable with that usual in North America....

It is obvious (from the trade statistics) that the existing trade is not only large enough to make it worthwhile, but that the United Kingdom does not secure nearly as much as she should....

The sale of goods by the method of appointing agents on commission is the policy adopted generally by United Kingdom firms in the Canadian market. While this method is moderately successful in many cases, there is no doubt that it places British goods at a disadvantage compared with United States products in competing classes. United States firms not only employ agents on commission; they also establish branch warehouses where stocks are kept and can be supplied at once. This is particularly necessary, for example, in machinery of every kind, so that spare parts may be readily available.

British goods have to compete, therefore, with United States firms carrying stocks on the spot and in addition with their agents on commission ... goods can be shipped usually on receipt of the order. This alone is instrumental in marketing large quantities of goods irrespective of price and quality....

... The British exporter has two cheap routes to Canada, one to Montreal and the other through the Panama Canal to Vancouver, but the element of time can be overcome only by the carrying of stocks in the country.

Unreliability in delivery, or the time taken to fill an order are two of the most difficult matters requiring solution....[36]

By way of comparison it is interesting to quote part of a leading editorial in *The Times* in 1956 entitled "The Export Lag."

... The unsatisfactory trends of the last few years may ... merely reflect inadequate adaptation to changed circumstances, essentially the return of competition. Obviously this would not be a fair comment to make of the whole of British exporting....

There is nevertheless an accumulating amount of evidence that the attitude of too large a part of British industry towards exporting is less aggressive, less enlightened and less far-sighted than that of its rivals. Complaints come from many markets in which British goods have done well since the war that quality is unsatisfactory, and style and design not adapted to local tastes; that service is not adequate; fixed prices are not quoted, and quotations for "servicing" are revised upwards when rivals do not do the same; that complaints are brushed aside without reasonable investigation; that inquiries are neglected; delivery promises too long; and that even these promises are broken. The old complaints of catalogues being in English, or in bad translations, with the information in British measures and currency, and of hurried visits to export markets in the Middle East or South America or even Europe by salesmen who cannot speak the local language are still only too often not merely repeated but justified....[37]

CHAPTER FIVE

MARKET REGULATION

1. PRIVATE REGULATION

IN A COMPETITIVE MARKET as conventionally defined in economic theory, changes in the relationship of prices and in the relationship of various non-price market variables would be expected to reveal themselves under the play of ordinary market forces. Consequently, in such a situation one could conclude that changes in Britain's share of the Canadian market have simply reflected the free play of market forces; and any apparently divergent trends between changes in relative prices and Britain's share of the market could be attributed to the influence of the many non-price variables affecting sales.[1] If, on the other hand, one envisages a market subject to arbitrary trade regulations of various kinds, then changes in Britain's share of the Canadian market may reflect not only changes in price and non-price variables but also in the control which this regulation exercises over the market. To what extent have British sales in Canada been influenced by arbitrary market restrictions, and what has been the incidence of these restrictions on Britain's share of the Canadian market during the past thirty years?

The essential quality of any market that is not competitive is that control is exercised over demand or supply.[2] Such control may arise through the private actions of producers, traders, and buyers among themselves, or through governmental policies. Thus, private regulation may lead to the exclusion of British goods by private Canadian interests, or a restriction of British supplies to the Canadian market by private British interests, or a combination of both. In the case of public controls, British goods may be excluded from Canada by measures taken by the Canadian government, or the supply of British goods to Canada may be restricted by measures taken by the British government. Such control, whether private or public, need not of course restrict trade; it may also seek to make the flow of trade larger than it would be if left on its own.

Many markets, it seems fair to say, are subject to some element of control and it is not to be expected that the various commodity markets relevant to this discussion can be neatly classified into those that are fully competitive and those that are not. Again there are difficulties because of a lack of satisfactory information and problems of interpretation. However, by examining the evidence available one can hope to gain some impression of the extent to which various markets have been regulated, and also to determine how this regulation is likely to have altered the size, composition, and direction of trade.

The private regulation of international trade is, it seems, mainly exercised in three ways. First, control can be exercised through intercorporate financial and management links. This might result in the regulation of the purchasing policies of Canadian buyers, such as subsidiary companies controlled abroad. It might also mean that the supply of British goods offered in Canada is controlled, as for example in the case of a British firm affiliated with a Canadian or American firm producing similar products. Secondly, suppliers in Britain and North America could seek to control trade with Canada through various kinds of market-sharing and patent-licensing agreements. Thirdly, effective trade regulation could arise as a consequence of oligopolistic markets—that is, markets dominated by relatively few sellers who, though not bound by any formal arrangements, are aware of their mutual interdependence and act differently than they would if they were operating in a competitive market situation.

In few countries of the world does foreign ownership and control of domestic production facilities loom as large as in Canada. As shown in Table XXXIV, in 1955 non-residents controlled some 57 per cent of Canadian manufacturing firms, about 66 per cent of mining, smelting, and petroleum exploration and development firms, and approximately 30 per cent of all companies in Canada. Table XXXIV also indicates that an overwhelming proportion of this foreign

TABLE XXXIV

NON-RESIDENT CONTROL OVER CANADIAN INDUSTRY

A. PERCENTAGE OF BOOK-VALUE OF CANADIAN COMPANIES CONTROLLED BY NON-RESIDENTS

	U.S.				Elsewhere, incl. U.K.			
	1926	1939	1948	1955	1926	1939	1948	1955
Manufacturing	30	32	39	47	5	6	4	10
Mining, smelting, and petroleum exploration and development	32	38	37	64	6	4	3	2
Railways	3	3	3	2	—	—	—	—
Other utilities	20	26	24	9	—	—	—	1
Total above plus merchandising and construction	15	19	22	26	2	2	3	4

B. CONTROL OVER SELECTED CANADIAN INDUSTRIES, 1955

	Percentage of capital employed Controlled in		
	Can.	U.S.	Elsewhere, incl. U.K.
Petroleum	20	74	6
Mining, smelting, refining	38	60	2
Manufacturing:			
Pulp and paper	46	43	11
Textiles	82	10	8
Chemicals	23	51	26
Transportation equipment	45	18	37
Electrical apparatus	18	68	14
Agricultural machinery	67	33	—
Primary iron and steel	92	8	—
Beverages	86	13	1
Automobiles and parts	4	96	—
Rubber	2	88	10
All other	47	45	8
Sub-total	48	42	10
Total of all above industries	41	51	8

TABLE XXXIV (cont.)

C. PERCENTAGE OF THE TOTAL SELLING VALUE OF CANADIAN FACTORY SHIPMENTS IN SELECTED INDUSTRIES MADE FROM UNITED STATES-CONTROLLED MANUFACTURING ESTABLISHMENTS, 1953

Motor vehicles	98	Grain mill products	29
Rubber products	78	Heating and cooking apparatus	29
Non-ferrous metal smelting		Paper products	29
and refining	70	Brass and copper products	27
Petroleum products	68	Toilet preparations	27
Motor vehicle parts	67	Canning and processing	24
Machinery—household, office, store	60	Hardware, tools and cutlery	23
Non-ferrous metal products	50	Miscellaneous manufactures	20
Electrical apparatus and supplies	50	Agricultural implements	20
Paints, varnishes, & lacquers	45	Aircraft and railway equipment	19
Soaps, washing compounds,		Petroleum and coke products	18
cleaning preparations	45	Dairy products	16
Medicinal and pharmaceutical		Castings, iron	15
preparations	41	Textile products (ex. clothing)	14
Sheet metal products	39	Iron and steel products, n.o.p.	14
Pulp and paper	39	Beverages	12
Chemicals and allied products	36	Bakery products and confectionery	10
Machinery, industrial	32	Primary iron and steel	7

SOURCES: Royal Commission on Canada's Economic Prospects, *Canada-United States Economic Relations,* prepared by I. Brecher and S. S. Reisman, Table 28, p. 105; Dominion Bureau of Statistics, *The Canadian Balance of International Payments, 1957,* pp. 51, 53.

control is vested in United States hands. United States preponderance has increased over the years, relative both to domestic and other foreign control, and is especially notable in such strategic sectors as manufacturing, petroleum exploration and development, and mining, smelting, and refining.

The extensive control of Canadian industry by non-residents, particularly in the manufacturing and primary resource sectors of the economy, means that purchasing policy for a large proportion of Canadian firms ultimately rests in the hands of foreigners, predominantly Americans. This in itself does not necessarily mean that trade has been diverted into uneconomic channels by arbitrary private control. In their operations firms presumably seek to maximize profits and consequently can generally be expected to purchase those goods best meeting their requirements at the lowest price regardless of source. Moreover, as already noted, production in Canada by United States subsidiaries of goods that might otherwise be imported from the United States may be a factor tending to increase Britain's share of the Canadian market, although the possible importance of this is greatly lessened because many of these subsidiaries rely heavily upon United States materials, parts, and components for their production. This dependence may, of course, reflect basic market factors and might be little different were the companies independent. Nevertheless, the distinct possibility remains that non-resident, largely American, control of much Canadian industry may impose certain artificial restrictions on many Canadian imports. In the words of one of the studies prepared for the Royal Commission on Canada's Economic Prospects:

As might be expected, because the relationships between parent and subsidiary are often close in personnel, plant design and product styling, they typically exhibit similar behaviour in their purchasing policies and practices. Accordingly, they will often use similar materials, parts and equipment and similar sources of supply as a matter of course and quite apart from any element of direction from the parent. Within this framework, however, there appears to be considerable latitude for many subsidiaries in their purchasing decisions. Many of the major companies apparently make a deliberate effort, as a matter of policy, to buy in Canada wherever supplies are available on a competitive basis with respect to price, quality and service. Indeed, a number of these companies have attempted to develop Canadian sources of supply, even at the cost of initial premium prices and other disadvantages. Among the reasons cited for such a policy are the desire for good customer and public relations, the need for equipment and supplies uniquely suited to Canadian conditions and the greater certainty and convenience associated with domestic supplies and services close at hand.

On the other hand, there are cases where the parent exercises close supervision over general purchasing and channels the subsidiary's requirements to itself and to its own suppliers. This is especially true where the global enterprise has developed surplus capacity and seeks to keep its plant operating at maximum levels.

It should be apparent that no simple generalization will explain adequately the whole range of purchasing behaviour. What is clear, however, particularly with respect to manufacturing enterprises, is the observable fact that imports from the parent, and from the parent's suppliers, remain high.[3]

A further complication arises as far as this investigation is concerned from the fact that certain United States companies which control a large share of Canadian industry also control a substantial share of United Kingdom industry. Some of the more obvious examples are motor cars, electrical apparatus and equipment, business machines, and farm machinery. Again it does not necessarily follow that trade has been diverted into artificial and uneconomic channels; but an element of arbitrary private control is obviously present. For example, it has been suggested to the writer that the recent upsurge in exports of British motor cars to Canada in part reflects a decision taken in Detroit to press North American sales of cars made by British subsidiaries of American companies. Similarly, the increase in Canadian imports of farm tractors and tractor engines from the United Kingdom reflects a decision by certain Canadian producers to import from British affiliates.

A recent study of American investment in Britain's manufacturing industries indicates that the net assets of British manufacturing firms in which American equity exceeded 25 per cent totalled over $1 1/3 billions in 1955. Of total United States investment in Britain, over one-fifth was accounted for by motor vehicles and equipment, a further fifth in the non-electrical machinery industry, somewhat less than an eighth in each of chemicals, primary metals, and electrical machinery and equipment, and smaller amounts in food products, rubber products, and other industries.[4] It is also clear that many leading United States companies have or have had financial affiliations with British firms in a wide range of industries including the following: basic chemicals, pharmaceutical products, toilet preparations and cosmetics, soap, synthetic fibres, engineering and electrical equipment (such as agricultural machinery, business machines, sewing machines, shoe machines, refrigeration equipment, electrical and electronic equipment), automobiles, trucks and components (roller bearings, automatic transmissions), precision instruments of all kinds, rubber products, moving picture films, abrasives, and glassware.[5] One of the conclusions, of considerable interest here, that the author draws is that "American representation is highly concentrated in the 'newer' ... British industries, the origin of which for the most part dates back to the inter-war period. Almost without exception, the rate of expansion of such industries is greater than that for industry as a whole. Yet, though new to this country, most of the industries concerned had been previously well established in the United States."

Later in this same study consideration is given to the influence of United States affiliated companies in Britain on Britain's external trade and balance of payments.[6] In general, it is concluded that "U.S. firms have played an important role in the U.K. drive for external solvency since 1945." It is also pointed out that in some product lines these affiliates have been important exporters to the United States and Canada. At the same time it is stated that

Whilst a number of U.S.-controlled firms, e.g., in the refrigeration, enamelling, industrial equipment, pump and kitchen equipment fields, claimed they competed with their parent companies, for the most part, there is some kind of market-sharing agreement in operation, which varies according to the currency availability position of the buyer and the relative costs and convenience of the seller. Thus, as might be expected, the U.K. branch unit or associate firm tends to specialize in supplying the European and Commonwealth (within the Sterling Area) markets, whilst the parent plan satisfies consumers in the Western Hemisphere.

All this verges on the subject of international cartel arrangements and their influence on British exports to Canada. This is a topic that lends itself to more detailed examination. Most of the evidence presented below is based on the substantial number of comprehensive United States studies which emerged at the end of World War II.[7] In addition, considerable reliance has been placed on the reports of the Canadian Combines Commissioner, including one report specifically concerned with the effect of cartel activities on Canada's international trade.[8] In the brief résumés of the evidence on cartel activities in individual industries which follow below, no attempt has been made to cover the entire range of products entering Canada's import trade. Nor should these summaries be regarded as being in any way exhaustive, authoritative, or complete for the industries that are considered. They are intended merely to illustrate the prevalence and the effect of cartel activities as far as Britain's export trade with Canada is concerned.

A. Inter-War Period

1. FIBRES AND TEXTILES

(i) *Wool, cotton, and their products.* Little evidence has been found suggesting cartel arrangements applying to trade in these products. The woollen and worsted industries as well as the clothing industry seem to be relatively competitive.[9] The Royal Commission on Textiles (1936) adduced some evidence indicating informal pricing agreements for cotton yarns, underwear, and carpets.[10] However, these regulations evidently applied only for several years in the mid thirties. During these years these agreements at times were disregarded by some members of the industries. In a few instances, however, such as in the case of cotton sewing thread where the J. & P. Coats and English Sewing Thread Company combine was dominant, there was an arrangement somewhat akin to that usually associated with international regulation of trade by private interests.[11]

(ii) *Synthetic fibres and their products.* The synthetic fibre industry in Canada was and is dominated by four foreign firms: Du Pont of the United States; Imperial Chemicals Incorporated and Courtaulds of Britain; Dreyfus Brothers of Switzerland.[12] Du Pont and Imperial Chemicals Incorporated operated through their jointly owned subsidiary, Canadian Industries Limited, and began producing nylon just before the war. Courtaulds, through their subsidiary, Courtaulds (Canada) Ltd., were the sole producers of viscose (rayon) yarns. The Dreyfus combine, through its subsidiary, the Canadian Celanese Corporation, controlled the production of cellulose acetate yarns. Both the Courtaulds and Dreyfus subsidiaries were formed in the late twenties. In every case the parent organizations had a monopoly in the production of the particular product in the American and British markets—indeed, one might almost say in the world market generally. No evidence has been found to suggest that the parent companies in Britain competed with their subsidiaries in Canada in providing synthetic fibres to the Canadian market.

At the product level there has probably been more competition. In the period before 1938, when Courtaulds and Canadian Celanese Corporation dominated the synthetic fibre market, only Canadian Celanese Corporation carried production beyond the yarn stage. Considerable weaving was done by firms who prior to 1930 had relied primarily on raw silk as their basic raw material. By the end of the thirties these firms were said to be shipping increasing quantities of fabrics abroad.[13]

2. IRON, STEEL AND THEIR PRODUCTS

(i) *Primary iron and steel products.* Extensive and highly complex cartel arrangements pervaded the primary iron and steel industry during the inter-war period.[14] The first International Steel Cartel formed in 1926 was not adhered to in general by producers in either the United Kingdom or the United States although these producers did participate in certain related arrangements such as the Tube Cartel and the Rail Cartel. After the failure of the first International Steel Cartel a second cartel was organized around various selling syndicates for individual products, these syndicates being co-ordinated by a series of management and comptoir committees. In addition, several independent cartels— for example, tubes, rails—co-ordinated their policies with the Steel Cartel's policies. The variety of products thus controlled included virtually all primary iron and steel products—strips and bands, semi-finished products, sheets, plates, structural shapes, bars, beams, rods, galvanized sheets, rails, scrap, tubes, tinplate, wire. With the advent of war the cartel was dissolved.

Unfortunately the various studies made of this cartel give no clear indication of the way in which it impinged on Canada's imports of primary steel products although it is generally considered to have exerted some influence.[15] It seems likely that somewhat different arrangements applied to each product. It is known that Britain's allocation of the international steel market was based on the share of this market that Britain commanded in 1934.[16] Although in general this was a relatively low base from Britain's point of view, it was a year in which Britain's exports to Canada loomed rather larger than usual, partly as a result of increases in Canadian tariff preferences. However, it does not follow that this improved Britain's position in Canada's market significantly. When the United States entered the cartel in 1938 her export trade was geared to her share of the export market in 1936—a year in which Britain's position in the Canadian market had again waned somewhat.[17]

Knowledge of the way in which two of the cartels affiliated with the International Steel Cartel regulated Canadian trade is somewhat more satisfactory and may be indicative of the marketing arrangements in other products. One of these affiliated organizations was the International Tube Cartel; the other the International Rail Makers' Association.[18] The Tube Cartel was organized between 1926 and 1929 and included the major producers in Canada, the United States, and the United Kingdom. Although officially dissolved in 1935, an informal agreement persisted until World War II. Evidence coming before the Canadian Combines Commissioner, as related in his report, suggests that Canadian producers agreed to restrict their production to particular sizes and classes of tubes in return for protection in the domestic market.[19] Some domestic consumers, according to the report, complained of being unable to obtain quotations from either United Kingdom or United States producers for these classes of restricted products.

The Rail Cartel had been organized at the turn of the century and both Britain and the United States eventually became members. The United States came in in 1904 on condition that Britain relinquish her exclusive right, as established in earlier agreements, to the Canadian and Newfoundland markets. Britain agreed to this and "it is stated that as a result they [the Americans] took practically all orders therefrom."[20] This cartel collapsed with World War I and was not resurrected until 1926. By 1929 both Britain and the United States were again members. Canadian producers accepted some orders under the agreement shortly before World War II.

(ii) *Manufactures.* There is much less evidence indicating private restriction on international trade in iron and steel manufactures than in primary products. Whether this merely reflects less public information or indicates a greater degree of competition is not clear. In view of the range of products and the large number of producers involved it is not unlikely that for many of these commodities at any rate there was a fair degree of competition. However, it is also evident that for a considerable number of important commodities restrictions did exist. Many of these restrictions were exercised through intercorporate financial and management links and through patent agreements. The agricultural machinery industry provides an example of the first of these kinds of control,[21] the roller bearing industry an example of the second.[22] Other commodities for which restrictive practices of one type or another are suggested include machine tools, typewriters, match-making machinery, sewing machines, diesel engines, pins, snap fasteners, aircraft, and grain disc separators.[23] However, very little authoritative information is available on these arrangements. One is unable to say how restrictive the practices were or what their impact was on the source of Canada's imports.

3. ELECTRICAL AND ELECTRONIC APPARATUS AND EQUIPMENT

The restrictive influence on international trade arising from intercorporate financial control and patent arrangements is especially apparent in this group of commodities. Among the many products affected were batteries, electric wires and cables, electric lamps, turbines, generators, heating devices, magnets, motors, refrigerators, vacuum cleaners, radio tubes, and radio sets.[24] Some of the predominant companies involved in these arrangements during the inter-war period were General Electric, Westinghouse, N.V. Phillips, Radio Corporation of America, the International Telephone and Telegraph Company, Marconi, Bell Telephone, Western Electric, and their international affiliates.[25] To describe the intricate web of market control for this group of products is a study in itself. Available evidence indicates that in the past where restrictions have occurred the Canadian market has typically been reserved either to Canadian corporations —most of which are subsidiaries of United States firms—or directly to United States corporations. For example, in the electric lamp industry extensive patent cross-licensing arrangements reserved the Canadian market to Canadian firms.[26] In the case of radio sets and tubes, Canada was assigned to the Radio Group (Radio Corporation of America-International General Electric-Westinghouse) as part of its exclusive territory.[27] Canadian patents on radio sets were subsequently pooled in Radio Patents Limited, while those on radio tubes were placed in a similar organisation, Thermionics, Limited. "The arrangements for the exchange of patents and licenses protect Canadian manufactures from outside competition, while the establishment of holding companies to control Canadian patents restricts competition among Canadian licensees."[28]

4. NON-METALLIC PRODUCTS

One of the clearer illustrations of the influence of private trade restrictions on Canada's foreign trade during the inter-war period is in the glass industry.[29] Cartel arrangements in this industry date almost from the beginning of the century. Throughout the twenties and thirties glass imports into Canada were influenced by a succession of formal and informal agreements. The major producers involved were Pilkington Bros. Ltd. of the United Kingdom, the Pittsburgh Plate Glass Company and the Libby-Owens-Ford Glass Company in the United States, and European producers associated under the International Plate Glass Convention. The market-sharing and price-fixing agreements, to which Pilkington was a party, evidently tended to stabilize Britain's share of the Canadian market and did not encourage expansion.[30] The same, however, was not true of the United States. For although United States producers of glass adhered to the agreements, United States and Canadian jobbers frequently brought lower-priced United States glass into Canada. In other words, the geographical proximity of the United States and Canada, the ease with which trade between the two countries could take place, the lower prices of United States glass, and the lack of control by United States producers over jobbers meant that the United States part of the agreement could only be partly enforced. From 1931 to 1939 the United States share of the Canadian market grew appreciably while the United Kingdom share remained about the same.

According to the Combine Commissioner's report, the effects of the cartel arrangements in the glass industry were rather dramatically demonstrated after the Ottawa tariff agreements came into effect in 1932. In the tariff reorganization, the principal plate glass items were freed under Imperial Preference rates. Subsequently automobile producers, who were trying to increase the empire content of their cars, found that British producers refused to sell them more than a small percentage of their glass requirements, even though these automobile companies were prepared to pay more than the price asked by United States glass producers.[31]

The evidence for other non-metallic products is less satisfactory. There are suggestions, however, that restrictive practices of one kind or another extended to various other glass products[32]—for example, optical goods, bottles, fibres, sheet glass—as well as to other kinds of non-metallic products—asbestos, cellophane, petroleum products, and matches. Except for matches, it is not clear how these restrictions may have affected British exports to Canada. In the case of matches Canadian production was made the monopoly of the Eddy Match Company—a joint subsidiary of the Diamond Match Company of the United States, Bryand and May of the United Kingdom, and Swedish Match. Canadian production only was sold in Canada.[33]

5. CHEMICALS AND PHARMACEUTICALS

Private regulation of international trade during the inter-war period was highly developed in the chemical and pharmaceutical industries. As far as the context of this essay is concerned the chief protagonists have been Du Pont in the United States and Imperial Chemicals Incorporated in Great Britain.[34] Control over most of the commodities in question has been exercised, in varying degree, through a combination of the three main elements of cartel regulation: marketing agreements, patent licensing, and intercorporate financial and management controls.

The story of the extension of international collusion in this industry to the Canadian market begins with the emergence of Imperial Chemicals Incorporated as the dominant chemical producer in Britain in the late twenties and the growing ascendancy of Du Pont in the United States at about the same time. In 1929 these two firms reached an understanding whereby Imperial Chemicals Incorporated was allocated the British Empire market excluding Canada and New-foundland, and Du Pont the market in the United States and Central America. It was agreed eventually to eliminate competition in the Canadian market by establishing a jointly owned subsidiary. The subsidiary, Canadian Industries Limited, was established after a series of company reorganizations by which the major Canadian producers of explosives and chemicals became either subsidiaries of Canadian Industries Limited or operating divisions within Canadian Industries Limited. The general effect of this arrangement, as summarized in the Combines Commissioner's report, was that Canadian Industries Limited was given exclusive rights in Canada to any process owned by either of the major stockholders. It was the sole distributor of products shipped to Canada by either Du Pont or Imperial Chemicals Incorporated, and was confined in its operations to the Canadian market.[35] The list of products embraced by these arrangements included a wide range of commodities coming within the confines of the chemicals industry; to mention but a few: paints, pigments, titanium, photographic supplies, plastics, cellulose, fertilizer, disinfectants, insecticides, anti-freeze, dyestuffs, hydrogen peroxide, explosives, and general chemicals.

One further point to be noted is that this complex web of control extended beyond the limits of Du Pont, Canadian Industries Limited, and Imperial Chemicals Incorporated. In part it reflected the various connections the parent organizations had with other cartels—for example, Imperial Chemicals Incorporated and Courtaulds.[36] In part also it reflected the power Canadian Industries Limited could wield to obtain the co-operation of various other Canadian manufacturers, actual or potential, of chemical products. For instance, Canadian Industries Limited made agreements with the Canadian International Paper Company, Proctor and Gamble, and Shawinigan Water and Power Company whereby these companies agreed to stay outside the preserve of Canadian Industries Limited in return for a similar concession by Canadian Industries Limited.[37]

Nor were the controls jointly fostered by Imperial Chemicals Incorporated and Du Pont the only ones interposed on Canada's trade in chemicals. In the case of soda ash, for example, the United States association Albasso was given jurisdiction over the Canadian market in its agreement with various European producers, including Imperial Chemicals Incorporated. Albasso, in turn, vested control of the Canadian market in the hands of a Canadian subsidiary of one of its members, later revising this arrangement to include certain United States producers in California.[38]

Other chemical products involved in private trade agreements include tanning materials, especially quebracho, for which two sales agents were delegated for North America and the Antilles;[39] borax and boracic acid, under the control of the International Borax Cartel;[40] pharmaceuticals—for example, British manufactures of insulin could not export to Canada under their patent rights;[41] oxygen plant and equipment, the British Oxygen Company being barred from Canada for certain products by patent licences.[42]

6. OTHER NOTABLE INSTANCES

In 1953 a United Nations study group published a list of well over one hundred products for which restrictive practices have been reported at one time or another since World War I.[43] To what extent Canadian imports of these products may have been restricted is not clear. None the less, the extensive nature of the list and the scope of those arrangements for which information is available suggests that Canadian imports of many of the products noted may on occasion have been circumscribed by restrictions of one kind or another.

B. Post-War Period

The spate of government enquiries in North America immediately after World War II provides most of the reliable information available on the extent and nature of private restrictions on international trade during the inter-war period. The fact that there have been no comparable enquiries since then has meant that there is much less information available on cartel practices since about 1948. On the whole it seems clear from the official inquiries that the advent of war in 1939 substantially altered many of the existing agreements, especially those to which enemy concerns were parties. Moreover, the fact is that for most of the years since 1939 there has been an acute shortage of most products, and this probably has meant that producers' interests have tended to be concentrated more on production problems and less on marketing problems. In addition, British producers after the war were pressed to give priority to sales in markets such as Canada which in pre-war years had sometimes been deliberately avoided. Also, after World War II British producers may have acquired a new awareness of the potential of the Canadian market both in the immediate future and in the longer run. As a result they may have been less willing to automatically exclude themselves from the area. Finally, the rather broader interpretation given to United States anti-trust laws recently in connection with foreign affiliations and agreements has led to at least the formal break-up of certain cartel arrangements.[44] One of the most important instances of this so far as this essay is concerned is the dissolution of Du Pont's and Imperial Chemicals Incorporated joint ownership of Canadian Industries Limited in 1954.[45] Both parent companies now have their own subsidiaries in Canada, though the extent to which they might eventually actively compete with one another and with United States and United Kingdom production is not clear. For the foregoing reasons as well as others, it seems likely that cartel restrictions since the war have been significantly less important than during the thirties.[46]

There are, however, indications that private restrictions on British exports to Canada have continued to exist. One reason for believing this is that the attitude of some British industrialists seems to have remained sympathetic to restrictive practices. Business leaders and various business associations continued to advocate the cartelization of international trade during the last years of the war.[47] There is evidence that to some extent this attitude may have carried over into post-war years.[48] This interest in cartel agreements may have stemmed not so much from short-run considerations, as from fear of the longer-run consequences of free and unmitigated competition on the relative position of British industry.[49]

Secondly, Mr. Dunning in the study already cited states that since 1945 "many hundreds" of licensing agreements between British and American firms have been concluded. In this connection he particularly mentions instrument firms, the petroleum refinery equipment industry, and the domestic electrical appliances, cosmetics, earth moving equipment, and machine tool industries.[50]

Thirdly, it should be remembered that even if British business attitudes were sympathetic to free competition, the scope for unilateral action was sometimes limited. In those instances where marketing agreements, pure and simple, prevail it might be relatively easy for British firms to withdraw and push their sales to the full. But as has been shown above, many of the cartel arrangements made during the inter-war years were based not only on marketing agreements but also on intercorporate financial and management links and patent-licensing arrangements. In many cases, for example in the chemicals industry, marketing agreements were supplemented by patent-licensing arrangements or some form of financial control to ensure that market agreements were more effective. Thus, some British concerns, before they could hope to expand their sales in Canada, might have been in the rather strange position of having to appeal to their American competitors for release from their patent-licensing agreements so that they, in turn, could attempt to push the American producer out of the Canadian market. Such an appeal might have evoked either an outright refusal from the Americans, or alternatively, a demand for concessions in Britain's traditional sterling markets, which might not have been acceptable to British producers. Nor is the situation much more plausible where companies are linked by financial and management ties. For example, how likely is it that a British company producing, for example, chemicals or synthetic fibres would strenuously push its sales in Canada in direct competition with its Canadian subsidiary?[51] To the extent, of course, that the subsidiary becomes an outlet for materials, parts, and components produced in Britain, as well as a selling agency for finished products, it may enhance the flow of trade.

In addition to these general grounds for expecting that something less than free competition has prevailed in the Canadian import market since World War II, there is also a certain amount of direct evidence pointing to this same broad conclusion. For instance, the Canadian Combines Commissioner's reports on dental supplies (1947) and optical goods (1948) found that Canadian buyers were unable to obtain supplies from Britain because of patent and marketing agreements. British producers were implicated in the Commissioner's report on resale price maintenance in the sale of china and earthenware (1954). In his report on the flat glass industry (1949) the Commissioner concluded that the formal restrictions between producers had abated, relative to pre-war, but that trade practices developed before the war have since become trade custom and thus maintained some restrictive control over the market.[52] The British sales of radio components in Canada continue to be impeded by patent regulations.[53] Similarly United Kingdom exports of pulp and paper machinery and refinery and chemical plant equipment to Canada are limited by patent licence arrangements.[54] Patent restrictions limit the sale of steel toes for safety boots.[55]

Another noteworthy source of information is a small but seemingly authoritative periodical, *Cartel,* published by the International Co-operative Association. It indicates that restrictive agreements have persisted in the glass industry;[56] in the television industry United States and British firms had a patent agreement (which was broken up in 1950 by United States anti-trust action) whereby the Western Hemisphere was allocated to United States producers;[57] the alkali cartel continued until 1951 when it was officially dissolved by a United States court order;[58] British and American firms control the distribution of 'newsreels',[59] American interests control the British Shoe Machinery Company;[60] the major British producers of containers, the Metal Box Company, is tied via financial links and patent licences to the Continental Can Company in the United States,[61] in the manufacture of water coolers one British company at least is precluded from selling in Canada by patent licences.[62]

In addition to the more formal private control exercised over Canadian imports, various kinds of informal arrangements, such as gentlemen's agreements and "trade practices," have probably also circumscribed Canada's trade. Virtually no comprehensive information is available on this aspect of this subject.

While the evidence adduced above is undoubtedly incomplete, it suffices to suggest some general conclusions regarding the impact of cartel restrictions on Britain's export trade with Canada since 1926:

(a) Between 1926 and 1939 producers in the United States, the United Kingdom, and Canada were involved in a variety of cartel arrangements. It has been estimated that from 40 to 50 per cent of total world trade in the late thirties was subject to some degree of arbitrary control by cartels.[63] It is apparent that a substantial share of Canadian foreign trade was subject to these controls but the exact extent of this control is not clear.

(b) As for Canadian imports, the typical cartel arrangement was one of four varieties:

(i) The Canadian market was allocated to United States producers with the understanding that other producers would not enter the Canadian market. In some instances the American producer would supply the Canadian market from United States plants; in others, United States producers would establish a subsidiary in Canada.

(ii) The Canadian market was allocated to existing Canadian firms. In some cases these firms were subsidiaries of United States firms.

(iii) British and United States producers shared the Canadian market through a jointly owned subsidiary producing in Canada for Canadian needs only. Both the United States and United Kingdom parent companies recognized the Canadian market as being outside their sales territory.

(iv) British and United States concerns shared the Canadian market with the understanding that each would supply a certain percentage of total Canadian demand.

The foregoing evidence is not sufficiently complete to allow one to say which of these varieties of cartel control was the most prevalent. But regardless of which type of restriction prevailed, it is apparent that to a considerable extent British suppliers during the inter-war years deliberately contracted out of the Canadian market, abandoning it either to United States or Canadian suppliers.

(c) Although there are reasons for believing that cartel restrictions have relaxed since World War II, compared to the inter-war years, it is evident that some product markets are still subject to some form of private control.

When the evidence of this section so far is compared to the statistics presented in chapter II above, one finds that some of those sectors of the Canadian market that have been dominated by foreign-owned subsidiaries or have been subject to cartel control of some kind have also been among the "newer" industries and the larger and fastest growing sectors of the Canadian market: for example, chemicals, synthetic fibres, iron and steel goods, vehicles, electrical equipment and supplies, electronic devices, glassware. To a considerable degree this may reflect the large-scale investment in these sectors for production and distributing facilities, technical development and research, and marketing. Another factor may be the dependence of both Canada and Britain in some of these industries upon industrial research and product development, both past and present, in the United States. For these and other reasons the establishment of United States subsidiaries in these sectors of Canadian industry has probably been encouraged. In addition, various protective devices, including the cartel arrangements mentioned above, have likely tended to arise in order to protect the heavy investments at stake. On the other hand, certain sectors, such as cotton and woollen textiles, where markets have apparently been less subject to private control and where foreign-owned subsidiaries have been comparatively unimportant, have been among the smaller and less dynamic sectors of the Canadian market.

Given this situation, it is possible that the incidence of private restrictive practices on Canadian imports has been enhanced over the years. Moreover, the nature of the restrictions has probably meant that British producers have been virtually excluded from participation in some of Canada's larger and more promising markets and have been significantly restricted in certain others. In short, the importance of these restrictions and their bias against British exports to Canada may have contributed appreciably to the decline in the share of Canadian imports coming from Britain over the past forty years.

There is an ancillary point to be added to these general conclusions. Is is sometimes alleged that monopolistic practices are more prevalent in the United Kingdom than in the United States. The extent to which this is true is apparently in doubt. Nevertheless, to the extent that it is true and to the extent that it has led to less initiative and enterprise on the part of the United Kingdom producers, higher production costs, less aggressive selling, and so on, United Kingdom producers may be at a disadvantage relative to United States producers when it comes to competition in foreign markets.

So much for cartel restrictions. Another type of private restriction deserving notice is that arising from oligopolistic markets—that is, a market wherein there is no formal collusion between sellers but where sellers are sufficiently few in number and sufficiently intelligent to recognize that their actions are interdependent. In these circumstances, each seller is aware that his actions will bring forth a response from his competitors and, as a consequence, each seller's actions are different from what they would be in a purely competitive market. There is virtually no empirical evidence available upon which to assess the importance of this factor. The only tangible evidence which the writer has encountered is a comment by a government official to the effect that some British sellers to Canada have failed to capitalize fully on their competitive price position in the Canadian market for fear of unleashing a strong campaign by domestic producers for higher Canadian tariffs. Notwithstanding the lack of evidence, it seems reasonable to suppose that the policies of many British exporters to Canada, potential as well as actual, are made with an eye to their effect on Canadian producers, many of whom depend heavily on United States materials, parts, and equipment. In so far as this is true, this situation is probably a further deterrent to increasing Britain's position in the Canadian market. For instance, an additional element of uncertainty is introduced into the situation: will any significant success on the part of British suppliers in penetrating the Canadian market be doomed to eventual failure because of the reaction it would evoke in governmental policies and in the policies pursued by competitors?[64]

Then too, the flow of exports from the United Kingdom to Canada may be impeded if British sellers give a higher priority to non-Canadian than to Canadian buyers. This question will be discussed at greater length in the next chapter. For the present, suffice it to say that the following comment would seem to typify the thinking of some British producers at least, exporters as well as non-exporters: "... the non-exporter is hardly likely to sacrifice some of his established good-will in the home market in order to try to create a new good-will with an export merchant or with overseas countries. He will tell himself that when bad times return his overseas customers or his merchant will be the first to cut orders down."[65]

2. PUBLIC RESTRICTIONS

The flow of British exports to Canada has been influenced not only by private restrictions but also by public restrictions arising from government policies in both Canada and Britain. Probably the most important public restriction is the

Canadian tariff. As is well known, no satisfactory method has yet been devised to measure tariff levels. Nevertheless, the data presented in Table XXXV give some rough indication of the rate of duty levied upon Canadian imports and of the proportion of imports entering the country duty free. According to these estimates almost three-fifths of Canada's imports from Britain at present are free of duty, and the average rate of duty on dutiable imports is about 16 per cent. A significantly smaller share—about two-fifths—of Canada's imports from the United States is free of duty, but the average rate on dutiable imports from the United States is about the same as the average rate on dutiable imports from Britain.

The figures shown in Table XXXV also suggest the main historical trends in Canadian tariff levels since 1900. Canadian tariffs generally were reduced somewhat from 1900 to 1929; significant increases were implemented during the early thirties; substantial decreases occurred between 1935 and the early fifties; and

TABLE XXXV

Selected Canadian Tariff Statistics, 1900-56*

| | Average ad valorem rate | | | | | | Free imports as percentage of all imports | | |
| | Dutiable imports | | | All imports | | | | | |
	U.K.	U.S.	Total	U.K.	U.S.	Total	U.K.	U.S.	Total
1901	25	25	28	18	12	16	26	50	40
1911	25	25	26	19	14	16	23	45	38
1920	22	23	23	16	14	15	22	38	35
1926	22	24	25	18	13	16	18	44	37
1929	26	23	24	21	14	16	21	40	35
1932	29	27	29	22	18	20	32	35	33
1935	26	27	28	14	16	16	54	40	42
1938	24	23	24	11	14	13	54	41	46
1948	17	16	18	8	9	9	55	42	48
1951	16	17	17	7	10	9	59	42	47
1956	16	17	18	7	10	10	55	38	42

Source: Dominion Bureau of Statistics, *Trade of Canada, Canada Year Book,* various issues.

* Fiscal years ending March 31, 1900-38; calendar years 1948-56.

this has been followed by a period of comparative stability in tariff rates. The tariff reductions after 1935 reflect in part the negotiation of lower rates and in part the impact of price inflation on duties levied in terms of specific amounts—that is, specific duties.

How have these tariff changes affected the competitive position of British suppliers in the Canadian market? Relative to domestic producers, the reductions occurring since the thirties have clearly enhanced the competitive position of British sellers. Indeed, the Canadian tariff facing British producers since World War II has been considerably lower than at any other time since the turn of the century. Moreover, Canadian tariffs have been comparatively stable and have not given rise to as much uncertainty as tariffs in certain other countries, for example, the United States.

The margins of tariff preference enjoyed by British producers over United

States and other foreign producers in the Canadian market were considerably increased by the Ottawa Agreements in 1932; and since the thirties these margins, generally speaking, have apparently decreased somewhat, though changes in preferential margins have differed considerably for particular commodity classifications.[66] Apart from the usual qualifications associated with average tariff figures, the statistics shown in Table XXXV are further qualified because the "very high duties levied on alcoholic beverages (largely offset by domestic taxes) bulk large in the duties collected" on imports from Britain.[67] Accordingly, in Table XXXVI the duties collected on alcoholic beverage imports from Britain have been omitted in calculating the average rate of duty. "For what they are worth, these general averages suggest that British goods enjoy a wider margin of preference now than they did in the 1920's, while rates on both British and American imports have fallen since 1939."[68]

According to Professor Young's study, changes in the preferential tariff margin

TABLE XXXVI

CANADIAN TARIFF RATES, EXCLUDING DUTIES ON ALCOHOLIC BEVERAGES, ON IMPORTS FROM BRITAIN AND THE UNITED STATES, SELECTED YEARS, 1926-53

| | Average ad valorem | |
	U.K.	U.S.
1926	14.0	13.3
1928	13.8	13.5
1939	7.3	13.0
1953	5.4	10.3

SOURCE: Royal Commission on Canada's Economic Prospects, *Canadian Commercial Policy*, prepared by J. H. Young (1957), Table 7, p. 55.

extended to Britain have varied widely from product to product. Relative to the late twenties, the margin has been reduced for such products as cotton textiles, certain kinds of electrical goods, engines and boilers, and machinery of a kind not made in Canada; it remains the same for various kinds of machinery made in Canada and it has been considerably broadened for automobiles, china tableware, and woollen fabrics. Professor Young concludes that "while many margins of preference have been narrowed during the post-war negotiations, the preferential margins which remain on a number of commodities are still significant and in some important cases substantially higher than they were before the changes introduced by the Ottawa agreements."[69]

Canada's import trade has over the years been practically free of all quantitative restrictions and foreign exchange controls except for the period from 1939 to 1950. During this latter period the quantitative and foreign exchange controls applied to Canadian imports were distinctly favourable to British producers and significantly increased the degree of discrimination in their favour. Emergency import restrictions were temporarily imposed on some of the products that Canada mainly imports from the United States, and these had been gradually eliminated by 1950. In 1949 Britain's share of Canadian imports was 11 per cent compared with 7 per cent in 1947. The share in 1947 seems to have been unusually small since it was over 10 per cent in 1946. Nevertheless, it is likely that Britain's share of Canadian imports during this period was somewhat larger than it would have been in the absence of controls.

In addition to tariffs, quantitative restrictions, and foreign exchange restrictions, imports may also be impeded by customs classification and valuation procedures. A recent study of this subject makes it clear that Canada's customs administration does restrict imports to some extent.[70] Restrictions of this kind were especially serious during the depressed thirties; but since that time they have been substantially reduced. There is no indication that this "invisible tariff" has discriminated against British suppliers during the period under review.

Another aspect of Canadian commercial policy requiring consideration is the purchasing policies pursued by the federal, provincial, and municipal governments. These policies—in so far as clearly defined policies exist—are usually closely kept secrets and are rarely if ever fully explained in public. Hence, it is difficult to comment on this matter with any assurance and much of what is said below is based on impressions gained from conversations with civil servants in Canada and Britain.

It is generally agreed that during the thirties the federal government followed a "buy Canadian" purchasing policy. Moreover, federal ministers did not hesitate to suggest that other governments and private purchasers in Canada should follow the same general policy. Immediately after World War II when shortages were everywhere in evidence, the government took a very liberal attitude toward imports from Britain. It seems unlikely that this resulted in a deliberate policy of diverting government purchases abroad; at the same time, it is probable that the general shortage of goods prevailing at the time rendered any remnants of the pre-war "buy Canadian" policy largely ineffective. Moreover, during this period the federal government actively encouraged Canadian imports from Britain.[71]

With the gradual disappearance of the abnormal post-war supply situation, a "buy Canadian" policy has evidently re-emerged as far as federal government departments are concerned. The degree to which it has been pressed has apparently varied somewhat over the years. Nevertheless, in recent years a standard clause has been written into all federal government contracts or specifications which reads in part as follows: "To the full extent to which the same are procurable, consistent with proper economy and the expeditious carrying out of this contract, Canadian labour, parts, and materials shall be used in this work."[72] These words leave little doubt about the basic intention of the federal government's purchasing policy. How seriously Canadian imports from Britain are restricted in the application of this general directive is an open question. It should be noted, however, that discrimination against foreign suppliers can arise not only through price discrimination but also in a wide variety of other ways—for example, in laying down specifications and in the procedures followed in calling for tenders. For purposes of this directive Canada is apparently defined to include the subsidiaries of foreign producers as well as "Canadian" producers.[73]

All things considered, then, it seems that the federal government's purchasing policies, with the possible exception of the immediate post-war years, have generally tended to discriminate against foreign suppliers. There is no evidence to suggest that these policies have directly discriminated more against British producers than against United States and other foreign producers. Indeed, when buying abroad, the federal government has apparently discriminated in favour of Britain as compared with the United States, assuming the quality of the goods and so on were the same. This policy, however, has possibly been more than offset by the indirect consequences of the discrimination in favour of domestic suppliers, including in this group foreign subsidiaries in Canada. Given the high proportion of these subsidiaries that are controlled in the United States, their great importance in Canada's industrial picture, and their generally heavy reliance on materials, parts, components, and finished goods imported from the United States, it follows that any advantage given domestic firms may have indirectly favoured imports from the United States rather than Britain.

The purchasing policies pursued by provincial and municipal governments are even more difficult to ascertain. One would expect that the political attractions of local purchases are at least as great for these governments as for the federal government. Consequently, these governments too have probably followed a "buy Canadian" policy. Apart from the direct effect of this discrimination, it has indirectly tended to favour imports from the United States rather than Britain for the same reasons as has federal purchasing. It must be added that some provinces, such as British Columbia, have been alert to advantages for their primary producers of providing Britain with more dollars, and in some cases special arrangements have been made to facilitate the exchange of local primary products against imports of British goods.[74]

So much for the policies pursued by Canadian governments. Turning to the influence of British government policy on British exports to Canada, one can usefully distinguish between those policies relating specifically to exports to Canada and those relating to exports generally. The latter are considered briefly in the next chapter. As for the former, all post-war British governments have clearly been anxious to see Britain's exports to Canada increase. This attitude has not resulted in legislation discriminating in favour of sales to Canada. For the most part the government of the day has relied upon informal persuasion and coercion to implement its policy. Ever since 1946 there has been an almost continuous "dollar drive," the intensity of which has varied from year to year. In addition to speeches by ministers, officials, business men, and others, an attempt has been made to marshal greater support by organizing an association of British and Canadian business men (at present known as the Dollar Exports Council and the Dollar-Sterling Trade Advisory Council) aided and abetted in their efforts to increase British sales in Canada by the appropriate government departments in London and Ottawa. Under the aegis of this group an exchange of trade missions and other activities have been arranged periodically. Moreover, during the post-war years when materials were under control, the British government's views on the desirability of exporting to Canada were reflected in the priorities established for the allocation of materials. With the abandonment of these controls, it has been necessary to rely on persuasion and other less forceful means. Although in general these measures may not seem very potent, on occasion they apparently are a factor. For instance, in 1953 it seems the Board of Trade played a role in ensuring satisfactory delivery dates when British producers were negotiating to supply much of the equipment that was eventually installed in the Toronto subway. In addition to these activities, the British government since the war has also revised the regulations governing the Export Credits Guarantee Department of the Board of Trade in order to foster more trade, for example, by reducing the risk faced by British sellers wishing to enter dollar markets or to increase their sales in these markets.

It must be added that during certain periods immediately after the war the favourable effect of these policies in British exports to Canada was offset to some degree by the unfavourable effect of certain other export policies of a more general nature. For example, during the period of bilateral trading, steel and other strategic goods were sometimes withheld from Canada in order that they would be available for use as an enticement to bring other countries into Britain's bilateral trading arrangements.[75] Another example is the policy of stressing the export of goods having a "high conversion" ratio—that is, the export of goods having more value-added domestically was pressed at the expense of goods having less value-added domestically.[76] Whether or not these policies led to some uneconomic use of British resources, they may have hampered British exports to Canada somewhat immediately after the war. Nevertheless, it is practically certain that they did not significantly affect the long-term trend of Britain's export trade with Canada.

Finally, there is the whole question of Britain's sterling area policy, and this is considered in the next chapter.

CHAPTER SIX

ALTERNATIVES TO SELLING IN CANADA

1. DISTRIBUTION OF BRITAIN'S INDUSTRIAL OUTPUT

AN EXAMINATION of those factors bearing more or less directly on the sale of British goods in Canada gives only a partial picture of Britain's export trade with Canada. Account must be taken of the fact that British suppliers individually and the British economy as a whole have always had several alternatives to exporting to Canada. One of these has been to sell at home; a second has been to sell abroad in countries other than Canada; and a third has been to produce less. To what extent, in the light of prevailing world economic conditions, have these alternatives or some combination of them been chosen in preference to exporting to Canada, and why have these alternatives been preferred?

These questions are very broad in their implications and lead to a wide range of considerations about the British economy and the world economy generally. Much has already been written on these matters elsewhere and, in any event, it is not feasible to try to explore questions of this scope within the present study. It is quite clear, nevertheless, that these more general questions are directly relevant and could be quite important in explaining the decrease in Britain's share of the Canadian market. Accordingly, several aspects of these questions of particular interest in the context of this discussion are briefly considered below.

It is appropriate to begin this line of enquiry with a brief statistical analysis of the geographical distribution of British production since the twenties. First, there is the question of how the national output has been divided between exports on the one hand and the home market on the other. Some figures bearing on this question are shown in Table XXXVII below.

Admittedly these figures are subject to a variety of limitations and a much more detailed analysis would be called for if one were to go into this matter fully. Nevertheless, in broad terms, the figures suggest that, compared with the twenties, Britain's home market during the thirties and since the war has been absorbing a larger share of the volume of output. At the same time, it seems that since World War II the domestic market has been absorbing a smaller share of total manufactures output than during the thirties.[1] It will also be observed from the figures that national income (constant dollars) and manufacturing production did not fall as much during the early thirties as the volume of exports; and by the end of the thirties both national income and manufacturing production were substantially greater than in 1929 whereas exports were almost 30 per cent less. Thus the decrease in the ratios shown for the thirties in columns (4) and (6) of Table XXXVII is accounted for mainly by the large decrease in exports occurring during the world-wide depression. During the postwar period the volume of British exports increased very substantially, though

TABLE XXXVII

SELECTED STATISTICS RELATING TO BRITISH PRODUCTION AND EXPORTS, 1924-57

(index numbers, 1924 = 100)

	Volume of total exports	Volume of manufactures exports	National income [*]	(1) ÷ (3)	Industrial production, manufactures	(2) ÷ (5)
	(1)	(2)	(3)	(4)	(5)	(6)
1924	100	100	100	100	100	100
1925	98	102	102	96	103	99
1926	88	106	102	86	100	106
1927	102	104	111	92	110	95
1928	104	108	112	93	110	98
1929	107	108	114	94	115	94
1930	87	87	113	77	110	79
1931	67	64	111	60	102	63
1932	67	66	111	60	103	64
1933	67	67	119	56	109	61
1934	72	73	123	59	120	61
1935	77	78	128	60	131	60
1936	79	79	133	59	144	55
1937	86	87	134	64	152	57
1938	76	76	134	57	148	51
1946	75	85	138	54	145	59
1947	83	95	139	60	158	60
1948	104	118	144	72	178	66
1949	114	131	151	75	190	69
1950	132	149	155	85	206	72
1951	132	150	162	81	215	70
1952	126	137	162	78	206	67
1953	128	138	168	76	219	63
1954	134	145	175	77	237	61
1955	144	157	181	80	253	62
1956	152	166	183	83	249	67
1957	155	170	186	83	255	67

SOURCES: K. S. Lomax, "New Index-Numbers of Industrial Production 1900-1938," *Times Review of Industry* (London & Cambridge Economic Bulletin no. 26), June 1958, p. v; Central Statistical Office, *Annual Abstract of Statistics, Monthly Digest of Statistics; Times Review of Industry* (London & Cambridge Economic Bulletin no. 26), June 1958; A. R. Prest, "National Income of the United Kingdom," *Economic Journal*, LVIII (March 1948), p. 55, Table II, p. 59; Central Statistical Office, *National Income and Expenditure*, 1957, Table 11, p. 7; 1958, Table 13, p. 9.

[*] Net national income at factor cost, 1900 prices, 1924-38; net national income at factor cost, 1938 prices, 1938-46; net domestic product at 1948 factor cost, 1946-57.

apparently not enough to re-establish the relationship prevailing between export and production during the late twenties.[2]

Looking only at exports, it is evident, first of all, that the value of British output going into exports is large relative to Canadian imports. In 1957, for instance, the value of total British exports converted at the market rate of exchange was about two-thirds larger than the value of total Canadian imports.

Apart from their size, there is also the question of how British exports have been distributed amongst the various markets of the world. This is broadly indicated by Table XXXVIII. According to these figures 4 to 6 per cent of total British exports were sold to Canada between 1924 and 1958. As for other export markets, the figures show that the proportion of British exports disposed of in the sterling area after 1945 was significantly above the pre-war share. From 1924 to 1929 the average share going to the sterling area was 41

TABLE XXXVIII

GEOGRAPHICAL DISTRIBUTION OF BRITISH EXPORTS, 1924-58

(percentages)

	By value					By volume	
	Sterling area (a)	Western Europe (b)	Canada (c)	U.S.A.	Other (d)	Canada (e)	World ex. Canada
1924	38	28	4	7	23	4	96
1925	40	27	4	7	22	4	96
1926	44	21	4	8	23	5	95
1927	42	25	4	6	23	5	95
1928	40	25	5	6	24	5	95
1929	39	26	5	6	24	5	95
1930	38	29	5	5	23	6	94
1931	38	30	5	5	22	6	94
1932	41	28	5	4	22	5	95
1933	40	28	5	5	22	5	95
1934	42	27	5	5	21	5	95
1935	43	27	5	5	20	5	95
1936	44	24	5	6	21	5	95
1937	43	25	6	6	20	6	94
1938	45	24	5	4	22	5	95
1947	49	23	4	4	20	6	94
1948	50	24	5	4	18	4	96
1949	52	22	4	3	19	4	96
1950	48	25	6	5	16	4	96
1951	51	24	5	5	15	4	96
1952	49	25	5	6	15	4	96
1953	49	27	6	6	12	5	95
1954	50	27	5	6	12	4	96
1955	50	26	5	6	13	4	96
1956	45	27	6	8	14	4	96
1957	45	27	6	7	15	4	96
1958	45	26	6	9	14		

SOURCES: Board of Trade, *Annual Statement of the Trade of the United Kingdom*, Central Statistical Office, *Annual Abstract of Statistics, Monthly Digest of Statistics; Times Review of Industry* (London & Cambridge Economic Bulletin no. 26), June 1958.

(a) 1924-38—all British countries excluding Canada and Newfoundland; 1938-58—sterling area.

(b) 1924-38—total trade with Sweden, Norway, Denmark, Benelux Countries, Germany, France, Switzerland, Portugal, Spain, Italy, Austria, Greece, and Turkey; 1938-58—non-sterling O.E.E.C. countries and dependencies.

(c) Including Newfoundland.

(d) Residual.

(e) Calculated using price index described in the Appendix below as a deflator, 1924-54, the official index of the average value of British exports to the dollar area, 1954 to 1957. 1938=100.

per cent, from 1930 to 1938 42 per cent, and from 1947 to 1958 49 per cent. Much of this increase was approximately offset by the decline in the share of British exports disposed of in "other" (non—European, non—North American) markets—the share for these markets declining from an average of 24 per cent for the years 1924 to 1929, to 21 per cent for 1930 to 1938 and 15 per cent for 1947 to 1958.[3] The share of exports sold in both western Europe and the United States, on the other hand, has been relatively constant. An average of 25 per cent of exports was sold in western Europe from 1924 to 1929 compared with 27 per cent from 1930 to 1938 and 25 per cent from 1947 to 1958 (26 per cent from 1950 to 1958). The corresponding figures for the United States are $6^{1}/_{2}$, 5, and $5^{3}/_{4}$ per cent respectively.

Some interesting changes are indicated by these figures for the period 1954 to 1958. During this time the share of British exports sold in the sterling area decreased from 50 per cent—close to a peak level for the period under review—to 45 per cent—a post-war low; the share sold in western Europe decreased slightly from 27 to 26 per cent; the share sold in Canada increased from 5 to 6 per cent—a level previously attained in 1953, 1950, and 1937; the share sold in "other" areas increased from 12 to 14 per cent; and the share sold in the United States increased from 6 to 9 per cent—a higher level than in any other year covered by the figures. This disparity in the change in the share of British exports sold in Canada and the United States is all the more interesting because total Canadian imports during this period increased 27 per cent compared with an increase of 25 per cent for total United States imports.

This general picture based on aggregative figures is brought into sharper focus when one consults somewhat more detailed statistics. First, if one compares British exports to Canada with British exports to other countries it is apparent that Canada has been an important market for British goods. As is shown in Table XXXIX, Canada has not only ranked well up on the list of buyers of

TABLE XXXIX

Share of British Exports Sold to Various Countries, 1937, 1956

(percentages; ranked in order of importance in 1956)

	1937	1956		1937	1956
United States	6	8	Netherlands	3	4
Australia	7	8	Sweden	2	3
Canada°	6	6	Irish Republic	4	3
India†	7	5	West Germany‡	4	3
South Africa	8	5	France	4	3
New Zealand	4	4	Denmark	3	3

Sources: Central Statistical Office, *Annual Abstract of Statistics*; *Monthly Digest of Statistics*.
° Including Newfoundland, 1937, 1956.
† Including Pakistan, 1937.
‡ Including East and West Germany, 1937.

British exports but also the share sold to Canada has not been much less than the share sold to the leading foreign buyer of British goods. It is also evident that British exports are highly diversified among many countries and that none is predominant.[4] In addition, the figures indicate that the share of exports sold to Canada did not change from 1937 to 1956. During the same period the share sold in the United States and Australia increased, but the share sold in certain other important sterling area and continental markets decreased.

Table XL shows the proportion of total British exports of particular product lines sold in Canada in 1937 and 1956. The figures indicate that some of the older consumer goods industries—for example, wool and woollen textiles, pottery, glassware and abrasives, clothing and footwear, and leather goods—have continued to channel a larger share of their exports into the Canadian market. In addition, it is apparent that some of the newer industries have expanded the share of exports sold in Canada more, and others less than certain of the older industries.[5] Of the sixteen product categories listed, half show an increase in

TABLE XL

Share of Total British Exports Sold in Canada, 1937, 1956

(percentage of total)

	1937	1956
Whisky	8	6
Wool and other animal hair and tops	4	8
Coal and coke	3	2
Chemicals (incl. oils, fats, resins)	4	3
Leather manufactures	9	9
Rubber manufactures	2	2
Woollen and worsted goods	13	15
Cotton goods	4	4
Synthetic fibre goods	9	1
Base and precious metal products	3	8
Iron, steel, metal manufactures	7	7
Machinery, non-electric	3	4
Electric machinery and apparatus	1	6
Clothing and footwear	6	10
Pottery, glass, abrasives	11	13
Road vehicles	2	4

Source: Board of Trade, *Annual Statement of the Trade of the United Kingdom*, 1938, 1956.

the share of exports sold in Canada. The increase shown for electrical equipment is the largest, though this showing is qualified by the fact that only a very small proportion of exports was sent to Canada before the war and now the share exported to Canada is about average by comparison with other product lines. Other categories showing increases in the share of exports going to Canada are wool and wooltops, woollen and worsted goods, base and precious metals, machinery, clothing and footwear, pottery, glass and abrasives, and road vehicles. All other product lines listed in Table XL either show no change in the share of exports going to Canada in 1937 and 1957 or a decrease, the latter including whisky, coal, chemicals, and particularly synthetic fibres.

The quantitative relationship between British exports to Canada, on the one hand, and total British exports and production, on the other, can be further illustrated by directly relating the size of certain hypothetical increases in British exports to Canada to total British exports and production. For instance, if from 1954 to 1958 the proportion of British exports sold in Canada had increased as much as the proportion of British exports sold in the United States (3 per cent), then, assuming the levels of total British exports and Canadian imports realized in 1958 and the official rate of exchange, British exports to Canada in 1958 would have been about 35 per cent greater than they were and Britain's share of Canadian imports would have been 14 instead of 10 per cent. Similarly, the *increase* in the share of British exports sold in the sterling area from 1924-9 (average) and 1930-8 (average) to 1947-58 (average) was greater than the *total* share of exports sold in Canada. Had the share of British exports sold in Canada increased by half the amount of this *increase* from 1924-9 (average) to 1947-58 (average)—4 per cent—British exports to Canada would have been about 45 per cent greater in 1958 than they were and Britain's share of the Canadian market would have been 15 per cent (assuming again the level of total British exports and Canadian imports realized in 1958 and official exchange rates). Looking at total British output, one finds various estimates suggesting that something like one-quarter or less of net British production during the post-war years has been destined for export.[6] On this assumption, some $1\frac{1}{2}$ per cent of total British output was destined for export to Canada. Assuming this relationship and the total levels of trade and production achieved during the post-war period, it follows that if a further $\frac{1}{2}$ of 1 per cent of total British output had been sold in Canada British exports in 1958 would have been about one-third greater than they were. Moreover, in view of the expansion in British output during the post-war period, a diversion of this magnitude for export to Canada could have been wrested from the expansion in British output while still leaving a greatly increased volume of goods available for sale at home and elsewhere.

The general point that emerges from all this is that exports to Canada have represented a small share of total British exports and an even smaller share of total British output. Consequently, assuming the levels of trade and production realized in past years, a marginal diversion of exports and output in the direction of the Canadian market as the total level of British exports and production were increasing could have produced a very large increase in British exports to Canada and the share of Canadian imports provided by Britain.

This simple arithmetic, of course, overlooks many difficulties and is not meant to imply that an increase in British exports to Canada could have been easily achieved or should have been pursued. Among the difficulties that are overlooked are all the problems obscured by using highly aggregative figures, the possible repercussions on the levels of trade and production of different patterns of trade and production, possible repercussions on the terms of trade and commercial policies, the variety of additional costs—for example, for distribution and selling—that might have been required to expand sales in Canada appreciably, and the time period one is prepared to allow for adjustment and the reckoning of net benefits.[7] Nevertheless, it is evident that Britain's total productive capacity has been very large in terms of the size of total Canadian imports. Consequently, it seems doubtful whether, in general, one can argue that British exports to Canada during the post-war period were restricted by an inability to supply if this is meant to suggest that a significant increase in British exports to Canada would have required more than a small share of Britain's aggregate productive capacity. Inability to supply can more reasonably be interpreted as arising from inadequate productive capacity for doing all the things that were deemed desirable and a preference for using the margin of resources that could have been employed to increase exports to Canada for other purposes thought to be of higher priority.[8]

In order to say whether it would be to Britain's advantage to increase—or for that matter, to decrease—exports to Canada one would need to evaluate the marginal benefits and marginal costs of exporting to Canada compared with the marginal benefits and marginal costs of using resources for other purposes. Exports are only an indirect means of acquiring goods and services to satisfy home demand; if the resources used to produce exports to Canada could be used to satisfy a greater volume of demand either by exporting to some other country or by directly producing the desired output domestically, it would be advantageous to reduce exports to Canada. Exports to Canada are beneficial from Britain's standpoint only so long as (a) the benefits derived from the marginal export to Canada exceed its costs, and (b) the benefits derived from the marginal export to Canada exceed its costs by a greater amount than the benefits costs margin attainable in any other use to which Britain might put the resources required to produce the marginal export to Canada. Among the benefits of exporting to Canada one would presumably wish to include the prospect of larger dollar earnings. In addition, there are the advantages of having a larger stake in an economy that has been growing more rapidly and has been more receptive to imports than many other economies in the world and an economy that to a considerable degree is complementary with the British economy. One might also wish to include various political advantages. On the cost side it would be necessary to take into account such advantages as those arising because of the need to adjust production to suit Canadian demand more satisfactorily, price concessions, the cost of overcoming present disadvantages in connection with advertising, distribution, stock-carrying, and other non-price factors, and the cost of disengaging from various international corporate affiliations that in the past have among other things provided men, money, technology, and protected markets to British industry.[9] In addition, it would be necessary to evaluate the relative risks and uncertainties associated with the Canadian market along with the possibility of adverse changes in the terms of trade, commercial policies, and the competitive practices of competing sellers. One would also need to assess the possible adverse repercussions in other foreign markets and the home market because of steps taken to increase exports to Canada. All this is a subject in itself and will not be further pursued here. Suffice it to say that, taking these and other considerations into account, it is by no means obvious that Britain would have been better off in the past had more resources been directed into exporting to Canada; nor is this proposition any more obvious for the present or the future.[10]

Finally, in light of the foregoing figures one may ask to what extent Britain's decreasing share of the Canadian market reflects disparities between the rates of economic growth in North America and Britain. It is evident from the statistics that Canada's gross national product and imports increased considerably more from 1926 to 1957 than British gross national product and exports, regardless of whether the comparison is made in value or in volume terms. It is also apparent that the disparity in the rate of growth between Canada and Britain over the past thirty-five years is appreciably greater than between Canada and the United States. Along these lines one might argue that a substantial part of the decrease in Britain's share of Canadian imports simply reflects the fact that Canadian and American output and foreign trade, by volume, have increased over two and a half times since 1926 and British output and exports have increased on the order of 80 per cent. In value terms and adjusting for exchange rate changes, the disparity is even greater. As a share of the value of total British exports, exports sold in Canada remained approximately the same—though this share reckoned in volume terms may have fallen off somewhat. Roughly maintaining this ratio was no mean feat considering the post-war increase in total British exports. Had British production grown more rapidly than it did it is conceivable, one might contend, that the proportion of output sold in Canada might have increased because of easier supply conditions; but even if this ratio had only been maintained, Britain's share of Canadian exports would have decreased less than in fact it did.

It is, of course, undeniable that if British output had increased more rapidly and a constant or rising share had been sold in Canada, exports to Canada would at present be larger than they are. One may question, however, if it is likely that a constant or rising share of a more rapidly increasing output would have been sold in Canada; there are a number of possible reasons why the share might have decreased, as in fact it appears to have done in volume terms. Indeed, from 1926-9 (average) to 1954-7 (average) the volume of British exports sold in Canada seems to have remained about the same despite a large increase in the volume of British output and an even larger increase in the volume of Canadian output and imports. Furthermore, it must be recognized not only that the rate of growth affects the level of exports but also that the level of exports affects the rate of growth. Thus, in order to assess the importance of disparities in growth rates one would need to consider the possibility that British economic growth would have been greater had exports been greater and, since exports can be used to pay for imports, that Britain might have imported more during the post-war period if the means of payment had been more plentiful. Neither possibility seems implausible when one recalls the surplus capacity in many sectors of the British economy during the inter-war period and the extensive trade and payments restrictions bolstered by liberal amounts of foreign aid during the post-war period. In addition, an explanation of the decrease of Britain's share of Canadian imports based on disparities in growth rates fails to give adequate weight to the fact, as illustrated above, that only a small share of British resources are devoted to producing exports for Canada. Consequently, even though British output has grown substantially less than Canadian imports it is quite possible that Britain's share of the Canadian market could have been at least maintained if only a part of the increase in total output that did occur had been channelled into exports for Canada. (Whether or not this should have been done is another matter that has already been referred to.)

In raising these points there is no wish to deny that disparities in growth rates may have contributed to a decrease in Britain's share of Canadian imports. It is neither a self-evident nor a complete explanation, however. Growth in the output of goods and services in a relatively open economy can itself be considerably influenced by foreign trade; and its significance so far as a particular foreign market is concerned can be overshadowed in importance, among other factors, by changes in the distribution of output and considerations relating to the relative size of the market in question. In other words, there is no necessary relationship, as far as any one market absorbing a small proportion of resources is concerned, between relative rates of economic growth and market shares.

2. The Attractions of Other Foreign Markets

In this section it is proposed to consider some of the reasons why sterling area and other foreign markets may in the past have been more attractive to British producers than the Canadian market. The attractiveness of different markets has, of course, varied appreciably from time to time and product to product. Here, however, only some of the more general considerations that arise in this connection are discussed.

One possibility is that price incentives have been such as to draw British production into these other markets. Available figures do not support this possibility; on the contrary they indicate that, on the basis of price movements only, British exports to Canada might have been expected to increase considerably more than British exports to most other countries, particularly since 1949. As shown in Table XLI, since 1949 prices of goods imported into Canada have risen appreciably more than prices of goods imported into most other Western countries, save the United States. Wholesale prices also increased more in the Western Hemisphere than in western Europe and the sterling area from 1949 to 1957.

The foregoing picture is, of course, considerably different when the comparison of price changes is made in terms of local currency. On this basis North American

TABLE XLI

Price Changes in Britain's Major Export Markets Selected Years 1937-57
(Index numbers expressed in U.S. dollars, 1937-8 = 100)

	1948	1949*	1951	1954	1957
Import prices					
Canada	208	234	251	234	257
U.S.	231	221	298	276	285
Latin America	205	200	205	198	216
Continental Europe	228	224	231	207	219
U.K. dependencies	212	214	205	197	209
Rest of sterling area	230	234	212	205	208
Wholesale prices					
Canada	184	189	217	211	224
U.S.	192	185	211	202	216
Latin America	202	192	225	219	230
Continental Europe	198	205	203	197	209
U.K.	170	176	173	178	197
Rest of sterling area	176	187	164	177	188

Source: International Monetary Fund, *International Financial Statistics*, monthly issues.

* Jan.-Aug. 1949.

prices, as indicated in Table XLII, have increased significantly less than western European and sterling area prices from 1937 to 1957. The relatively rapid increase in domestic prices in Britain's major markets in some respects may have blunted incentives to export to North America even though North American prices, when converted into sterling, increased even more. Nevertheless, the fact remains that earnings in foreign currency can be converted into local currency, which means that in comparing relative price movements in different countries effective foreign exchange rates must be taken into account. Thus, although there may be particular products which have been drawn off to markets other than Canada because of price considerations, it appears that in general price *per se* has not been a major factor channelling British exports into these other markets. Indeed, the relatively favourable prices obtainable in Canada have possibly been one of the more attractive features of the Canadian market.[11]

TABLE XLII

PERCENTAGE CHANGE IN WHOLESALE PRICES, DOMESTIC CURRENCY,
FOR SELECTED COUNTRIES AND YEARS

	Decrease, 1929-38	Increase, 1937-57
Canada	17	111
U.S.	17	110
U.K.	12	239
Union of South Africa	11	189
Belgium	24	308
France	0	3114
Germany	23	128
Netherlands	28	269
Norway	+2	205
Sweden	7	182
Switzerland	25	81
Australia	11	234
New Zealand	+4	163
India	n.a.	281

SOURCES: United Nations, *Statistical Yearbook*, 1953, Table 157; International Monetary Fund, *International Financial Statistics*, June 1958, country tables; *Times Review of Industry* (London & Cambridge Economic Bulletin no. 26), June 1958.

A second way in which the existence of these other markets might affect Britain's sales to Canada would be if as a result of the relationships that developed between private institutions these other markets fell within the British orbit while Canada remained outside. Much of the evidence available on this point has already been marshalled in chapter v. All things considered there seems little doubt that during the past forty years institutional relationships have generally favoured British sales in other markets, notably the rest of the Commonwealth, rather than in Canada. It is worth noting that some of the industries where this factor has probably been of less importance, such as textiles and leather goods, have sold a larger share of exports in Canada than some of the newer industries, such as chemicals and synthetic fibres, where fairly close international relationships of one sort or another have existed in the past between private institutions.

Thirdly, there is the question of what impact official policies relating to foreign trade and investment may have had on the geographical pattern of Britain's overseas trade. British government policies prior to World War I can be regarded as mainly laissez-faire in nature. Free trade was largely accepted as the basic principle of commercial policy and foreign investment was regulated primarily by private commercial considerations. World War I marked a turning point. Since then the government has more actively influenced foreign trade and investment. During the twenties commercial policy was not as liberal as it had been pre-war, and with the adoption of Imperial Preference in 1932 the traditional free trade policy was finally thrown over. Similarly, official or semi-official control has been continuously exercised over foreign lending since World War I except for a few years during the late twenties. This general trend toward government control and restriction has, of course, not been unique to Britain. Other governments, both Commonwealth and foreign, have followed similar policies; indeed, in many cases the policies of these other governments were less liberal to begin with and official interference and restriction were carried further during the inter-war period than in Britain.[12]

There are reasons for believing that the effective result, regardless of the intended result, of these official policies with respect to foreign trade and investment during the inter-war period was to make the Canadian market less attractive to the British producer compared with the other major markets open to him. In the first place, in so far as these inter-war policies in Britain were protectionist in nature, designed to provide relief and to maintain the *status quo* in the face of new conditions rather than to promote an adjustment to these conditions, the competitive position of British industry relative to foreign markets was undermined; and the protectionist policies pursued by other countries enhanced this development. It is likely that each additional setback to Britain's relative competitive ability had greater repercussions on her position in the Canadian market than on her position in other Commonwealth and foreign markets. During this period these other markets, particularly those in the rest of the Commonwealth, were probably less competitive than the Canadian market. For one thing, American products have always been more readily available and acceptable in Canada than in most of these other areas; for another, Canada's domestic industry was more highly developed than in most Commonwealth countries and some other countries. Thus, where official policies tended to undermine the ability of British industry to compete internationally by sheltering it or discriminating against it, it is probable that these policies also effectively redirected the geographical pattern of British trade into less competitive markets and therefore away from Canada.

But inter-war governmental policies also played a more direct role in hampering the growth of British exports to Canada. One example is the policy of Imperial Preference which was extended and intensified in 1932, to a considerable extent by raising tariffs against non-Empire countries.[13] One unexpected result of this policy was that it significantly stimulated the flow of direct investment into Canada from the United States.[14] In an effort to penetrate the Empire tariff wall surrounding Canada as well as other Empire countries,

American companies decided to establish branch plants, subsidiaries, and other market outlets within Canada. In some cases it was intended that these plants and subsidiaries would supply not only the Canadian market but also other Empire markets at the lower preferential tariff rates. (The Canadian automobile industry is an illustration of an industry which was established and expanded with an eye to both the Canadian and Empire markets.) As new plants and subsidiaries, induced into Canada as a result of Imperial Preference, came into production and established plants expanded, it was only natural that the impact of these developments should have been felt first and most profoundly in the Canadian markets.

A second illustration of inter-war policies which directly affected the flow of British goods into overseas markets is provided by British policies relating to overseas investment. During the fifteen years prior to World War I, a period when British government policy was basically non-interventionist and British investors were virtually free to choose where they would lend their money, about two-thirds of the very substantial flow of foreign funds into Canada came from Britain. Moreover, in 1913 Canada was the most important borrower of British funds in the Commonwealth save Britain herself.[15] After World War I the export of British capital was influenced in varying degree but more or less continuously by government policies exercised through official and semi-official agencies. Very roughly, these policies can be said to have given priority to borrowers whose currency after 1931 was linked to sterling and also to borrowers who gave some assurance—in some cases a specific undertaking—that the borrowed funds would be used to make purchases in Britain and so directly stimulate British exports.[16] Canada was not a sterling country. Moreover, for a number of reasons, it was probably more difficult to prescribe where funds borrowed by Canada could be spent than in the case of borrowing by other Commonwealth countries. Consequently, Canada was in a less favourable position vis-à-vis the London capital market. Thirdly, and perhaps most important, during practically the whole inter-war period it was cheaper for Canadians to borrow in New York than in London.[17] In addition, Canada had a large and ever increasing supply of domestic savings which competed for Canadian investment opportunities.[18] Some of this saving was used to buy back Canadian securities held in London—a particularly profitable transaction from 1919 to 1924 and from 1931 to 1933 when the pound was discounted in terms of the Canadian dollar. The situation was different for countries in the rest of the Commonwealth. They were less favourably received in New York than was Canada; and their domestic supply of savings remained comparatively small. For these and other reasons, Britain's foreign investment during the inter-war period tended to be concentrated increasingly in Commonwealth areas (including the colonies) other than Canada. British investment in Canada, on the other hand, came to a virtual standstill at the 1914 level while domestic and United States investment in Canada continued to grow.[19] Important qualitative differences are also apparent. In the late thirties British investors still held the largest interest in such enterprises as the railroads but American and Canadian interests were dominant in the newer mining and manufacturing activities and in the newer public utilities. As a result of these various developments, those inducements to commodity trade arising from foreign investment tended mainly to enhance Britain's trade with what is now the sterling area and other countries rather than her trade with Canada. In Canada, on the other hand, increasing reliance upon United States and domestic investment, particularly in the more dynamic sectors of the economy, tended to increase Canada's relative dependence upon Canadian and American sources of supply.

After World War II and the division of the western world into soft and hard currency areas some of these tendencies were reinforced. The fact that Canada was a hard currency area whilst the sterling area and western Europe were soft currency areas may in itself have accentuated the decline in Britain's share of Canadian imports. Because of discrimination against dollar goods the pressure on British industry to be fully competitive in dollar markets was further reduced; the high degree of protection provided by measures designed to conserve dollars made soft currency markets more attractive and profitable than the competitive conditions to be met in Canada; and the relatively small amount of British investment flowing to Canada further diminished Britain's position in the Canadian market.

There is little doubt that compared with the foreign trade and investment policies pursued by other countries, Canadian policies, especially since 1945, have been relatively liberal. Canadian tariffs, particularly since World War II, have been lower than those imposed by most other countries in the sterling area, Europe, and the Americas; there have been no quotas or currency restrictions of consequence since about 1949, and those imposed between 1947 and 1949 applied mainly to goods imported from the United States; compared with efforts elsewhere, there has been little sustained and vigorous effort to foster domestic manufacturing artificially in Canada through commercial policy; foreign investment has been accorded much the same rights and privileges as domestic investment and has been free from the threat of expropriation. It cannot be contended that Canadian foreign trade and investment policies have been more restrictive vis-à-vis the United Kingdom than the policies of those areas which receive the bulk of Britain's exports. However, it can be argued—and in the writer's view quite convincingly—that because Canada's foreign trade and investment policies have been relatively more liberal, the Canadian market has been more highly competitive than most other markets open to British goods. Thus, one might say that Canadian policy has been injurious to United Kingdom trade in that it has been too liberal; had it been less liberal, especially as far as United States trade and investment are concerned, Britain's share of Canadian imports now might well be higher.

Several considerations supporting this contention might be mentioned. First, the general reductions in tariffs since the late thirties may have somewhat reduced the margin of effective tariff preference enjoyed by British suppliers in the Canadian market. Secondly, relatively competitive market conditions together with rapid economic growth have tended to encourage rapid economic change in such matters as technology, distribution, production methods, and institutional organization. This environment has possibly been less attractive to British exporters than the less changeable environment that may have been found elsewhere.

A third consideration of this sort concerns the relative difficulty facing the British seller in Canada, as opposed to other markets, with respect to such non-

price factors as product differentiation, salesmanship, and delivery. British suppliers have probably found it less difficult to meet market competition in regard
to these various non-price factors in sterling area and other markets than in
Canada. This is not to say that British producers have made less effort in Canada
than elsewhere to compete effectively in terms of these non-price factors. Indeed,
United Kingdom sellers may have paid at least as much attention to these aspects
of trade in Canada as in other countries. The principal difference has probably
been that consumers in these other markets have not been permitted freedom
of choice to as great an extent as have Canadian consumers. Hence, because
of the trade barriers imposed by producers themselves, by governments, and
by distance, the consumer and investor in Australia, New Zealand, India, and
other countries has not been given the opportunity to choose freely between
American or British products imported on a non-discriminatory basis; the Canadian, on the other hand, has always had this choice clearly before him, although
even in Canada Imperial Preference has continued to discriminate in Britain's
favour.

As already noted, during the years prior to 1939 when there was less discrimination against American goods in many of these other markets, United
States exports to markets outside North America grew more rapidly than
United Kingdom exports. Moreover, in many of these markets some types of
United States products were preferred by many buyers during these pre-war
years. One example of this is automobiles. After 1939 restrictions on dollar
imports virtually eliminated imports of North American automobiles and most
consumers have been forced to buy substitutes. Generally speaking, therefore,
immediate post-war trade restrictions in these countries to some extent overran
consumer preferences favourable to North American products. Consequently,
competition between British and American suppliers in such matters as the styling
and design of products, salesmanship, servicing, delivery, and credit was virtually eliminated in many of the markets where British exports were concentrated.
In Canada, on the other hand, competition in non-price matters has consistently
been keen and has frequently been crucial in determining a seller's success. On
these grounds alone, if on no other, many British producers probably had a
considerable incentive to avoid the hard Canadian market and to concentrate
on the softer markets of the world, particularly during the immediate post-war
period. As post-war restrictions discriminating against dollar goods have been
reduced and eliminated this incentive has been weakened.

It remains, finally, to refer briefly to the costs of entry faced by suppliers
proposing to sell in a market for the first time or to expand beyond a marginal
position.[20] In a perfectly competitive market, entry is free from institutional,
financial, and legal constraints. As demonstrated in chapter v, restrictions of
this kind have sometimes circumscribed possible initiatives by British sellers in
the Canadian market. These barriers in some cases could presumably have been
breached, but usually only at a significant cost.

Apart from entry costs of this kind, there are also those that arise because
products are sold under conditions of monopolistic competition. Under these
conditions, unlike pure competition, a producer's costs and the demand for his
product are not independent of each other. For example, the prospective British
entrant into the Canadian market must incur the cost of "making a market" for

his goods, as it were, through advertising, salesmanship, and promotion. Established tastes must be worn down and new preferences established. Products must be readapted to the market. In addition, it is necessary to establish a system of distribution which is at least the equal to that of established suppliers. Delivery, spare parts, service, and so on must come up to the established market standards and perhaps even exceed it. Also, it is necessary for the entrant to "prove" his staying power. He must demonstrate that he is there to stay and that there is little question of supplies being cut off because the supplier has failed. The nature of these non-price factors in some cases makes it unfeasible to consider entering or expanding in local markets. To provide adequate distribution facilities, servicing, and advertising for certain products such as automobiles and machinery, it may be necessary to think in terms of tackling the entire Canadian market or even the entire North American continent. Thus costs of entry may have to be met on a very large scale.

Under these conditions a prospective entrant may initially face a substantial cost disadvantage in relation to established sellers. Confronted with many market uncertainties, the entrant in addition will frequently have to commit himself to meeting heavy costs of entry. Initially, while sales remain small, these costs may be relatively high on a per unit basis. Thus, he may not be able to compete effectively until sales have reached a certain size and certain once-for-all entry costs have, in part at least, been written off against past sales.

For these reasons there seems little doubt that entry into the Canadian market or a substantial expansion beyond a small operation would frequently involve high costs from the standpoint of individual British producers and the British economy generally. Consider the position of a British producer well established in sterling area markets, but with no significant foothold in Canada. It is quite conceivable that such a producer might decide to try to divert more output towards Canada because of long-term market considerations, such as the growth potential of the Canadian market. That is, long-term prospects in the Canadian market might be thought sufficiently more attractive than traditional markets to entice the producer to incur the costs of entry necessarily required to establish himself in the Canadian market. At the same time, it seems rather unlikely that producers would take such a step simply on the basis of marginal and uncertain price and income changes. A producer who is already well established in both sterling area markets and Canada or in Canada only may perhaps be more sensitive to small price and income changes. Moreover, those suppliers on the verge of entering the Canadian market anyway may finally be brought in by such devices. Further, the cost of entry into Canada has probably varied considerably with the level of economic activity; during those postwar years when there was a dearth of supplies, 1945-8 and 1950-3, the cost of entry may well have been comparatively modest. These qualifications having been noted, the fact remains that the sensitivity of sales to marginal changes in income and prices is reduced the higher and more persuasive the costs of entry. Or in more technical language, barriers to entry reduce price and income elasticities. In addition, these barriers introduce certain discontinuities into the analysis which are usually assumed away in the traditional analysis based on marginal changes and continuous functional relationships.

The relevance of these observations in the present context is readily apparent.

From the foregoing analysis it is evident that many British suppliers have been well established in sterling area and other markets and not as well established in Canada; that entry into many sectors of the Canadian market has entailed meeting the costs a newcomer faces where monopolistic competition prevails; and that in some sectors of the Canadian market, including several more prosperous ones, entry has been circumscribed by institutional, financial, and legal restrictions.

3. EFFECT OF STERLING AREA RESTRICTIONS IN 1952 ON BRITISH EXPORTS TO CANADA

In order to gain further understanding of the influence that conditions in Britain's major markets may have had on British sales in Canada, it is useful to examine the trade statistics in some detail for the years from 1951 to 1954. During this period, it will be recalled, several important sterling area countries imposed restrictions on imports from Britain. Australia, for example, the largest sterling area importer of British goods, in 1946-7 had generally exempted sterling area imports from import licensing. In March 1952 import licensing was again extended to cover imports from all countries.[21] The quotas established under these licensing arrangements limited imports of many kinds of equipment and raw materials for industrial use to 60 per cent of their value in the base period July 1950 to June 1951, and limited imports of consumer goods to 20 per cent of their value in the base period. A third category of products, "capital development goods," was made subject to administrative control.[22] Restrictions on imports from non-dollar countries (other than Japan) were gradually relaxed during 1953 and relatively few remained after April 1954.[23] Less drastic restrictions were also imposed by New Zealand and South Africa; and these too were relaxed during the latter part of 1953.[24]

At the same time as these restrictions were being imposed demand in Britain's home market was deliberately being restricted through monetary and fiscal policies.[25] Thus, it is fair to say that from the end of the first quarter of 1952 until late in 1953 sterling area demand for British products was appreciably reduced. In so far as relatively easier conditions in these other markets were exercising a debilitating effect on British exports to Canada and to the extent that this could have been corrected by restraining sterling area demand, one would expect to see some evidence of the changes made in March 1952 in the trade statistics relating to this period.

With this in mind, Table XLII has been prepared. The figures shown under the heading "British exports" are based on British export statistics and those shown under "Canadian imports" on Canadian import statistics. The Table compares changes in British exports to Canada and to sterling area countries, by quarters, from 1951 to 1954 and changes in Canadian imports from Britain and from other countries, by quarters, from 1951 to 1954.

For a number of reasons the evidence leaves room for uncertainty. First, the restrictions applied for a relatively short period and it is doubtful whether their effects would fully manifest themselves in so short a time. Secondly, comparison is made difficult with 1950 and 1951 because of the substantial price changes that followed the outbreak of war in Korea. Thirdly, some seasonality is evident

TABLE XLIII

Influence on Sterling Area Import Restrictions in 1952-3 on British Exports to Canada

(index numbers, first quarter 1952 = 100)

		1950	1951 I	II	III	IV	1952 I	II	III	IV	1953 I	II	III	IV	1954 I	II	III	IV	1955
British exports																			
Total, value	C	125	113	162	155	114	100	120	140	146	135	187	152	149	125	144	119	135	139
	S	66	71	81	87	96	100	77	68	76	78	76	79	89	86	86	87	82	92
	%*	12	10	13	11	8	6	10	13	12	11	16	13	11	9	11	9	11	10
Metals & engineering products	C	128	95	165	130	113	100	133	145	140	130	215	143	153	125	145	98	113	125
	S	67	66	74	79	91	100	81	71	82	84	79	77	88	87	87	88	82	96
	%*	11	9	13	10	7	6	10	12	10	9	16	11	10	8	10	7	8	8
Canadian imports																			
Total, value	B	148	135	194	163	116	100	137	144	147	140	112	176	167	129	170	141	135	147
	O	82	100	121	110	106	100	111	106	116	106	129	118	110	99	119	107	112	127
	%†	15	11	13	12	10	8	10	11	10	11	11	12	12	11	11	11	10	9
Iron & products	B	184	129	220	147	131	100	176	173	158	153	237	209	200	155	232	137	118	139
	O	66	87	108	96	90	100	114	92	100	105	132	107	89	94	114	87	82	118
	%†	18	9	13	10	9	6	10	12	10	9	11	12	14	11	13	10	9	7
Non-ferrous metal products (including electrical equipment)	B	116	100	141	157	116	100	140	142	139	136	160	172	158	123	153	155	158	153
	O	78	107	118	104	106	100	102	108	135	116	142	141	149	120	127	132	161	152
	%†	22	14	17	22	16	15	20	19	15	17	16	18	15	15	18	17	14	15
Textiles & fibre products	B	142	175	235	187	99	100	100	118	117	145	151	152	122	116	114	119	101	120
	O	87	135	147	106	88	100	87	79	111	115	102	80	82	82	87	77	91	99
	%†	45	36	44	49	31	27	31	41	29	35	41	52	41	39	36	42	30	33

Sources: Board of Trade, *Report on Overseas Trade*, monthly issues; Dominion Bureau of Statistics, *Trade of Canada*, monthly issues.

Symbols: C—to Canada; S—to sterling area; %*—exports to Canada as percentage of exports to sterling area; B—from Britain; O—from all countries except Britain; %†—imports from Britain as a percentage of imports from all other countries.

in the figures which further complicates comparison. Fourthly, at least one large and exceptional order was filled during this period, that is, equipment for the Toronto subway which began operations in March 1954, and this somewhat distorts the picture of British exports to Canada. Finally, economic conditions in Canada varied, the pace of economic activity and inflationary pressures generally tending to taper off after the second quarter of 1953.

Subject to these and other qualifications, the figures collected in Table XLII suggest that the sterling area restrictions may have enhanced British exports to Canada somewhat. British exports to the sterling area decreased rather sharply after the first quarter of 1952, and exports to Canada increased notably during the latter part of 1952. As sterling area exports recovered toward the end of 1953, exports to Canada began to lag. The ratio of Canadian to sterling area exports generally increased slightly during the period of the restrictions. These trends are somewhat more pronounced for metals and engineering goods than for all goods. Traces of the same tendency can be found in Canadian import statistics. This statistical evidence is supported by the fact that some government and Dollar Export Council officials as well as business men apparently believe the restrictions augmented British exports to Canada.

Although some improvement may have occurred, the difficulty of being very confident on this point indicates that at best the extent of the improvement was rather limited, particularly when account is taken of the relative severity of the restrictions. Moreover, although Canadian imports from Britain increased significantly during the period in question, it is noteworthy that Britain's share of Canadian imports, even in product lines important to British suppliers, was unexceptional. Further, such increases in British exports to Canada as did occur may simply have reflected a shortening of order books and a temporary step-up in deliveries to Canada as a consequence of the restrictions, rather than a diversion of trade.

Sterling area restrictions during this period to a considerable extent were applied through direct controls and one cannot say how effective a policy based entirely upon indirect price and income measures might have been. To have brought about a corresponding cut-back in sterling area demand, indirect measures would probably have had to be rather severe, partly because the impact of indirect measures would have been less immediate and more uncertain. For these reasons and others, one might suspect that indirect measures, even of a rather stiff nature, might not have been any more effective, at least in the short run.

It is appropriate to recall here that during the inter-war period, when there was hardly an excess of demand for British output, the share of British exports sold in Canada also declined. It seems inadequate, therefore, to regard such difficulties "as delays in delivery and lack of incentive to venture upon the risks of export trade" as simply the "concomitants of inflation."[26] Although the post-war inflation of sterling and other "soft currency" markets probably enhanced difficulties of this sort, the reports of the Balfour Committee indicate that somewhat similar problems hampered British exports even during the depressed twenties.[27] This suggests that some of the basic problems encountered in Britain's export trade with Canada since the war have been long standing, deep seated, and complex and cannot be attributed simply to excess demand.[28]

CHAPTER SEVEN

CONCLUDING COMMENTS

IN THE COURSE of this discussion an attempt has been made to provide a rounded, comprehensive explanation for the decrease since World War I in the proportion of goods sold in Canada that come from Britain. Underlying this immediate purpose has been the more general objective of trying to gain a clearer understanding of the determinants of international trade in the modern world economy by examining in some detail the various factors influencing one small but significant segment of world trade.

Probably the firmest conclusion to emerge from the analysis, important even though it may seem trite, is that many factors have contributed to the decrease in Britain's share of Canadian market sales. The relative importance of these factors has varied widely from product to product and from year to year. Accordingly generalization is both difficult and hazardous, and simple explanations relying on one or two factors are likely to be inadequate.

Subject to this important qualification, a number of broad conclusions might be drawn from the preceding discussion. First, there is little evidence of a high correlation between changes in Britain's competitive price-cost position and Britain's share of Canadian market sales. The most impressive illustration of this is the relatively minor effect, so far as one can tell, that the substantial devaluations of sterling in 1931 and again in 1949 had on Britain's share of Canadian imports. In neither case was there much substitution of British production for other foreign production as a result of the greatly improved competitive price position of British producers. Nor apparently did the higher sterling profits obtainable from Canadian sales because of the devaluations induce British sellers to divert goods from other markets on any large scale. Furthermore, comparisons of absolute price levels, though very difficult to make, suggest that some British producers since 1949 have tended to rely upon prices that are somewhat below the conventional price ranges in order to offset in some degree various nonprice disadvantages. In short, the usual text-book picture of relatively high elasticities and nice adjustment between the flow of trade and price incentives, *per se*, propelled by the forces of competition is not very apparent from the statistics for the past thirty-five years. This is not to say that these incentives have been inoperative; nor is it so say that prices and costs cannot be, and on occasion may have been, relatively high or low. Nevertheless, it seems reasonably clear that such incentives as have arisen since the 1920's because of prices and costs have been largely swamped by other market influences.

Secondly, the analysis suggests that income variations may also be of secondary importance in explaining the phenomenon in question. Despite something like a fourfold increase in Canada's gross national product (constant dollars) and the volume of all Canadian imports, the volume of British goods sold in Canada during the mid fifties seems to have been little different than in 1913—though it appears to have increased somewhat beyond this level since then. There is some indication that British exports to Canada in some years since World War II may have been hampered by strong demand in non-dollar markets. It is apparent, however, that as the pressure of this demand has abated in recent years there has been little recovery in Britain's share of the Canadian market, even during the period 1952-4 when sales in sterling area markets were restricted by government measures. Moreover, excess aggregate demand has only been in evidence since 1939 and the decrease in Britain's share of Canadian market sales has been a long-term development.

Thirdly, it seems that the long-term decrease in Britain's share of Canadian market sales is to be primarily explained in terms of the structure of Canadian demand, the size and pattern of foreign investment in Canada, Britain's relatively unfavourable position in terms of non-price market variables, private and public restrictions on the flow of trade, and certain government policies enhancing the relative attractiveness of sterling area markets for British producers. These market factors have been highly interdependent and the relative importance of each has varied from time to time.

The incidence of structural changes in Canadian demand and in foreign investment in Canada has been considerable. Broadly speaking, Canadian demand has grown in such a way that demand for those products which loomed large in British exports to Canada during the twenties has grown less than demand for other kinds of products. Thus the Canadian market over the long term has, as it were, tended to grow away from British producers. This development may have been somewhat enhanced by Britain's decline as an entrepot. In the short term the structure of Canadian demand has largely accounted for the tendency of Britain's share of Canadian sales to increase in periods of recession and to decrease in periods of expansion, though the level of British exports to Canada has naturally tended to be higher in periods of expansion and lower in periods of recession. As for foreign investment in Canada, this has increasingly come from the United States and over the years United States investment in Canada has become much larger than that of Britain. The importance of this change has been appreciably increased because a high proportion of American investment has been direct investment accompanied by a rich variety of entrepreneurship, risk-bearing, and technology, and has been concentrated strategically in some of the fastest-growing sectors of the economy.

Britain's export trade with Canada has also been undermined by the competitive and diversified nature of the Canadian market relative to other markets, the importance of non-price competition, the costs of entry to be met within this competitive and ever changing framework, and the failure of British sellers to measure up to the standards of distribution, selling activity, and so on established by these market conditions. These conditions have been fostered by a variety of factors including Canada's relatively rapid economic development, the "openness" of the Canadian economy, Canada's physical size and geographic location next to the United States, and the relative emphasis in North American society on mass production methods, rapid technological advance, enormous selling effort, and an environment of change and novelty. Within this context, the inadequacies of the distribution system—with all that this implies—open to

British goods seem to have been especially serious in hampering British exports to Canada.

In addition, the sale of British goods in many of the larger and more prosperous sectors of the Canadian market in the past has frequently been encumbered by trade restrictions of various kinds. Some of these have been of private origin arising out of international market-sharing arrangements, inter-corporate financial affiliations, and international patent-licensing agreements. Others have resulted from government policies, especially commercial policies. In general, Canadian commercial policy has discriminated somewhat in favour of domestic production. As explained above, this may have resulted in some indirect discrimination against imports from Britain, even though government policy has directly discriminated in favour of British production as opposed to other foreign production, and the degree of this direct discrimination has apparently not changed very much.

Finally, British foreign economic policy since World War I in some ways has tended to increase the attraction of the sterling area, compared to Canada, both as a place to sell British goods and a place to invest British capital.

In conclusion, brief reference might be made to some of the implications of these general conclusions as far as certain issues in present-day discussions of international economics are concerned.

The conventional theory of international trade has been largely constructed on the basis of three variables—price, income, and quantity—and the basic assumptions of pure and perfect competition. The limited relevance and significance of this model has been widely recognized.[1] At the same time, it seems fair to say that writings on international economics have contined to emphasize price and income analysis based on competitive assumptions. In part this has reflected the difficulty of incorporating other variables and assumptions into the analysis. In part, it may also have reflected an understandable aversion to the complicated, untidy, highly qualified, and frequently indeterminant discussion which may often result when one attempts to broaden the analysis beyond its conventional confines. The present study, unfortunately, reveals many of these problems all too well. Yet it is doubtful if problems of this kind can be avoided simply because they are difficult and do not lead to precise answers. As Professor Chamberlin has observed, "the only defensible scientific attitude seems to be to 'let the chips fall where they may', to give full importance to the indeterminate as well as to the determinate, and carefully to avoid the temptation of formulating problems with the objective of assuring a determinate answer."[2]

It has been argued by some that failure to extend analysis beyond its conventional limits is less important in international economics than in domestic economics because of the composition and structure of international trade.[3] While this may be true, it does not follow that these other factors are unimportant in international trade; and one general conclusion of this study is that they definitely have been important in the case of Britain's export trade with Canada.

All this is not meant to detract from the basic importance of traditional analysis. Moreover, it must be fully recognized that the many variables influencing sales are closely interdependent and that considering them separately is largely a matter of analytical convenience. Any attempt by a seller, for example, to improve his distribution facilities may mean higher costs and prices unless offsetting economies appear. In terms of the familiar two-dimensional diagram relating total cost and total revenue to different levels of output, there will be a different set of cost and revenue curves for every combination of non-price variables; and a change in any of these non-price variables will generally lead to changes in both costs and prices and the level of output at which the firm maximizes profits. On the buyer's side choice among differentiated but functionally substitutable goods requires a weighing of the price and non-price characteristics of different goods. Because of this interdependence, comments to the effect that prices are too high or too low frequently mean very little. Similarly, an analysis of trade based on only price and income effects may be deficient, just as prior to the thirties economic analysis frequently suffered because inadequate attention was given to income as a determinant of trade.

As far as elasticity is concerned, no one would deny that there may be situations where trade flows are highly responsive to price and income changes. At the same time, however, it is quite possible that the relative importance of price and income variations may be overshadowed by other market factors.[4] In the preceding discussion a number of reasons have been suggested why in the case of Britain's export trade with Canada one might expect the flow of trade to be relatively unresponsive to price and income changes, especially when these changes are of marginal magnitudes.

Along this line of thought there is also the question of what light this analysis might shed on Britain's "dollar shortage." In so far as this shortage was a consequence of lagging exports to dollar countries, the implication of the present study is that it arose partly because of deeply seated long-term factors and is not to be explained simply in terms of post-war inflationary pressures. Further, because of the considerable differences between Canada and the United States mentioned in chapter I, one has some reason to doubt the basic importance of such factors as United States commercial policy, the size and self-sufficiency of the American economy, changes in the terms of trade, and the degree of complementarity between the British and American economies. The present study tends to support those who have emphasized such factors as changes in demand patterns, the role of foreign investment, the importance of non-price factors in influencing sales, rapid technological progress, and the relative propensities of societies to foster and adjust themselves to rapid change in all phases of economic activity. It also indicates the possibility that private trade restrictions may have impaired dollar earnings in the past.

To what extent these factors may have influenced the general decrease in Britain's share of world trade cannot be inferred from this study though some of the variables that might be considered in this context are suggested. Moreover, it is one thing to try to explain the decrease in Britain's share of Canadian imports; it is quite another to suggest that Britain's share of the Canadian market should have been different from what it has been. This latter question has been only briefly referred to above. As was pointed out, before one could conclude that Britain's share of the Canadian market should have been greater (or less) than it has been one would need to demonstrate that the net return from using British resources for exports to Canada would have been greater (or less) than the net return that was earned or might have been earned by using these resources for other purposes. In these terms it is by no means self-evident that Britain would have been better off during the past forty years had a larger share of resources been devoted to exporting to Canada.

Finally, brief mention might be made of recent discussion about the possibility of diverting Canadian imports from the United States to Britain. As indicated in chapter II, the trade figures suggest that about 40 to 50 per cent of Canadian imports consist of goods which Britain is in a weak position to supply, at least in the short run, because of a lack of production facilities. Thus, to achieve a given amount of diversion in total Canadian imports, diversion of almost twice this amount would be required in product lines where, in the short term at least, diversion is at all possible. The difficulty of achieving a large diversion in this sector of Canadian imports is readily apparent when one considers the characteristics of Canadian trade and the nature of the basic market forces that have made it what it is. On this basis it seems most unlikely that diversion on significant scale could be achieved by means of a combination of weak and marginal policy measures. Instead, strong measures would seem to be required capable of overrunning the deeply rooted natural market forces that have been at work over the years. It is only in terms of such measures and the high costs which they might entail that the prospective benefits of diversion can be realistically evaluated.

ANGLO-CANADIAN TRADE:

PRICES AND THE TERMS OF TRADE, 1924-54 °

In RECENT YEARS the amount of detailed statistical information available on price changes in international trade has been considerably enlarged. Presumably this has been a consequence of the belief held by various investigators that more detailed data will result in more penetrating analysis than can be expected from consideration of total export and import figures alone without regard to differences between areas and commodity groups. Average value and terms of trade indexes relating to commodity trade between Canada and the United Kingdom are presented in Table A below. These index numbers represent a net addition, albeit modest, to the detailed information available from other sources.[1]

The procedure followed in constructing the average value series is outlined in section I below. In section II certain questions relating to the terms of trade movements indicated by these figures are briefly considered.

I

The average value series shown in Table A were computed from figures recorded in the *Annual Statement of the Trade of the United Kingdom* (Board of Trade).[2] To compute the series, average value index numbers based on average values in sterling were calculated for those commodity classifications listed in volume IV of the *Annual Statement* which met the following conditions: (*a*) both value and quantity data were recorded for all years within the period relating to a given base year; and (*b*) the value of trade exceeded a certain minimum amount in any one of the years within this period.[3] On this basis (including exceptions) the individual average value series taken together represent over 70 per cent of the total value of United Kingdom exports to Canada in each base year and 80 per cent of the total value of imports.

Trade classifications for which separate series were not calculated were included in the aggregate series in one of two ways. In most cases the year-to-year average value change was assumed equal to that recorded for all commodities represented by an individual series. In some instances, however, it seemed more appropriate to assume that the average value change was the same as that indicated by the individual series for one or more products manufactured from the same basic material (for example, cotton).[4]

The individual average value index numbers were combined to form Laspeyre-type series weighted by the relative importance, by value, of the various commodities in five base years—1924, 1930, 1936, 1948, 1952—the series for each

TABLE A

INDEX NUMBERS RELATING TO UNITED KINGDOM FOREIGN TRADE

(1924 = 100)

| | U.K. trade with Canada | | | | U.K. world trade (e) | |
| | Average value | | Terms of trade | | Terms of trade | |
	U.K. exports (a)	U.K. imports (b)	Net barter (c)	Income(d)	Net barter (c)	Income (d)
1924	100	100	100	100	100	100
1925	101	111	91	88	98	97
1926	91	105	87	90	101 ·	89
1927	89	99	90	105	100	101
1928	90	95	95	129	99	102
1929	88	92	96	136	98	105
1930	82	80	103	130	107	93
1931	73	62	118	118	119	79
1932	72	65	111	91	120	80
1933	73	58	126	108	122	83
1934	79	57	139	124	119	86
1935	78	61	128	125	118	92
1936	81	66	123	125	114	90
1937	87	84	104	117	108	92
1938	89	69	129	116	118	89
1948	258	200	129	125	100	104
1949 (f)	278	233	119	123	101	117
1950	314	270	116	167	94	125
1951	412	313	132	157	85	112
1952	361	332	109	140	91	114
1953	379	301	126	186	100	128
1954	376	289	130	163	98	133

(a) U.K. commodity exports to Canada, the produce and manufactures of the U.K.
(b) U.K. retained commodity imports from Canada.
(c) Average value of exports ÷ average value of imports.
(d) Value of U.K. exports ÷ average value of U.K. imports.
(e) Derived from data shown in the Times Review of Industry, (London & Cambridge Bulletin no. 20), Dec. 1956, p. xvi.
(f) Figures for 1949 and later years include Newfoundland as part of Canada.

weighting period then being linked together to form a continuous series. In order to assess the degree of distortion associated with the common "index number problem," the average value change between base years was calculated using the weights appropriate to both the beginning and the end of each period (for example, the change between 1924 and 1930 was calculated using both 1924 weights and 1930 weights). The series seem reasonably satisfactory from this standpoint.

II

While no attempt has been made to analyse the statistics shown in Table A in any detail, a number of points suggested by the figures are worth noting.

1. *Terms of Trade and Exchange Rate Variations*

During the period 1924-54 the pound-Canadian dollar exchange rate underwent four distinct peace-time revaluations. In 1931-2 and in 1949 the pound depreciated in value; in 1924-5 and in 1933 the pound appreciated in value. Price changes occurring in Britain's trade with Canada as well as changes in the net barter terms of trade during these years are shown in Table B. According to these figures, Britain's terms of trade with Canada deteriorated from 1924 to 1926 (when the pound appreciated in value) and from 1948 to 1950 (when the pound depreciated in value). On the other hand, Britain's terms of trade improved from 1930 to 1932 (when the pound depreciated in value) and improved further from 1932 to 1934 (when the pound appreciated in value). There

TABLE B

ANGLO-CANADIAN EXCHANGE RATES: AVERAGE VALUE AND TERMS OF TRADE INDEX NUMBERS

	U.K.—Canada exchange rate* $/£	U.K. trade with Canada		Terms of trade Net barter
		Average value		
		U.K. exports	U.K. imports	
1924	446.71	100	100	100
1925	483.05	101	111	91
1926	485.50	91	105	87
1930	486.56	100	100	100
1931	468.86	89	78	114
1932	397.93	88	81	109
1933	458.55	89	73	122
1934	499.26	96	71	135
1948	403.00	100	100	100
1949	375.69	108	117	92
1950	304.41	122	135	90

* Dominion Bureau of Statistics.

is, therefore, no evidence of a predictable relationship between an exchange rate depreciation or appreciation and the terms of trade. This result, which is consistent with theoretical reasoning on this point, agrees with the empirical findings of Professor Kindleberger. Everything depends on the size of the demand and supply elasticities about which, as Professor Kindleberger points out, "generalizations good from country to country, or even for the same country from time to time, have little validity."[5] It must, of course, be fully acknowledged that variations in the pound-Canadian dollar exchange rate during these years occurred at times when, perhaps typically, the economic climate in both countries was disturbed and complex. Many fundamental economic developments were in progress at about the same time and the cross-currents generated by other factors make it virtually impossible to identify statistically, with any confidence, the influence solely attributable to exchange rate variations.

2. *Terms of Trade and Britain's "Dollar Shortage"*

In considering Britain's so-called "dollar shortage," many post-war writers have placed considerable emphasis on deteriorating terms of trade as a factor accounting for Britain's balance-of-payments difficulties.[6] As far as Britain's trade with Canada is concerned, the figures shown in Table A indicate that Britain's net barter terms of trade during the post-war years were slightly more favourable than during the thirties and appreciably more favourable than during the twenties. This picture, of course, relates only to bilateral trade and does not mean that, taking Britain's foreign trade as a whole, adverse terms of trade have not contributed to Britain's "dollar shortage"—including the Canadian "dollar shortage." The figures do indicate, however, that in so far as an adverse change in Britain's terms of trade has been a factor in causing the "dollar shortage," one must look to Britain's terms of trade with countries other than Canada.

3. *Terms of Trade between Primary Products and Manufactures*

Trade between Canada and the United Kingdom to a very large extent consists of an exchange of Canadian raw and processed commodities for British finished manufactures. Moreover, the proportion of these commodities in the total export trade of each country with the other has not altered significantly over the years, though, of course, there have been considerable shifts in the relative importance of individual commodities. It is therefore interesting to observe in Table A that Britain's net barter terms of trade with Canada during the post-war boom were somewhat more favourable than during the depressed thirties. And during both the thirties and the post-war years Britain's terms of trade with Canada were substantially more favourable to Britain than during the twenties. This evidence is at variance with two generalizations sometimes implied or stated in this connection, namely, that there is a secular tendency for the terms of trade to favour primary producers at the expense of manufacturers and that the terms of trade move against primary producers and in favour of manufacturers during depressions and *vice versa* during booms.

4. *Terms of Trade and the Volume of British Exports to Canada*

Mr. R. L. Marris in an article in 1955, using simple regression analysis relating to Britain's foreign trade with all countries, showed that there is a close "historical association" between Britain's terms of trade and the volume of her exports.[7] He suggested that the curves he obtained by plotting Britain's net barter and income terms of trade against the volume of her exports from 1921 to 1954 might be viewed in one of two ways: "as qualified estimates of the static transformation curves of the textbooks"; or as "a picture of what normally happens to the purchasing powers of U.K. exports during the course of a recession associated with a world-wide shift in the terms of trade between primaries and manufactures." Following up this analysis, the writer applied the same statistical technique to data relating to Anglo-Canadian trade. Very little correlation was found to exist between the terms of trade and the volume of British exports to Canada. This suggests, when account is taken of the nature of Britain's trade with Canada and the properties of the static transformation curve, that before either of the interpretations indicated by Mr. Marris can be accepted it is necessary to investigate the question on a much less aggregative basis.

NOTES

CHAPTER ONE

1. The possible significance of this has been lucidly explained by Sir Dennis H. Robertson, *Britain in the World Economy* (London: George Allen and Unwin Ltd., 1954), pp. 57 ff.

2. For example in judging the effectiveness of devaluation in overcoming a balance of payments deficit, consideration of whether the sum of the export and import demand elasticities is greater than one may be considerably less important than knowing whether the elasticities are likely to be large enough to bring about a substantial change in the deficit.

3. Of the two volume series of United Kingdom exports to Canada shown in Table II, the second is probably the more accurate. Both series are, of course, subject to all the qualifications associated with adjusting value figures for price changes over long periods of time.

4. Admittedly, these figures for the United States include United States exports to Canada. Exclusion of these would not materially change the picture, although the growth in the United States' share as well as its size would be somewhat less. It might also be noted that at various times since World War I, and especially since World War II, United States access to large world markets has been seriously curtailed through various trade and payments restrictions. With freer access to these markets, say equivalent to that enjoyed in Canada, the United States share of world exports might conceivably be higher than indicated by these figures.

CHAPTER TWO

1. This exercise admittedly relates to the question of Britain's share of total Canadian consumption rather than to the question of Britain's share of Canadian imports which is the main concern of this study. It is, however, relevant to the latter question if other foreign suppliers are deemed to have access to sectors of Canadian demand where British access seems limited—an assumption that is plausible when the composition and size of Canadian imports from other countries, particularly in the Western Hemisphere, are taken into account.

2. Bank of Canada, *Statistical Summary* (Financial Supp. 1957), p. 109.

3. This conclusion corresponds to that arrived at by a number of studies of Britain's export trade with all countries, for example, J. M. Letiche, "Differential Rates of Productivity Growth and International Imbalance," *Quarterly Journal of Economics*, LXIX (Aug. 1955), pp. 388 ff; H. Tyszynski, "World Trade in Manufactured Commodities, 1899-1950," *Manchester School of Economic and Social Studies*, XIX (Sept. 1951), pp. 288 ff.

4. These calculations are similar to those made by H. Tyszynski in "World Trade in Manufactured Commodities, 1899-1950," pp. 272 ff; I. Svennilson in *Growth and Stagnation in the European Economy* (Geneva: United Nations, 1954); Robert E. Baldwin in "The Commodity Composition of Trade: Selected Industrial Countries, 1900-1954," *Review of Economics and Statistics*, XL (Supp., Feb. 1958), pp. 50 ff; and Stephen Spiegleglas in "World Exports of Manufactures, 1956 vs. 1937," *Manchester School of Economic and Social Studies*, XXVII (May 1954), pp. 111 ff. Some of the difficulties associated with such calculations are referred to by R. E. Baldwin in the article cited and by Professor Gottfried Haberler in a comment on Baldwin's paper in *Review of Economics and Statistics*, XL (Supp., Feb. 1958), pp. 3-5.

5. Alfred E. Kahn, *Great Britain in the World Economy* (New York: Columbia University Press, 1946), p. 230; Committee on Industry and Trade, *Survey of Overseas Markets* (London: H.M.S.O., 1925), p. 451, ". . . the United States has established to a much greater extent than before the war direct trading with non-European sources of supply of raw materials which were formerly handled through Europe. The importance of Europe as an agent in this intermediary trade has therefore declined. . . ."

6. Ronald J. Wonnacott, *An Input-Output Analysis of the Relationship of the Canadian and U.S. Economies,* Harvard Economic Research Project, Aug. 1958 (mimeo).

7. Cf. recent moves in the United States to curb patent restrictions on the export of radio and television goods from the United States to Canada.

CHAPTER THREE

1. For example, Canadian statistics are incomplete and scattered for years prior to 1926.

2. From 1924 to 1926 the British wholesale price index for manufactures decreased by 10 per cent; from 1926 to 1929 is decreased a further 7 per cent. *Times Review of Industry* (London & Cambridge Economic Bulletin no. 26), June 1958. The General Strike, of course, occurred in 1926. Although this may have distorted British prices to some extent, these distortions were not considered sufficiently important to invalidate the use of 1926 as a base year for the comparisons presented here.

3. For further discussion on commercial policy see chapter v.

4. For tramp freight rates see L. Isserlis, "Tramp Shipping Cargoes and Freights," *Journal of the Royal Statistical Society*, CI, pt. 1 (1938), p. 122; I.M.F., *International Financial Statistics*, XI, no. 6 (June 1958), p. 35. For railway revenue per ton-mile see U.S. Dept. of Commerce, *Historical Statistics of the United States, 1789-1945, Statistical Abstract of the United States*, various issues. It should be noted that the foregoing data on ocean freight rates relate to tramp ships rather than to ocean liners. Liner freight is important to trade between Canada and the United Kingdom and these rates are monopolistically controlled.

5. Pp. 50 ff.

6. Although the Canadian import price index series includes imports from the United Kingdom, the preponderance of Canadian imports from the United States means that the index closely approximates an index of prices of United States exports to Canada. The price increase from 1938 to 1948 shown for British exports to Canada has been calculated using 1936 weights. Had 1948 weights been used the increase shown would have been somewhat greater.

7. As the data do not pertain to total Canadian sales, nothing can be said about changes in Britain's share of total Canadian sales in Canada. It is possible that the incidence of devaluation, both in 1931 and 1949, may have fallen mainly upon Canadian production rather than upon imports from other countries.

8. It is sometimes argued that the 1949 devaluation was rendered ineffective by domestic price increases in the United Kingdom after 1949. Although there has been some loss of the price advantage gained by devaluation through domestic price increases, it is evident from the foregoing figures that only a part of this advantage has been lost.

9. *The Dollar Shortage* (New York: John Wiley and Sons, 1950), p. 160.

10. It does not follow, of course, that commodities selling at the same price are the same in all other respects.

11. This applies to a situation comprising a large number of buyers and sellers whether under conditions of pure competition or monopolistic competition—that is, the "large group" of competitors referred to by Professor Chamberlin in his *Theory of Monopolistic Competition* (Cambridge: Harvard University Press, 1950). It is assumed, too, that when individual profits are maximized the national return from exporting is maximized.

12. *Special Register Information Service* (S.R.I.S.), Sept. 9, 1953: Tariff Board, *Canadian Wool-Cloth Industry* (Woollens and Worsteds) (Reference no. 116), 1955, pp. 40 ff.

13. S.R.I.S., July 4, 1952; May 6, 1954.

14. S.R.I.S., July 4, 1952; June 25, 1952; Feb. 10, 1953; April 13, 1956; March 13, 1956.

15. S.R.I.S., Oct. 3, 1955.

16. S.R.I.S., Oct. 27, 1950; Jan. 2, 1951.

17. S.R.I.S., June 4, 1951; May 20, 1958; Oct. 4, 1955; Aug. 31, 1955.

18. S.R.I.S., Jan. 21, 1955; Nov. 22, 1954; March 8, 1954; July 26, 1954; July 17, 1957; Tariff Board, *Waterproof Footwear and Rubber-soled Canvas Footwear* (Reference no. 121), 1957, pp. 23 ff.

19. S.R.I.S., Aug. 23, 1954.

20. S.R.I.S., June 29, 1950; March 15, 1955; June 19, 1952.

21. S.R.I.S., March 15, 1955.

22. "A general comparison with United Kingdom prices is not possible, since few United Kingdom appliances are in the market. However . . . United Kingdom prices have not usually been competitive." (*S.R.I.S.*, Jan. 30, 1952, p. 5.) A *News Chronicle* survey in Trinidad before devaluation in 1949 is reported to have found British prices on this type of commodity as much as 100 per cent higher than United States and Canadian products. The 1949 devaluation would not, of course, have wiped out differentials of this magnitude. *Economist*, May 7, 1949, p. 825.

23. Royal Commission on Canada's Economic Prospects, *The Electronics Industry in Canada*, prepared by Canadian Business Service Limited (1956), *passim*; *The Canadian Electrical Manufacturing Industry* (1956), prepared by Clarence L. Barber, *passim*; F. A. Knox *et al.*,

The Canadian Electrical Manufacturing Industry (Canadian Electrical Manufacturers Association, 1955), p. 26.

24. *Economist*, Oct. 23, 1954, Supplement, "Motoring for Million." This review asserts that U.S. automobiles "give the most motor car for the money in the world," p. 19. "The price of a full-sized automobile in Canada is lower than anywhere else in the world outside of the U.S., measured both by actual prices at retail and in terms of labour income." Royal Commission on Canada's Economic Prospects, *The Canadian Automotive Industry*, prepared by The Sun Life Assurance Company of Canada (1956), p. 33.

25. E. T. Sara, "British and Foreign Steel Prices," *Times Review of Industry* (London & Cambridge Economic Bulletin), June 1953.

26. "Iron and Steel," *Productivity Team Report* (Anglo-American Council on Productivity, 1952), p. 108 and Appendix M.

27. Tariff Board, *Pipes and Tubes of Iron or Steel* (Reference no. 119), 1957, p. 27.

28. Tariff Board, *Basic Iron and Steel Products* (Reference no. 118), 1957, p. 46. In this connection see also Duncan Burn, *The Structure of British Industry* (Cambridge: University Press, 1958), vol. I, pp. 292 f.

29. Tariff Board, *Basic Iron and Steel Products* (Reference no. 118), Appendix F, pp. 286 ff.

30. *S.R.I.S.*, March 24, 1958.

31. Tariff Board, *Zinc and Zinc Products* (Reference no. 122), 1957, p. 45.

32. "Machine Tool Manufacture in the Western Bloc," *Times Review of Industry*, Dec. 1954, p. 102.

33. "The Machine Tool Industry," *Planning*, XV (Dec. 20, 1948), p. 190.

34. P. 45.

35. See p. 4. This conclusion is also indicated by *S.R.I.S.*, May 13, 1950; March 4, 1952. See also *Report on the British Tool, Machine Tool and Scientific Instrument Section Exhibition at the Canadian Industrial Trade Fair* (Toronto, 1950), pp. 44-6.

36. *S.R.I.S.*, Feb. 24, 1951; Oct. 11, 1956; Oct. 29, 1954; May 15, 1958; June 22, 1951; June 20, 1951; July 5, 1957; June 9, 1954; Oct. 29, 1951; Jan. 10, 1955; Sept. 15, 1954; Dec. 9, 1957; *Report of a Visit to the U.K.*, 1955, Petroleum Industry; *S.R.I.S.*, May 21, 1952; July 26, 1955; Oct. 5, 1953; July 25, 1952; April 22, 1955.

In connection with many of the foregoing industries see also the Board of Trade *Report of the United Kingdom Engineering Mission to Canada, 1948* (London: H.M.S.O., 1949). "... the Mission is satisfied that over a wide range of engineering products the prices now being quoted to Canada are competitive. ... for all but mass-produced equipment, the United Kingdom manufactures has little to fear from foreign competition so far as prices are concerned. ..." The fact that even prior to devaluation prices compared favourably suggests that after devaluation British prices would have compared even more favourably.

37. *S.R.I.S.*, April 12, 1954; Feb. 29, 1952; *Report of the Directors of the Canadian Metal Mining Association on the Mission to the United Kingdom*, Canadian Metal Mining Association, Nov. 1955. (British manufacturers have a decided price advantage when competing with Canadian and American production. This would range from 10 to 30 per cent according to the type of equipment and machinery involved. This factor of price certainly constitutes the main selling point for British manufacturers selling in Canada.) *S.R.I.S.*, May 4, 1956.

38. Royal Commission on Canada's Economic Prospects, *The Canadian Industrial Machinery Industry*, prepared by Urwick, Currie Limited, pp. 13-14.

39. *Agricultural Machinery: A Report on the Industry* (London: Political and Economic Planning, 1949), p. 74.

40. *Financial Times*, Nov. 20, 1954, p. 1.

41. This general picture of the trend of Britain's competitive price position on agricultural machinery during the post-war years is supported by the Board of Trade *Report of the British Agricultural Machinery Mission to Canada, 1949* (London: H.M.S.O., 1949).

42. "The Locomotive Building Industry," *Planning*, XII (April 1947), p. 9.

43. *Locomotives: A Report on the Industry* (London: Political and Economic Planning, 1951), p. 49.

44. Royal Commission on Canada's Economic Prospects, *The Electronics Industry in Canada, passim, The Canadian Electrical Manufacturing Industry, passim*; Knox *et al.*, *The Canadian Electrical Manufacturing Industry, passim*; *S.R.I.S.*, Aug. 12, 1954, Dec. 4, 1951, July 18, 1958.

45. Royal Commission on Canada's Economic Prospects, *The Canadian Electrical Manufacturing Industry*, pp. 69-71.

46. See for example, *Economist*, Jan. 7, 1950, p. 43; *Financial Times*, Nov. 4, 1955, p. 1.

47. P. 6. For a similar view see *S.R.I.S.*, April 29, 1954.

48. P. 45.

49. *S.R.I.S.*, Nov. 26, 1954; Nov. 30, 1954; Sept. 19, 1952; May 21, 1958; April 14, 1958; March 15, 1957.

50. *S.R.I.S.*, Feb. 27. 1951; Jan. 24, 1952; Feb. 20, 1952; June 15, 1955; Jan. 17, 1955; Aug. 26, 1955; March 16, 1956; July 22, 1957.

51. *S.R.I.S.*, May 10, 1957; May 4, 1956; Jan. 25, 1956; Jan. 17, 1955; April 25, 1957; March 16, 1956.

52. J. B. Heath, "British-Canadian Industrial Productivity," *Economic Journal*, LXVII (Dec. 1957), Table III, p. 674.

53. Although the *Economist* is a journal of opinion, it is noteworthy that a perusal of its writings during the post-war years gives the impression that the turning point in Britain's relative price position came with devaluation in 1949. Prior to devaluation it was alleged that "North Americans find almost all British prices too high" and this theme was frequently reiterated. By 1950 the emphasis was reversed. In fact by the end of the year (1950) the question was put whether British prices in dollar markets should not be raised, and it was asserted that they "could rise perceptibly without cancelling out Britain's competitive advantage." This change in outlook coincides roughly with the showings of the indexes marshalled in the previous section and creates some limited presumption in their favour. See *Economist*, April 16, 1949, p. 697; May 7, 1949, p. 825; Nov. 4, 1950, p. 700; Dec. 9, 1950, p. 1019; Jan. 28, 1956, p. 331 (Annual Report, Lloyd's Bank).

54. J. B. Heath, "British-Canadian Industrial Productivity," *Economic Journal*, LXVII (Dec. 1957), pp. 665 ff.

55. *Ibid.*, Table III, p. 674.

56. National Industrial Conference Board Inc., *Production Costs Here and Abroad*, Studies in Business Economics, no. 61 (1958), pp. 21 ff., Table 4, p. 37.

57. Knox *et al.*, *The Canadian Electrical Manufacturing Industry*, Table 2.17, p. 40.

58. *Ibid.*, p. 40; Heath, "British-Canadian Industrial Productivity," p. 669.

59. For example, newsprint and copper, *Financial Times*, Jan. 13, 1955, p. 1; *Statist*, Jan. 8, 1955, p. 40.

60. Pp. 45 above; Knox *et al.*, *The Canadian Electrical Manufacturing Industry*, Table 2.16, p. 39.

61. Heath, "British-Canadian Industrial Productivity," p. 670.

62. *Ibid.*, Table III, p. 674.

63. The report of the National Industrial Conference Board, *Production Costs Here and Abroad*, already referred to, indicates that on average the unit cost of materials of firms producing similar products in Britain and the United States was somewhat higher in Britain in 1956-7.

64. *Production Costs Here and Abroad*, Table 1, p. 23; Table 4, p. 37.

65. In calculating the amount of taxable profit in the three countries, certain differences exist in such matters as depreciation allowances. Consequently, the profit base to which the tax rate is applied is somewhat different in the three countries. Such differences are, however, quite modest, especially when considered over a number of years and when related only to manufacturing industry.

66. Heath, "British-Canadian Industrial Productivity," p. 675. "... it appears that Canadian real gross investment in plant and machinery aggregated 1926-38 per head of numbers employed in 1938 was about double the British over the same period . . . ."

67. According to Mr. Heath's estimates, *ibid.*, p. 675, "the higher aggregate investment in Canada was not due in the main to a difference in the importance of the highly capitalized industries."

68. M. Fleming, "External Economies and the Doctrine of Balanced Growth," *Economic Journal*, LXV (June 1955), pp. 241 ff.

69. Allyn Young, "Increasing Returns and Economic Progress," *Economic Journal* XXXVIII (Dec. 1928), pp. 527 ff.

70. Britain's advantage in this respect may be somewhat less than these figures suggest because of the greater variety of markets to which British producers cater compared to North American producers.

71. J. Jewkes, "The Size of the Factory," *Economic Journal*, LXII (June 1952), p. 245; G. Rosenbluth, "Industrial Concentration in Canada and the U.S.A.," *Canadian Journal of Economics and Political Science*, XX (Aug. 1954), p. 336.

72. Marvin Frankel, *British and American Manufacturing Productivity* (Urbana: University of Illinois, 1957), chap. v.

73. T. M. Ridley, "Industrial Production in the United Kingdom, 1900-1953," *Economica*, N. S. XXII (Feb. 1955), pp. 1 ff; K. S. Lomax, "New Index-Numbers of Industrial Production, 1900-1938," *Times Review of Industry* (London & Cambridge Economic Bulletin no. 26),

June 1958; Central Statistical Office, *Monthly Digest of Statistics;* Dominion Bureau of Statistics, *Canadian Statistical Review,* 1957 Supp. and monthly issues; Royal Commission on Canada's Economic Prospects, *Canadian Secondary Manufacturing Industry,* prepared by D. H. Fullerton and H. A. Hampson, Table 14.

74. Royal Commission on Canada's Economic Prospects, *Canadian Secondary Manufacturing Industry,* chap. 4.

75. Knox *et al., The Canadian Electrical Industry,* p. 43; Royal Commission on Canada's Economic Prospects, *The Canadian Industrial Machinery Industry,* prepared by Urwick, Currie Ltd., p. 16.

76. National Industrial Conference Board, *Convertibility and Foreign Trade,* Studies in Business Economics, no. 45 (1954), pp. 90 ff.; *Production Costs Here and Abroad* (1958).

77. These conclusions are also indicated in an article by John H. Dunning, "United States Manufacturing Subsidiaries and Britain's Trade Balance," *District Bank Review* (Sept. 1955), pp. 27 ff. Dunning explicitly notes how much lower costs are in the United Kingdom than in North America. Quite a number of United States subsidiaries in Britain are said to be manufacturing at costs from one-third to one-half below those of their parent companies.

78. *American Investment in British Manufacturing Industry* (London: George Allen & Unwin Ltd., 1958), pp. 151 f.

CHAPTER IV

1. For example, Ontario and Quebec together absorb about 85 per cent of total steel supplies in Canada. The favourable freight differential provides protection to the products of Stelco, Dofasco, and Atlas in much of this market, the degree of protection varying with products and areas. Tariff Board, *Basic Iron and Steel Products* (Reference no. 118), pp. 20-43; *Pipes and Tubes of Iron or Steel* (Reference no. 119), pp. 19-25.

2. Walter Isard and Merton J. Peck, "Location Theory and International and Interregional Trade Theory," *Quarterly Journal of Economics,* LXVIII (Feb. 1954), pp. 101 ff.; Walter Isard, "Location Theory and Trade Theory: A Short-Run Analysis," *Quarterly Journal of Economics,* XLVIII (May 1954), pp. 305 ff.; W. Beckerman, "Distance and the Pattern of Intra-European Trade," *Review of Economics and Statistics,* XXXVIII (Feb. 1956), pp. 31 ff.

3. All-cargo air service now exists for such products as consumer goods and machine tools. This is especially helpful in making spares available more quickly.

4. For example, the "bridge subsidy" and the "agreed charges" arranged between suppliers and carriers of steel. Tariff Board, *Basic Iron and Steel Products* (Reference no. 118), p. 41.

5. Board of Trade, *Report of the British Agricultural Machinery Mission to Canada, 1949* (London: H.M.S.O., 1949), pp. 40 f.; *Board of Trade Journal,* Nov. 28, 1953, p. 1128. In this connection it is noteworthy that steps have been taken to open a direct sea route from Manchester to Chicago and ports on the Canadian Great Lakes. *Financial Times,* March 2, 1956, p. 1.

6. Board of Trade, *Exporting to Canada* (London: H.M.S.O., 1951), pp. 31-3.

7. Dollar Export Board, *Dollars and Industry,* A Record of the Dollar Convention, 1951, *passim.*

8. Board of Trade, *Report of the United Kingdom Engineering Mission 1948* (London: H.M.S.O., 1949), p. 14. A variety of "British Trade Weeks" have been sponsored by Canadian governments; see *Board of Trade Journal,* Sept. 12, 1953, p. 547.

9. *Financial Times,* Feb. 27, 1956, p. 4; Dollar Exports Board, *Dollar Sales, Advertising and Sales Promotion* (London, 1950), p. 19.

10. *Dollars and Industry.* Several speeches made by business men at the Dollar Convention in 1951 specifically noted that the Canadian and American markets were different in certain ways.

11. See, in this connection, "British Merchandise in U.S. Markets," *Banker's Magazine,* no. 1344 (March 1956), p. 230 ff.

12. This is implied at several points in Dollar Exports Board, *Advertising and Sales Promotion; Dollars and Industry,* p. 68; *Board of Trade Journal,* June 3, 1950, p. 1166, March 25, 1950, p. 607; Knox *et al., The Canadian Electrical Manufacturing Industry* (Canadian Electrical Manufacturers' Association, 1955), p. 7.

13. See, for example, *Report of the British Agricultural Machinery Mission to Canada, 1949* (London: H.M.S.O., 1949), p. 14.

14. *Board of Trade Journal,* Aug. 16, 1952, p. 298.

15. Cf. screw threads, *Board of Trade Journal,* June 21, 1952, p. 1250; Aug. 16, 1952, p. 298.

16. Board of Trade, *Report of the United Kingdom Engineering Mission, 1948; Dollars*

and Industry, passim; Dollar Exports Board, *Dollar Sales: Capital Goods* (London, 1950). In the case of cotton textile machinery, for example, U.S. producers give assistance in planning plant layout and installing equipment.

17.   To overcome this obstacle some British firms have been forced to provide a full set of blueprints in North America before sales could be made. *Dollars and Industry*, p. 67.

18.   *Report on the British Tool, Machine Tool and Scientific Instrument Section Exhibition at the Canadian Industrial Trade Fair* (Toronto, 1950), p. 25.

19.   See chapter II above.

20.   See *Dollars and Industry*, p. 70.

21.   *Exporting to Canada*, p. 26.

22.   *Board of Trade Journal*, June 28, 1947, p. 1070; Feb. 26, 1949, p. 402.

23.   *Ibid.*, Nov. 27, 1948, p. 1022; Feb. 26, 1949, p. 431.

24.   A typical comment: "But it has to be recorded with regret that Trade Commissioners have found that, in spite of extreme good-will from possible customers, and notwithstanding well intentioned efforts by many U.K. manufacturers, as well as by the Export Promotion Department of the Board of Trade, all their efforts have too often been rendered nugatory and an impasse has been reached simply because discussions and negotiations never passed the paper stage and because there was no actual merchandise to be seen, tried, tested and explained to potential customers by a qualified representative of the U.K. company which manufactured it." *Ibid.*, May 15, 1948, p. 965.

25.   "During the past year representatives of U.K. firms have visited the Dominion, many of them for the first time . . . [there is a] comparative lack of touch of British firms with their countrymen in the Dominion": *ibid.*, Jan. 20, 1938, p. 97: "The time has long passed when long-distance methods will do . . . the way British firms now in Canada handle business can bring only disappointment": *ibid.*, July 24, 1930, p. 89: "The U.K. does not secure nearly as much [trade] as she should [with Canada]": Committee on Industry and Trade, *Survey of Overseas Markets* (London: H.M.S.O., 1924), p. 318. See also *Economist*, March 5, 1927, p. 483; "Commercial History and Review of 1929," Feb. 15, 1930. Board of Trade officials in conversation with the writer admitted that the Canadian market had been "neglected during the inter-war period." See also section 2 below.

26.   T. E. Pennie, "The Influence of Distribution Costs and Direct Investments on British Exports to Canada," *Oxford Economic Papers*, N.S. VIII (Sept. 1956), p. 232.

27.   J. C. Brearley and M. S. Segall, "Wholesaling in Canada," *Marketing in Canada*, ed. E. J. Fox and D. S. R. Leighton (Homewood, Ill.: Richard D. Irwin Inc., 1958), pp. 145, 147.

28.   See *Dollar Sales: Capital Goods*, pp. 23 ff.; Dollar Exports Board, *Dollar Sales: Consumer Goods*, pp. 25 ff.; *Exporting to Canada*, chap. 3.

29.   *Dollar Sales: Consumer Goods*, p. 25. They are not even mentioned as a possibility in the booklet on capital goods.

30.   Brearley and Segall, "Wholesaling in Canada," pp. 144-5.

31.   Pennie, "The Influence of Distribution Costs and Direct Investments on British Exports to Canada," p. 238.

32.   *Ibid.*, p. 239.

33.   See various Productivity Team reports and G. Hutton, *We Too Can Prosper* (London: George Allen and Unwin, Ltd., 1953), *passim*: reports of various U.K. export missions sent to Canada and the U.S. and published by the Board of Trade; *Economist*, March 18, 1939, p. 551, July 2, 1949, p. 7, July 11, 1953, p. 79; various reports and articles in the *Board of Trade Journal*—e.g., March 15, 1952, p. 533.

34.   "No area in the world where the product must be so nicely adapted to the needs of the consumer [as in North America]," *Board of Trade Journal*, July 16, 1949, p. 103; "[the Canadian] is a shrewd buyer who looks for value, and only buys when he has found it," *ibid.*, March 15, 1952, p. 533. Some typical comments from *Dollars and Industry*: "the American buyer expects and gets a high degree of spoon feeding" (p. 69); "[the Canadian farmer] perhaps more than any other potential customer in the world is interested only in buying a sound article at a competitive price" (p. 72); "the normal deliveries acceptable in [Britain] will not be acceptable in Canada" (p. 48). "Both [capital and labour in British industry] accept the notion of a non-competitive industrial order, closed to irritating newcomers and accepting technical advances only at a pace that does not involve either loss of investment or displacement from jobs for those who are committed to older methods . . . ," *Economist*, July 2, 1949, p. 7. It is interesting to note that some firms who have been exposed to the competitive North American markets have found, apparently to their surprise, that their ability to compete in the British market has improved as a result.

35.   Board of Trade, *Report of the United Kingdom Engineering Mission, 1948*, p. 29.

36. Committee on Industry and Trade, *Survey of Overseas Markets* (London: H.M.S.O., 1925), pp. 318 f. Another portion of the Committee's report is equally interesting and although written in tne twenties is relevant even today. See *Final Report of the Committee on Industry and Trade* (London: H.M.S.O., 1929), section VI, pp. 157-245.

37. *The Times*, April 10, 1956, p. 11.

CHAPTER FIVE

1. This includes in the term competition not only the common case of pure competition, but also the case of monopolistic competition where the number of buyers and sellers is large (Professor Chamberlin's "large group").

2. E. H. Chamberlin, *The Theory of Monopolistic Competition*, 6th ed. (Cambridge: Harvard University Press, 1950), p. 7, p. 65.

3. Royal Commission on Canada's Economic Prospects, *Canada-United States Economic Relations*, prepared by Irving Brecher and S. S. Reisman, p. 145.

4. John H. Dunning, *American Investment in British Manufacturing Industry* (London: George Allen & Unwin Ltd., 1958), p. 53.

5. *Ibid.*, pp. 59-78.

6. *Ibid.*, pp. 291-8.

7. For example, Ervin Hexner, *International Cartels* (Chapel Hill: University of North Carolina Press, 1945), George W. Stocking and Myron W. Watkins, *Cartels or Competition?* (New York: The Twentieth Century Fund, 1948); George W. Stocking and Myron W. Watkins, *Cartels in Action* (New York: The Twentieth Century Fund, 1947); Edward S. Mason, *Controlling World Trade* (New York: McGraw-Hill Book Co. Ltd., 1946); U.S. Senate Committee on Military Affairs, Sub-committee on War Mobilization (Kilgore Committee), Monograph no. 1, 78 Cong., 2nd Sess.; *Economic and Political Aspects of International Cartels*, prepared by Corwin D. Edwards (Washington: Government Printing Office, 1944); Corwin D. Edwards, "International Cartels as Obstacles to International Trade," (*American Economic Review*, XXXIV, Supplement (part 2, March 1944), pp. 330 ff.

8. Report of the Commissioner, Combines Investigation Act, *Canada and International Cartels* (Ottawa: King's Printer, 1945).

9. Lloyd G. Reynolds, *The Control of Competition in Canada* (Cambridge: Harvard University Press, 1940), pp. 8 f., pp. 21 ff.

10. *Ibid.*, p. 15; *Report of the Royal Commission on the Textile Industry* (Ottawa: King's Printer, 1938), pp. 61 f.

11. Alfred Plummer, *International Combines in Modern Industry*, 3rd. ed. (London: Sir Isaac Pitman and Sons Ltd., 1951), pp. 61-2.

12. Hexner, *International Cartels*, pp. 380 ff.; Stocking and Watkins, *Cartels in Action*, pp. 512 f.; Reynolds, *The Control of Competition in Canada*, p. 7.

13. *Report of the Royal Commission on the Textile Industry*, pp. 48 f.

14. See Ervin Hexner, *The International Steel Cartel* (Chapel Hill: University of North Carolina Press, 1943); Stocking and Watkins, *Cartels in Action*, chap. v.; *Canada and International Cartels*, pp. 31 ff.

15. *Canada and International Cartels*, p. 32.

16. *Economist*, Jan. 18, 1936, p. 116.

17. *Report of The Federal Trade Commission on International Steel Cartels* (Washington: G.P.O., 1948), p. 102.

18. See Hexner, *The International Steel Cartel*; *Canada and International Cartels*, pp. 32 ff.; *Report of The Federal Trade Commission on International Cartels*, chaps. iii, iv.

19. *Canada and International Cartels*, p. 33.

20. Plummer, *International Combines in Modern Industry*, p. 161.

21. *Agricultural Machinery: A Report on the Industry* (London: Political and Economic Planning, 1948), p. 72.

22. Simon N. Whitney, *Antitrust Policies* (New York: Twentieth Century Fund, 1958) I, pp. 454 ff.; *Cartel*, Oct. 1957, p. 136.

23. United Nations Organization, *Restrictive Business Practices* (New York: U.N.O. Economic and Social Council, 1953), Supplement 11 A, p. 10, Annex A, p. 46.

24. Hexner, *International Cartels*, pp. 354 ff.; *Canada and International Cartels*, pp. 22 f.; and the following reports of the Monopolies and Restrictive Practices Commission: *Report on the Supply of Electric Lamps* (London: H.M.S.O., 1951), p. 23; *Report on the Supply of Insulated Electric Wires and Cables* (London: H.M.S.O., 1952), p. 54; *Report on the Supply and Export of Certain Semi-Manufactures of Copper and Copper-Based Alloys* (London: H.M.S.O., 1955), p. 57.

25. Edwards, *Economic and Political Aspects of International Cartels, passim; Canada and International Cartels*, pp. 22 f.

26. *Canada and International Cartels*, pp. 22 f.

27. *Ibid.*, pp. 23 f., 48 ff.

28. *Ibid.*, pp. 23-4.

29. *Ibid.*, pp. 8 f.; Report of Commissioner, Combines Investigation Act, *Flat Glass* (Ottawa: King's Printer, 1949), pp. 8 ff.; *Cartel,* July 1950, pp. 26-7.

30. *Canada and International Cartels*, p. 8.

31. *Ibid.*, p. 9.

32. Hexner, *International Cartels*, pp. 363 ff., 354.

33. *Ibid., passim; Canada and International Cartels*, pp. 24 f.

34. See Hexner, *International Cartels*, pp. 296 ff.; *Canada and International Cartels*, chap. I; Stocking and Watkins, *Cartels in Action*, chaps. IX-XI.

35. *Canada and International Cartels*, p. 20.

36. Hexner, *International Cartels*, p. 382.

37. Stocking and Watkins, *Cartels in Action*, p. 459.

38. *Canada and International Cartels*, pp. 21 f.

39. Hexner, *International Cartels*, p. 280.

40. *Ibid.*, p. 304.

41. Monopolies and Restrictive Practices Commission, *Report on the Supply of Insulin* (London: H.M.S.O., 1952), p. 9.

42. Monopolies and Restrictive Practices Commission, *Report on the Supply of Certain Industrial and Medical Gases* (London: H.M.S.O., 1956), p. 44.

43. United National Organization, *Restrictive Business Practices,* Supplement 11 A, p. 10, Annex A, p. 46.

44. *Cartel,* April 1956, pp. 66 ff.

45. *Financial Post,* Feb. 27, 1954, p. 17.

46. A number of instances where restrictions have apparently lapsed are indicated by some of the reports of the Monopolies and Restrictive Practices Commission: *Semi-Manufactures of Copper and Copper-Based Alloys,* p. 57; *Insulated Electric Wires and Cables,* p. 54; *Electric Lamps,* p. 23.

47. G. W. Stocking and M. W. Watkins, *Cartels or Competition?,* pp. 355 ff.

48. W. Diebold, *Trade and Payments in Western Europe* (New York: Harper and Bros., 1952), chap. XIV; Michael L. Hoffman, *New York Times,* Jan. 15, 1950, p. 15, "British business concerns have been extremely active in the post-war movement to revive international cartels or to construct new ones, according to cartel experts [in Geneva].... Some of the fields in which British initiative to form cartel agreements has been discovered are coke, electric meters, non-ferrous metals and cables."

49. Diebold, *Trade and Payments in Western Europe,* pp. 282 f.

50. Dunning, *American Investment in British Manufacturing Industry,* p. 193. This general view is corroborated by a survey conducted by the National Industrial Conference Board and reported upon in *Foreign Licensing Agreements,* Studies in Business Policy, no. 86 (New York, National Industrial Conference Board Inc., 1958), Table 3, p. 14.

51. The Canadian Industries Limited example illustrates two interesting considerations. First, although large-scale direct investment may stimulate trade, it may also result in the elimination of trade. Second, the broader application of the United States anti-trust laws may simply result in greater competition between the Canadian subsidiaries of United Kingdom and United States firms. The degree of competition between the parent organizations may be little changed.

52. Report of Commissioner, Combines Investigation Act, *Flat Glass,* p. 75.

53. S.R.I.S., Market Digest on Radio Components, Dec. 4, 1951; Market Digest on Radio and Television Components, July 18, 1958.

54. S.R.I.S., Market Digest on Pulp and Paper Machinery, July 25, 1952; *Report of Visit to the U.K.,* 1955, Petroleum Industry.

55. S.R.I.S., Market Digest on Industrial Protective Clothing, Feb. 27, 1956.

56. *Cartel,* Jan. 1950, p. 26.

57. *Ibid.*, Jan. 1951, p. 78.

58. *Ibid.*, April 1951, pp. 138 ff.

59. *Ibid.*, Jan. 1953, pp. 89 ff.

60. *Ibid.*, July 1954, p. 120.

61. *Ibid.*, Oct. 1955, p. 137.

62. *Ibid.*, April 1956, p. 69.

63. Cited by E. S. Mason, *Controlling World Trade,* p. 26.

64. Although it is true that in the final analysis governmental policies depend upon government actions, it is only realistic to recognize that these policies can be and frequently are considerably influenced by pressures exerted by domestic producers.

65. Working Party Report, *Pottery* (London: H.M.S.O., 1946), p. 29.

66. Most of what is said here on this subject is based on Royal Commission on Canada's Economic Prospects, *Canadian Commercial Policy,* prepared by J. H. Young (1957), pp. 54-6.

67. Royal Commission on Canada's Economic Prospects, *Canadian Commercial Policy,* p. 55. It has been estimated that the average margin of preference on British goods entering Canada under preferential tariffs was 11 per cent in 1929, 23 per cent in 1937, and 12-13 per cent in 1948. On all British goods entering Canada during these years the margin is estimated at 7, 20, and 10-11 per cent respectively. These estimates indicating a reduction in the average margin of preference since the thirties may, however, be misleading since they appear to include the high duties levied on alcoholic beverages. These duties are largely matched by domestic taxes. Also, they are mostly specific duties and have been affected by price changes. Sir Donald MacDougall and R. Hutt, "Imperial Preference: A Quantitative Analysis," *Economic Journal,* LXIV (June 1954), Table I, p. 241.

68. Royal Commission on Canada's Economic Prospects, *Canadian Commercial Policy,* p. 55.

69. *Ibid.,* p. 56.

70. G. A. Elliott, *Tariff Procedures and Trade Barriers* (Toronto: University of Toronto Press, 1955).

71. For example, by exhibiting "in reverse"—that is, by emphasizing Canada as a buyer rather than as a seller—at post-war British industries fairs, and by encouraging British exports to Canada through the activities of Canada's Trade Commissioners in London.

72. Royal Commission on Canada's Economic Prospects, *Canadian Commercial Policy,* p. 70.

73. It has been suggested that one reason some British firms established subsidiaries in Canada was to make themselves eligible for contracts arising from the St. Lawrence Seaway project.

74. For example, fishing equipment and railway equipment.

75. *Board of Trade Journal,* Feb. 26, 1949, p. 411, p. 431; Feb. 19, 1949, p. 347.

76. "It is better to export finished goods containing steel than to export steel as such." *Economic Survey for 1947* (London: H.M.S.O., 1947), Cmnd. 7046, p. 23. It has also been argued that in the immediate post-war years when the economy was closely controlled too much emphasis was placed on increasing exports of "traditional" products and not enough on expanding exports of "newer" products. See, for example, "First-Aid for Exports," *Planning,* June 22, 1945.

CHAPTER SIX

1. It may be observed here that there seems to be considerable agreement that the import content of British exports has declined since the twenties. In part this decline is thought to reflect a trend toward a lower import content in most commodity categories. A larger part of the decline is attributed to a shift in the composition of British exports away from commodities incorporating a high proportion of import content—for example, cotton textiles and yarn—to commodities embodying relatively less import content—for example, engineering products. Mr. W. Z. Billewicz has estimated that in 1946 the import content of exports was between 14 and 21 per cent. A. E. G. Robinson, "The Problem of Living within Our Foreign Earnings," *Three Banks Review* (March 1954); W. Z. Billewicz, "The Import Content of British Exports," *Economica,* N.S. XX (May 1953), p. 162. It is also noteworthy that, in terms of value, exports expressed as a percentage of gross national product appear to have been larger since 1948 than during the late twenties.

2. Whether or not the distribution between the home market and exports was an appropriate one is another question and one that would require a much more comprehensive analysis than is possible here.

3. This decline no doubt is at least partly due to post-war difficulties in eastern Europe, the East, and South America.

4. An index of market concentration is calculated by the Dominion Bureau of Statistics. The greater the number of markets to which a country caters and the more nearly equal are the shares of trade of various markets in a country's trade, the smaller will the index number of concentration be, subject to the condition that the index number will always be between 0 and 100. For 1957 the index number is 62 for Canadian exports, 26 for United States exports, and 18 for British exports. Dominion Bureau of Statistics, *Review of Foreign Trade 1957,* Table 6, p. 17, p. 45.

5. The high figure shown for non-ferrous metals is largely accounted for by palladium and platinum trade and represents mainly a transfer of goods within the operations of the International Nickel Company.

6. It has been estimated that in 1924-5 about 21-24 per cent of British net output went into exports and about 16½-20 per cent in 1930-1; G. W. Daniels and H. Campion, "The Relative Importance of British Export Trade," *London and Cambridge Economic Service,* Special Memorandum, no. 41 (Aug. 1935). For other estimates pertaining to the pre-war period see E. C. Snow, "The Relative Importance of Export Trade," *Journal of the Royal Statistical Society,* XCIV, pt. III (1931), pp. 373 ff.; Mr. Leak, "Discussion on Methods Used in Different Countries for Estimating National Income," *Journal of the Royal Statistical Society,* XCVII, pt. IV (1934), p. 548. The assumed figure of 25 per cent probably errs on the high side for the post-war period.

7. For instance, some costs, such as "costs of entry," might have been low during the early post-war years, compared to pre-war, because of the strong demand situation in Canada; others might have been comparatively high.

8. Harry G. Johnson, *The Overloaded Economy* (Toronto: University of Toronto Press, 1952).

9. John H. Dunning, *American Investment in British Manufacturing Industry* (London: George Allen & Unwin Ltd., 1958), *passim.*

10. For discussion pertaining to this subject see, for example, Austin Robinson, "The Future of British Imports," "The Problem of Living within Our Foreign Earnings," and "The Cost of Agricultural Import-Saving," *Three Banks Review,* March 1953, March 1954, and Dec. 1958; "Growth and Balance of Payments: A Symposium," *Bulletin of the Oxford University Institute of Statistics,* XVII (Feb. 1955), particularly the contributions by Johnson, Marris, and Henderson; R. L. Marris, "The Purchasing Power of British Exports," *Economica,* N.S. V (June 1953).

11. In this connection, see also Table XXI above.

12. Alfred E. Kahn, *Great Britain in the World Economy* (New York: Columbia University Press, 1946), especially pt. III; H. W. Arndt, *The Economic Lessons of the Nineteen-Thirties* (London: Oxford University Press, 1944); W. Arthur Lewis, *Economic Survey, 1919-1939* (London: George Allen and Unwin, 1949).

13. See Arndt, *The Economic Lessons of the Nineteen-Thirties,* pp. 105 ff.; W. K. Hancock, "Problems of Economic Policy, 1918-1939," *Survey of British Commonwealth Affairs,* II (London: Oxford University Press, 1940), pp. 198 ff.

14. Herbert Marshall, Frank A. Southard, and Kenneth W. Taylor, *Canadian-American Industry* (New Haven: Yale University Press, 1936), pp. 199 ff.

15. Report of a Study Group of Members of the Royal Institute of International Affairs, *The Problem of International Investment* (London: Oxford University Press, 1937), pp. 255 ff.; "British Capital Abroad," *Economist,* Nov. 20, 1937, pp. 360 f.

16. "British Capital Abroad," pp. 359 ff.; *The Problem of International Investment,* chapter x; Hancock, "Problems of Economic Policy, 1918-1939," pp. 177 ff.; R. B. Stewart, "Great Britain's Foreign Loan Policy," *Economica,* N.S. V (Feb. 1938), pp. 45 ff.

17. *The Problem of International Investment,* p. 164.

18. Hancock, "Problems of Economic Policy, 1918-1939," p. 180.

19. *Ibid.,* p. 187.

20. Donald Bailey Marsh, *World Trade and Investment* (New York: Harcourt, Brace and Co., 1951), pp. 335 ff.

21. International Monetary Fund, *Fourth Annual Report on Exchange Restrictions,* 1953, p. 54.

22. Board of Trade, *Board of Trade Journal,* March 22, 1952, p. 617; *Economist,* March 22, 1952, pp. 744 ff.

23. Board of Trade, *Board of Trade Journal,* Feb. 21, 1953, p. 383; July 11, 1953, p. 79; Sept. 19, 1953, p. 593; Feb. 27, 1954, p. 438.

24. *Economist,* March 22, 1952, pp. 744 ff.; International Monetary Fund, *Fourth, Fifth and Sixth Annual Report on Exchange Restrictions,* 1953, 1954, 1955, relevant country surveys; United Nations, *Economic Survey of Europe in 1954* (Geneva, 1955), p. 85.

25. For example, *Economist,* Feb. 2, 1952, p. 257; March 15, 1952, p. 625; April 18, 1953, p. 169.

26. *Economist,* annual statement by Sir Oliver Franks of Lloyd's Bank, Jan. 28, 1956, p. 330.

27. See above, pp. 68, 85-6.

28. An interesting account of how export needs and internal capital development may have come into conflict has been written by Ragnar Nurkse, "The Relation between Home Invest-

ment and External Balance in the Light of British Experience," *Review of Economics and Statistics*, XXXVIII (May 1956), pp. 121 ff.

CHAPTER SEVEN

1. For example: "It seems to me that the theory of international trade . . . requires further development in two main·directions. The theory of imperfect competition and the theory of short-run oscillation (business cycle theory) must be applied to the problems of international trade"—G. Haberler, *The Theory of International Trade* (London: William Hodge and Co. Ltd., 1937), preface; "At the moment, the main gap (in international economics) appears to be in the slight degree to which the theory of imperfect competition has been applied in the international field . . . revision (is required in) the assumption of mobility of resources within countries (which underlies the notion of elastic supply curves) and of a high degree of competition in international trade, which makes for elastic demand . . ."—C. P. Kindleberger, *The Dollar Shortage* (New York: John Wiley and Sons, 1950), p. 10; ". . . nowadays everyone is willing to admit that the traditional theory of value based on the assumption of perfect competition is highly unrealistic and that competition in practice is very imperfect"—Joan Robinson, "The Impossibility of Competition," *Monopoly and Competition and Their Regulation,* Papers and Proceedings of a Conference held by the International Economic Association, ed. Edward H. Chamberlin (London: Macmillan and Co. Ltd., 1954), p. 245; T. Balogh and P. P. Streeten, "The Inappropriateness of Simple 'Elasticity' Concepts in the Analysis of International Trade" and "Exchange Rates and National Income," *Bulletin of the Oxford University Institute of Statistics,* XIII (March 1951), pp. 65 ff., and XIII (April 1951), pp. 101 ff; Irving B. Kravis, " 'Availability' and Other Influences on the Commodity Composition of Trade," *Journal of Political Economy,* LXIV (April 1956), pp. 193 ff.
2. Edward H. Chamberlin, "Monopolistic Competition Revisited," *Economica,* N.S. XVIII (Nov. 1951), p. 356.
3. P. T. Ellsworth, *International Economics* (New York: Macmillan and Co., 1938), pp. 434-5; W. Edwards Beach, "Some Aspects of International Trade under Monopolistic Competition," *Explorations in Economics,* Notes and Essays Contributed in Honour of F. W. Taussig (New York: McGraw-Hill Book Co. Inc., 1936), p. 105.
4. Saying that the elasticity of demand for exports with respect to price is small or zero is the equivalent of saying that at the margin price is of minor or no importance as a determinant of sales and that the quantity demanded is to be explained mainly or entirely by other factors. The same can be said about income elasticity.

APPENDIX

* Copyright, 1959, by The President and Fellows of Harvard College.

1. For example, Rosemary Hutt, "British Exports to The United States, 1948-1955," *Review of Economics and Statistics,* XXXIX (Feb. 1957), pp. 65 ff.; C. P. Kindleberger, *The Terms of Trade* (New York, 1956); Adler, Schlesinger, and Van Westerborg, *The Pattern of United States Import Trade since 1923* (New York, 1952); *Board of Trade Journal* (London: H.M.S.O.), 168 (May 14, 1955), p. 1053; Central Statistical Office, *Monthly Digest of Statistics.*
2. The construction of average or unit value series is discussed by Kindleberger, *The Terms of Trade, passim,* especially Appendix A, pp. 315 ff., Appendix B, pp. 353-62.
3. This minimum amount, which was not the same for exports and imports, was also different for various base years to allow for changes in price levels. In a few cases, where special circumstances seemed to warrant it, exceptions were made to these general conditions. Most of 'these exceptions led to the inclusion of items which would otherwise have been excluded.
4. This latter method was used mainly for exports, particularly textile products and machinery items.
5. *The Terms of Trade,* p. 174.
6. For example, J. R. Hicks, "An Inaugural Lecture," *Oxford Economic Papers,* N.S. 5 (June 1953); R. F. Harrod, "Imbalance of International Payments," *Staff Papers,* International Monetary Fund, III (April 1953), p. 33.
7. R. L. Marris, "The Purchasing Power of British Exports," *Economica,* N.S. XXII (Feb. 1955), pp. 13 ff. See also D. J. Morgan and F. W. Paish, "The Purchasing Power of British Exports Further Considered," *Economica,* N.S. XXII (Nov. 1955), pp. 329 ff.; R. Marris, "The Purchasing Power of British Exports—A Rejoinder," *Economica,* N.S. XXIII (Feb. 1956), pp. 67 ff.

INDEX

9 781487 573324